Frontiers in Economic History

Economic historians have contributed to the development of economics in a variety of ways, combining theory with quantitative methods, constructing new databases, promoting interdisciplinary approaches to historical topics, and using history as a lens to examine the long-term development of the economy. Frontiers in Economic History publishes manuscripts that push the frontiers of research in economic history in order to better explain past economic experiences and to understand how, why and when economic change occurs. Books in this series will highlight the value of economic history in shedding light on the ways in which economic factors influence growth as well as social and political developments. This series aims to establish a new standard of quality in the field while offering a global discussion forum toward a unified approach in the social sciences.

María Vázquez-Fariñas
Francisco Cabrera-Gallardo
Editors

Business Trajectories in the History of Spain

Sectors, Figures and Transformations

Springer

Editors
María Vázquez-Fariñas
Department of Economic Theory and Economic History, Faculty of Economics and Business Studies
University of Málaga
Málaga, Spain

Francisco Cabrera-Gallardo
Department of Economics
University of Jaén
Jaén, Spain

ISSN 2662-9771 ISSN 2662-978X (electronic)
Frontiers in Economic History
ISBN 978-3-032-16213-7 ISBN 978-3-032-16214-4 (eBook)
https://doi.org/10.1007/978-3-032-16214-4

This Springer imprint is published by the registered company Springer Nature Switzerland AG
The registered company address is: Gewerbestrasse 11, 6330 Cham, Switzerland

Contents

List of Figures

List of Tables

Companies and Entrepreneurs: An Economic History Perspective

María Vázquez-Fariñas and Francisco Cabrera-Gallardo

Abstract The study of business history constitutes a fundamental tool for understanding processes of economic, social, and cultural change. Analysing the trajectories of companies and entrepreneurs allows us to recognise that the economy is not an abstraction, but rather the outcome of decisions, strategies, and organisational dynamics embedded within specific historical contexts. This perspective helps to unravel the interaction between individual initiative, institutional structures, and technological transformations, providing a more comprehensive understanding of economic development. Furthermore, business history encourages reflection on entrepreneurial culture and the mechanisms of adaptation in response to the challenges posed by globalisation, digitalisation, and structural crises. Its study not only broadens our understanding of the economic past but also offers insights into contemporary forms of management, innovation, and corporate social responsibility. In this way, business history establishes itself as an interdisciplinary field linking economics, sociology, history, and management, contributing to an understanding of the firm as both an agent of change and an institution with social significance extending beyond purely economic dimensions.

M. Vázquez-Fariñas (✉)
Department of Economic Theory and Economic History, Faculty of Economics and Business Studies, University of Málaga, Málaga, Spain
e-mail: maria.vazquez@uma.es

F. Cabrera-Gallardo
Department of Economics, University of Jaén, Jaén, Spain

PhD Program in Economic and Business, University of Málaga, Málaga, Spain
e-mail: fcabrera@ujaen.es

M. Vázquez-Fariñas, F. Cabrera-Gallardo (eds.), *Business Trajectories in the History of Spain*, Frontiers in Economic History,
https://doi.org/10.1007/978-3-032-16214-4_1

1 Introduction: Understanding Companies and Entrepreneurs Through History

The study of companies and entrepreneurs—and, consequently, of business history—constitutes a fundamental tool for promoting the dissemination of business culture among specialists in the field as well as the general public. Moreover, it serves as an essential instrument for fostering an entrepreneurial spirit among those who aspire to establish companies and build their professional careers within the sphere of entrepreneurship. Analysing and understanding the life trajectories of entrepreneurs throughout history allows their experiences to be incorporated into business organisation and enriches decision-making processes, which invariably unfold under complex circumstances, beyond structural or organisational variables (Vázquez-Fariñas et al., 2021).

Delving into the biographies of company leaders and the history of their organisations provides a key avenue for approaching economic reality. Confronting fluctuations in commercial activity, technological challenges, or political changes demonstrates that the economy is not an abstract process, but rather a succession of human decisions embedded within specific social, cultural, and institutional frameworks. This perspective seeks to offer readers a dynamic understanding of economic processes and companies, regardless of their size or scope.

The main objective of this collective work is to explore, from a long-term and multidisciplinary perspective, the evolution of entrepreneurship, corporate organisation, and business culture in Spain. The volume aims to:

1. Reassess the historical role of entrepreneurs and companies as agents of economic and social change.
2. Analyse the mechanisms of adaptation and resilience in Spanish business history across major turning points—from the Ancien Régime to the liberal revolution, and from industrialisation to the modern service economy.
3. Contribute to international debates on business historiography, by situating Spanish case studies within broader frameworks of modernisation, globalisation, and institutional development.

By combining regional and sectoral studies, this work provides a multifaceted view of how Spanish capitalism evolved, not as a linear or uniform process, but as a complex interaction between continuity and innovation.

In addition, this volume responds to the growing international interest in comparative business history, offering valuable empirical evidence and conceptual reflections for researchers concerned with how different institutional contexts shape entrepreneurial behaviour and business organisation.

The knowledge of companies and their protagonists therefore fulfils several essential functions:

1. It enables tracing the evolution of markets, observing how firms have adapted to globalisation, digitalisation, and the technological transformations characteristic of each period.
2. It provides valuable management lessons: from success stories, revealing the importance of innovation, strategic vision, and the calculated assumption of risk; and from failures, which expose common mistakes and provide opportunities for learning.
3. It serves as a source of motivation, exemplified by the trajectories of Andrew Carnegie, John D. Rockefeller, Henry Ford, Estée Lauder, Steve Jobs, Bill Gates, Amancio Ortega, Jeff Bezos, and Elon Musk, whose biographies demonstrate how creativity, perseverance, and passion can transform ideas into entrepreneurial realities.
4. It contributes to understanding the social and cultural role of companies beyond their economic dimension, as they influence politics, culture, and collective values while reflecting the aspirations of the societies in which they operate.

Taken together, these functions illustrate the historiographical and analytical potential of business history and provide an appropriate framework for situating this volume within a broader comparative perspective.

Spain constitutes an ideal setting for exploring the long-term evolution of companies and entrepreneurs because its economic trajectory brings together multiple characteristics that are analytically revealing. The country combines early modern institutional experimentation, a delayed but intense industrialisation process, diverse regional economic structures, alternating periods of openness and protectionism, and a long history of interaction with international capital and technology. This complexity makes Spain a particularly rich laboratory for examining how entrepreneurs respond to structural constraints, institutional change, and shifting global dynamics.

In Spain, business history has grown remarkably in recent decades, although its academic consolidation was somewhat delayed, particularly from the 1970s onwards. Since then, the field has expanded exponentially, with a proliferation of conferences, publications, and research projects that have considerably broadened our understanding of companies and their protagonists. Nevertheless, the discipline continues to face significant methodological challenges, among them limited access to primary sources due to the reluctance of many firms to open their archives. Despite these challenges, the vitality of research in the field remains unquestionable, and the present work serves as clear evidence of that (Matés-Barco & Caruana, 2021).

Building on this expanding academic landscape, the present volume contributes to the consolidation of Spanish business history within international historiography. This book offers a renewed perspective on business trajectories in Spain from the eighteenth century to the present, examining the country's economic and industrial evolution during the transition from a traditional agrarian economy to a modern industrialised society, considering both nationwide transformations and regional specificities, with predominance of small and medium-sized enterprises. The book highlights the dynamic interaction between entrepreneurship, capital formation, and institutions, analysing the role of families, foreign investors, and public policies in shaping Spain's business structure. Far from reproducing simplistic narratives of economic backwardness, the chapters emphasise the agency of entrepreneurs, the strategic use of foreign capital, and the significance of institutional innovations that sustained industrial growth.

This volume also contributes to the wider field of international business history by providing evidence that enriches ongoing global debates on entrepreneurship, institutional development, and corporate evolution. Spain represents a particularly valuable case within comparative business history because it combines features of late industrialisation, strong state intervention, persistent regional diversity, and a long-term interaction with foreign capital. By examining these dynamics across different periods and sectors, the book offers empirical material that dialogues with international scholarship on varieties of capitalism, family business resilience, multinational investment, and the historical foundations of managerial practices. In doing so, the volume positions Spanish business history not as an exceptional or isolated trajectory, but as an integral part of broader global patterns of economic transformation.

Therefore, the themes addressed illustrate the diversity of conceptions and approaches of Spanish and foreign entrepreneurs and companies over the past centuries. To this end, a group of renowned specialists has been brought together, whose extensive experience enables a multidimensional approach. Through various perspectives, the contributors analyse specific cases of firms and entrepreneurs with the aim of providing a synthesis of the role historically attributed to them.

Following this introductory chapter, the studies comprising the volume are organised both chronologically and thematically, illustrating the diversity of actors, sectors, and institutions that have shaped Spanish business history. The chapters include:

- Institutions of Pre-Industrial Origin: Rafael Barquín Gil (National University of Distance Education) and Pablo A. Martín-Grande (King Juan Carlos University) analyse the functioning of the *pósitos*, municipal grain banks between the sixteenth and nineteenth centuries that reveal the interaction of public regulation and economic practice in food security.
- Entrepreneurial Emergence in Political Transformation: Antonio Pinto-Tortosa (University of Málaga) examines Antequera's local bourgeoisie during the early stages of the liberal revolution (1835–1836), illustrating how certain social groups began to develop entrepreneurial activities in a context of profound political and economic transformation.
- Industrialisation and Foreign Investment: Mercedes Fernández-Paradas and José J. Luque García (both from the University of Málaga) explore the influence of French capital in the gas industry through the case of *Lebon et Cie.*; Leonardo Caruana (University of Granada) and Julio Tascón (University of Oviedo) reconstruct the trajectory of *Hullera Vasco-Leonesa*—one of the longest-lived coal mining companies-; and Víctor M. Heredia-Flores (University of Málaga) traces

the Heredia family in Málaga's steel sector. These chapters demonstrate how foreign capital, family entrepreneurship, and industrial innovation shaped regional and national development.
- Companies and Politics: Jorge Lafuente del Cano and Pedro Pablo Ortúñez Goicolea (both from the University of Valladolid) study Leopoldo Calvo-Sotelo's trajectory, exemplifying the permeability between business and political power and highlighting the role of business experience in shaping political leadership.
- Services and Modernisation: Marta Laguna-García (University of Valladolid) and Carlos Larrinaga Rodríguez (University of Granada) analyse the evolution of the Spanish hotel industry throughout the twentieth century; Juan Manuel Matés-Barco (University of Jaén), María Vázquez-Fariñas (University of Málaga), and Mariano Castro-Valdivia (University of Jaén) focus on Pedro Durán Farell in the energy sector; and Francisco Cabrera-Gallardo (University of Jaén / University of Málaga) examines *Construcciones Calderón*, highlighting challenges of sustainability, digitalisation, and financing. These chapters illustrate the adaptation of enterprises to tourism, energy, and construction challenges in the twentieth century, reflecting both professionalisation and technological innovation.

This thematic and chronological organisation allows for cross-chapter comparisons, highlighting patterns of entrepreneurial behaviour, capital mobilisation, and institutional interaction. It strengthens the overarching narrative by connecting individual case studies to broader economic and social trends, offering readers not only historical detail but also analytical insight into the processes that have shaped Spanish business over the centuries.

The following sections further develop this analytical structure: Section 1.2 addresses the structural and methodological dimensions underpinning the study; Section 1.3 situates the volume within the long-term evolution of Spanish economic history; and Section 1.4 offers concluding reflections that tie together the book's thematic and methodological coherence.

2 Structural and Methodological Dimensions

Understanding the evolution that gradually transformed business organisational forms, the figure of the entrepreneur, and the environment—which invariably conditions entrepreneurial activity—is essential for analysing Spanish economic history. Until a few decades ago, entrepreneurial initiatives were almost entirely agrarian or artisanal, operating within small associations or family units. With the advent of industrial capitalism, these initiatives gradually shifted towards more complex structures, including companies with corporate frameworks. Organisational transformation not only implied larger company size but also internationalisation, diversification, and pursuit of competitiveness. In this regard, Spanish companies of the nineteenth and twentieth centuries had to adapt to increasingly intense technological, financial, and market changes, making business history a process of continuous adjustment to evolving realities (Carreras & Tafunell, 2021; Fernández-Paradas & Larrinaga Rodríguez, 2021).

The figure of the entrepreneur has been in constant evolution, serving simultaneously as a historical agent and a catalyst of change in the economic structure. On the one hand, entrepreneurs are actors dedicated to founding and managing companies wherever market opportunities arise, typically risking part of their private capital. On the other hand, entrepreneurial action is conditioned by social and institutional networks, a key focus for microhistorical studies in economic history. The interplay between individual initiative and environmental constraints demonstrates that innovation and strategic decision-making cannot be understood in isolation from context.

The innovative capacity of entrepreneurs, closely linked to the conditions of each period, highlights the importance of historical contextualisation in business studies. Real business cases must be analysed alongside their social, political, legal, and financial environments to understand the factors shaping opportunities and limitations. In Spain, there is not yet full consensus regarding the economic significance of the entrepreneur or the conditions that may have enhanced or hindered their impact. Nevertheless, recent studies indicate that entrepreneurial activity has generally had a positive effect on GDP growth and labour productivity, especially in periods of economic liberalisation and industrial expansion (Hernández-Barahona et al., 2025).

Special attention must be given to institutional, technological, and cultural environments underpinning historical entrepreneurial contexts. These cannot be understood independently of political structures, regulatory frameworks, and financial mechanisms. Historically, Spanish business dynamics were shaped by conservative values, low risk tolerance, and limited institutional support for entrepreneurship (Hernández-Barahona et al., 2025; Tortella & García Ruiz, 2013). From the twentieth century onwards, the figure of the entrepreneur gained prominence, reflecting the increasing role of the state, international capital flows, and foreign business networks (Carreras & Tafunell, 2021).

For the study of companies and entrepreneurs from the Ancien Régime to the present, focusing solely on individual cases is insufficient. It is necessary to consider the multitude of internal and external factors that determine entrepreneurial opportunities in each historical period. In recent decades, entrepreneurial culture in Spain has expanded compared with earlier centuries, though this growth has been cyclical rather than linear, reflecting periods of expansion and contraction. Spanish companies have had to adapt over time to market internationalisation, foreign competition, technological change, and shifts in capital availability. These constitute essential determinants for understanding the evolution of the Spanish business fabric.

Moreover, examining business structures across time reveals recurring patterns in corporate organisation, financing strategies, and intergenerational management. Family firms, foreign capital, and state intervention often coexisted in complex arrangements, influencing both success and failure. For example, the chapters on *Hullera Vasco-Leonesa* and the Heredia family illustrate how family capitalism adapted over decades to industrial and technological changes, while foreign investment in the gas industry demonstrates the critical role of external capital and institutional partnerships.

In sum, over the centuries under analysis, business forms, institutional and cultural contexts, and the entrepreneur figure have undergone constant evolution. Companies are not merely economic actors, but historical and social realities embedded in networks, markets, and institutions. Studying individual cases in combination with comparative analyses across sectors and periods allows a deeper appreciation of the complexity, diversity, and adaptability of entrepreneurial processes in Spain.

Regarding the methodological framework, this volume integrates case studies within a coherent comparative perspective. It combines qualitative and historical research methods with a systematic approach to primary and secondary sources:

- Primary Sources: Company archives, notarial and administrative documents, press reports, private correspondence, and institutional records.
- Secondary Sources: Economic and business history literature, historical datasets, and regional studies.

Analysis is conducted using multiple complementary approaches:

1. Comparative analysis across time periods, sectors, and regions to identify patterns of adaptation and continuity.
2. Microhistorical and biographical methods tracing entrepreneurial agency, leadership styles, and family firm dynamics.
3. Quantitative and econometric tools, applied to financial data, prices, and production figures, enabling cross-chapter comparisons of profitability, market integration, and investment strategies.
4. Interdisciplinary engagement, incorporating economics, management studies, sociology, and cultural history, to understand companies' social, political, and institutional embeddedness.

This methodological plurality allows readers to link individual agency with structural economic and institutional factors, producing a cohesive, cross-chapter analytical framework. The methodology also ensures that each chapter contributes to the overarching narrative of Spanish business evolution while retaining rigour and specificity. Tables, figures, and timelines summarise key indicators, improving clarity and enabling pedagogical utility. In addition, comparative frameworks are used to link individual entrepreneurial trajectories to broader macroeconomic and institutional transformations, providing an integrated perspective that combines qualitative narrative and quantitative reasoning. By analysing companies across sectors and centuries, the volume offers readers insights into patterns of organisational change, innovation, and institutional interaction.

3 Historical Contextualisation of Business

This section contextualises the chapters within the broader framework of long-term Spanish economic history. To fully comprehend the entrepreneurial experiences documented in this volume, it is essential to situate them within their historical, economic, and institutional contexts. Spain's business history spans more than four centuries, during which both socio-economic structures and entrepreneurial practices evolved significantly. Entrepreneurs progressively transformed their activities, and an entrepreneurial spirit gradually consolidated, influencing the development of business organisational forms and shaping the interaction between the public and private sectors within an interconnected capitalist system (Comín & Martín Aceña, 1997).

Institutional, governmental, and political transformations consistently shaped the conditions for entrepreneurial activity. Analysing these processes helps us understand how companies developed within the cultural, social, and political frameworks of each period (Comín & Martín Aceña, 1996). The historical trajectory of Spanish companies illustrates the complex interplay between state policies, private initiative, and international influences, highlighting the necessity of contextualising micro-level business actions within macroeconomic trends.

During the period in which the *pósitos* (grain banks) began to operate, Spain was governed by an absolute monarchy, with an economic model rooted in enlightened mercantilism. Strong state intervention coexisted with early forms of economic liberalisation, and the Crown actively promoted new technologies through royal manufactories and privileged companies dedicated to foreign trade. These institutions expanded commercial networks and facilitated capital flows, yet individual entrepreneurs remained dependent on the approval of a hierarchical system. In this context, the state itself promoted the creation of large companies that, in practice, operated under near-monopolistic conditions. The main motivation was to revitalise the economy across the various territories of the Spanish empire. Mixed public–private capital arrangements often constrained real entrepreneurial autonomy, revealing the early tension between state guidance and market initiative (Benaul & Sánchez, 2003; Cortés-Basurto, 2008).

The structural rigidity of the Spanish economy, combined with a reliance on foreign capital, limited domestic investment capacity and technological innovation, creating a lag in industrialisation compared to other European countries (Fontana, 2002). However, even within these constraints, entrepreneurial experimentation occurred, laying the groundwork for industrial and commercial initiatives in later centuries.

With the arrival of the nineteenth century, Spain gradually industrialised, developing textile, steel, railway, and mining sectors. The emergence of large business corporations was closely linked to the expansion of the banking system and international trade (Del Rey-Reguillo, 2003; Fernández-Paradas & Larrinaga Rodríguez, 2021). As indicated above, both entrepreneurs and the Spanish economy were heavily dependent on foreign investment, often facilitated through concessions, monopolies, or tariffs. This "incipient capitalism" provided the framework within which companies studied in this volume—such as *Lebon et Cie* and *Hullera Vasco-Leonesa*—operated, demonstrating how foreign capital and institutional arrangements shaped entrepreneurial opportunities (Comín & Martín Aceña, 1996).

At the same time, the need to modernise led to the establishment of institutions such as the *Sociedades Económicas de Amigos del País* and the first engineering schools, though access was limited to the elite. These developments, although limited in scope, contributed to modernising education and professional formation, supporting the evolution of family businesses into more structured enterprises, some of which have persisted to the present day (Carreras & Tafunell, 2021; Maluquer de Motes, 2016).

By the early twentieth century, the Spanish business landscape had begun to show clear signs of modernisation. Spain's non-participation in World War I created opportunities for diversification into new sectors, stimulating the formulation of international networks and enhancing domestic investment opportunities (Valdaliso, 2005; Valdaliso & García, 2013). Large companies continued to rely on public capital, often complemented by private investment closely linked to the state. This growing business development was accompanied by the establishment of legal and regulatory frameworks to provide stability, encouraging further investment and facilitating interactions between banks, companies, and public authorities (Tortella & Núñez, 2021).

Following the economic devastation caused by the Civil War (1936–1939), Spain entered a period of international isolation and autarky. This context proved decisive in shaping the way entrepreneurs organised their business structures, operating within a regulated capitalist system characterised by strong state intervention, whether through nationalised or semi-public enterprises. The state sought to stimulate the economy through large strategic companies tasked with reindustrialising the country, while private entrepreneurs depended on state concessions and licences to carry out their economic activities, illustrating the persistent influence of institutional frameworks on entrepreneurial behaviour (Martín Aceña & Comín, 1991; Matés-Barco, 2023; Toboso-Sánchez, 2007).

The end of international isolation in the 1960s initiated sustained economic growth, driven by liberalisation, foreign investment, and increased mobility for private capital (Caruana et al., 2011; Del Rey-Reguillo, 2003). Entrepreneurship expanded, business associations proliferated, and Spanish firms increasingly engaged with international markets (Prados de la Escosura, 2017). The democratic transition and integration into the European Economic Community during the 1980s further opened opportunities for diversification, competition, and technological modernisation, encouraging the emergence of more competitive and innovative corporate structures (Vázquez-Fariñas, 2023).

This transformation represented a challenge for some companies, while at the same time it stimulated the strengthening of large business groups. It also promoted the emergence of a more competitive and technologically advanced corporate structure, capable of adapting its processes to innovation. Public Administration encouraged entrepreneurship and facilitated access to knowledge through the creation of new universities and technology parks (Tortella & García Ruiz, 2013).

Since the beginning of the twenty-first century, Spain's business ecosystem has reached a level comparable to other European economies, benefiting from harmonised European regulations and directives. Entrepreneurs have remained committed to innovation and digitalisation, while also integrating social responsibility and sustainability into corporate strategy (García-Tabuenca et al., 2012). The evolution of Spanish companies demonstrates the persistent interaction between private initiative and public policy, showing how entrepreneurial agency, institutional frameworks, and international exposure collectively shape long-term economic outcomes.

To illustrate these processes, Table 1 summarises the principal economic trends and business dynamics in Spain from the sixteenth century to the present. It combines long-term GDP and industrial output series with contextual information on dominant sectors, foreign investment, and institutional patterns.

In addition, the following timeline (Fig. 1) provides a synthetic overview of the main economic, institutional, and entrepreneurial transformations that frame the

Table 1 Key economic indicators and trends in Spanish business history

Century	GDP growth	Industrial output	Major sectors	Foreign investment	Notes
Sixteenth–seventeenth	Low, subsistence economy	Minimal	Agrarian	Limited	Mercantilist crown control
Eighteenth	Moderate	Textile, grain	Textile, steel, urban trade	Emerging	Expansion of *pósitos*, proto-industrialisation
Nineteenth	Moderate–high	Mining, textiles, railways	Textiles, coal, steel, transport, banking	Increasing	Industrialisation with foreign capital
Twentieth (pre-1936)	High	Steel, energy, services	Mining, steel, energy	Moderate–high	Diversification, banking growth
1939–1959	Low	Strategic industries	Construction, energy	Limited	Autarky, state intervention
1960–1975	High	Tourism, services, manufacturing	Tourism, manufacturing, energy	High	Liberalisation, industrial growth
1980–2000	Moderate–high	Modern industries	Technology, services, construction	High	EU integration, digitalisation
2000+	Moderate	Digital economy	Services, technology, finance	High	Corporate social responsibility

Source: authors' elaboration based on Carreras & Tafunell (2021); Comín & Martín Aceña (1997); Hernández-Barahona et al. (2025); Maluquer de Motes (2016); Prados de la Escosura (2017); Tortella & García Ruiz (2013); Vázquez-Fariñas 2023

1500–1700 | Imperial economy and mercantilist regulation

- Expansion of overseas trade and crown monopolies; early manufacturing guilds; limited private entrepreneurship.

1700–1800 | Reform and proto-industrialisation

- Bourbon reforms; creation of commercial companies; beginnings of modern credit institutions.

1800–1850 | Liberal revolution and early industrialisation

- Abolition of guilds; emergence of private banks and railway companies; first large-scale mining ventures.

1850–1914 | Integration into global capitalism

- Expansion of steel, textile, and energy sectors; rise of family firms and foreign investment; professionalisation of management.

1914–1939 | War, crisis, and restructuring

- Economic nationalism; emergence of state-owned enterprises; diversification into new industries such as chemicals and electricity.

1939–1959 | Autarky and reconstruction

- State intervention through INI; limited foreign trade; persistence of family ownership.

1960–1975 | Developmentalism and modernisation

- Economic liberalisation; tourism and services boom; expansion of multinational subsidiaries.

1975–2000 | Democracy, European integration, and globalisation

- Privatisation of public firms; financial modernisation; internationalisation of Spanish corporations.

2000–2025 | Digital transformation and sustainability

- Rise of technology firms; new entrepreneurial ecosystems; growing emphasis on corporate social responsibility and green innovation.

Fig. 1 Chronological timeline of key milestones in Spanish business and economic history (1500–2025). Source: authors' elaboration based on Carreras & Tafunell (2021); Maluquer de Motes (2016); Prados de la Escosura (2017); Tortella & García Ruiz (2013)

case studies analysed in this volume. It is designed to help readers visualise long-term continuities and ruptures and to facilitate cross-chapter comparisons.

The chapters in this volume illustrate these broader historical dynamics through specific cases across sectors, regions, and periods (Table 2). The study of the *pósitos* (Chap. 2) shows how pre-industrial institutional frameworks constrained and

Table 2 Chapters' organisation

Chapter	Sector / case	Period	Key theme	Contribution to volume
2	*Pósitos*	Sixteenth–nineteenth c.	Public–private dynamics	Early institutional entrepreneurship
3	Antequera bourgeoisie	1835–1836	Emergence of local entrepreneurs	Microhistorical perspective on liberal reforms
4	*Lebon et Cie.*	1841–1925	Foreign investment	Role of multinationals in industrialisation
5	*Hullera Vasco-Leonesa*	Nineteenth–twentieth c.	Industrial growth, family business	Resilience and adaptation in mining
6	*Heredia steel*	Nineteenth c.	Family entrepreneurship	Long-term industrial projects and decline
7	Calvo-Sotelo	Twentieth c.	Executive–politician interface	Technocratic leadership and policy impact
8	Hotels	Twentieth c.	Services sector, modernisation	Hospitality and tourism entrepreneurship
9	Pedro Durán Farell	1950–1970	Energy sector, governance	Managerial innovation and individual agency
10	*Construcciones Calderón*	1949–2020	Construction sector	Intergenerational adaptation, sustainability challenges

Source: authors' elaboration based on the contents of the volume

channelled entrepreneurial behaviour, highlighting state–private collaboration and market regulation. Analysis of the bourgeoisie in Antequera (Chap. 3) highlights the micro-level impact of liberal reforms and property transitions on local entrepreneurship, thus showing localised entrepreneurial emergence within political transformations. Industrial sector of the nineteenth century (Chaps. 4, 5 and 6) exemplifies the role of foreign capital, family firms, and managerial expertise in mediating technological and market changes. Cases of business–politics interaction (Chap. 7) and services and modernisation (Chaps. 8, 9 and 10) demonstrate how companies navigated regulatory environments, globalisation, and sectoral innovation in the twentieth century, examining the diversification of business activities, the emergence of technocratic elites, and the adaptation of traditional companies to global markets. This structure not only ensures internal coherence but also reflects the historiographical evolution of Spanish business history—from the study of institutions and industries to that of management, entrepreneurship, and innovation. Although each chapter focuses on specific cases, together they illustrate patterns of entrepreneurship, institutional interaction, and sectoral evolution across Spanish history.

In addition, taken together, these chapters illustrate the interconnectedness of entrepreneurial initiative, institutional contexts, and structural economic transformations, providing readers with a multi-scalar perspective that links individual agency with broader historical and economic trends. By situating each case within its period-specific structural and institutional context, the volume fosters a deeper understanding of the complexity, continuity, and change that characterise Spanish business history.

Beyond the historical contextualisation, this section also reinforces the comparative and methodological coherence of the volume. The chapters share a common analytical approach that integrates qualitative and quantitative methods, comparative historical analysis, and biographical reconstruction. Together, they allow for cross-sectoral and cross-regional comparisons of entrepreneurial behaviour and institutional adaptation. In addition, to enhance the pedagogical dimension and accessibility of the book, visual aids such as timelines, maps, and summary tables have been incorporated throughout the chapters. These elements support teaching and facilitate the understanding of complex historical and economic transformations for academic and general audiences alike.

All in all, this collective volume contributes to recent historiographical debates in several ways. First, it reinforces the idea that Spanish business history cannot be understood in isolation from its European context. The circulation of capital, technology, and managerial ideas demonstrates the permeability of Spanish capitalism and its interaction with international dynamics.

Second, it challenges traditional narratives that emphasise backwardness or dependency, showing instead a more nuanced picture of adaptation, learning, and selective modernisation.

Third, by incorporating microhistorical and biographical approaches, the book reintroduces the individual entrepreneur as a key analytical unit, without neglecting structural and institutional factors. This dialogue between the personal and the systemic allows for a richer understanding of how business practices evolve across time.

Finally, the volume opens new methodological and comparative perspectives, encouraging future research to link business history with political economy, sociology, and innovation studies.

4 Conclusions

At present, there is a growing interest in understanding the structural roots of the Spanish economy and the evolution of its entrepreneurial actors. This book fills historiographical gaps by integrating diverse cases, regional approaches, and a comparative perspective spanning more than two centuries, while reflecting the context of each period. Its collective nature—with contributions from both established specialists and new generations of researchers—ensures academic rigour and a plurality of perspectives.

From a methodological standpoint, this volume is grounded in a qualitative and descriptive approach based on historical research methods applied to the study of companies. Work with primary documentary sources (business, notarial, administrative, and press archives), combined with a critical review of specialised literature, makes it possible to reconstruct processes of formation, consolidation, and crisis of different firms. A structured analytical strategy has been followed in several phases:

gathering and selecting information; critically examining data; comparing cases; and formulating conclusions that transcend the particular to offer interpretations of broader significance.

The adopted perspective seeks, on the one hand, to contextualise each company within its economic, political, and social environment, and on the other, to highlight the interaction between individual actors (entrepreneurs, families, managers) and collective institutions (markets, the state, foreign capital). This approach enables us to observe how business decisions were shaped by regulatory frameworks, political circumstances, and technological transformations, while also recognising the active role entrepreneurs themselves played in shaping those contexts.

It should be noted that the cases analysed here are not intended to constitute an exhaustive compendium of Spanish business history. Rather, their selection responds to criteria of representativeness and historical significance: each chapter sheds light on a sector, a region, or a specific issue which, taken together, contribute to reconstructing a broader picture. This approach allows for the identification of recurring patterns—such as the importance of family capital, the influence of foreign investment, state intervention, and the persistence of traditional institutions—and places them in dialogue with experiences from other countries, thereby endowing the work with a valuable comparative dimension.

Through the analysis of real Spanish companies across different regions, sectors, and historical moments, this book illustrates how general frameworks previously outlined are made concrete, diverge, or transform into specific business realities. This linkage between the general and the particular provides an interpretative map that facilitates a deeper assessment of the companies and entrepreneurs examined throughout the volume.

Therefore, the historiographical contribution of this work lies in building bridges between business history and economic history, linking case studies with the macroeconomic and political dynamics of over two centuries. At the same time, it proposes a methodological framework that can be replicated in other sectoral or geographical contexts. Its interdisciplinary nature—engaging in dialogue with economics, sociology, management, and cultural history—enriches interpretation and repositions business studies as a key tool for understanding long-term economic and social change. In doing so, the volume not only synthesises previous findings but also introduces new empirical evidence and methodological perspectives that expand the boundaries of Spanish and European business history.

In this way, the work offers not only a collection of case studies but also a historiographical reflection that underscores the relevance of entrepreneurship as a historical agent. At the same time, it invites readers to rethink traditional narratives of Spanish backwardness by highlighting the diversity of trajectories and the adaptive capacity that characterised economic actors.

Finally, the conclusions drawn in this introductory chapter set the stage for the analyses developed in the following contributions. Each case study deepens one of the thematic or chronological lines introduced here—from early modern grain banks to twentieth-century energy and construction firms—illustrating the diversity of entrepreneurial responses to institutional and technological change. The coherence among chapters, despite their variety, lies in the shared goal of understanding how business actors have contributed to shaping Spain's economic modernisation.

Building on these historical analyses, the volume also offers insights that are highly relevant to contemporary economic and business challenges. Several of the long-term patterns identified in the chapters—such as the interaction between state and market, the importance of technological adoption, the role of family capital, and the capacity of firms to reorganise in moments of crisis—resonate strongly with current debates on the energy transition, digitalisation, artificial intelligence, and the pursuit of sustainable business models. Understanding how past entrepreneurs navigated institutional uncertainty, technological shifts, and global competition offers valuable lessons for analysing the structural transformations currently reshaping the Spanish and European economies.

In this way, this book not only broadens knowledge about the companies analysed but also invites reflection on the role of private initiative in economic modernisation and in the construction of historical memory. Through representative cases, comparative approaches, and solid methodological grounding, it offers readers a valuable resource for both academic and general audiences, on the conviction that understanding the history of companies and entrepreneurs is also to understand the foundations upon which our present rests and our future is projected. It is therefore intended not only for scholars and students of business and economic history but also for professionals, policymakers, and readers interested in understanding the historical foundations of Spain's economic transformation.

5 Competing Interests

The authors have no conflicts of interest to declare that are relevant to the content of this chapter.

References

Benaul, J. M., & Sánchez, A. (2003). El legado industrial del Antiguo Régimen. En *VII Encuentro de Didáctica de la Historia Económica* (pp. 1–44). Retrieved August 22, 2025, from https://epub.sub.uni-hamburg.de/epub/volltexte/2009/2091/pdf/S15.pdf

Carreras, A., & Tafunell, X. (2021). *Between Empire and Globalization: An Economic History of Modern Spain*. Palgrave Macmillan. https://doi.org/10.1007/978-3-030-60504-9

Caruana, L., Larrinaga, C., & Matés-Barco, J. M. (2011). La pequeña y mediana empresa en la edad de oro de la economía española: estado de la cuestión. *Investigaciones de Historia Económica, 7*, 322–333. https://doi.org/10.1016/j.ihe.2010.10.001

Comín, F., & Martín Aceña, P. (1996). *La empresa en la historia de España*. Civitas.

Comín, F., & Martín Aceña, P. (1997). La empresa en la Historia de España. *Revista de Historia Económica / Journal of Iberian and Latin American Economic History, 15*(1), 221–223. https://doi.org/10.1017/S0212610900006443

Cortés-Basurto, M. Á. (2008). Reseñas. Ma. del Pilar Martínez López-Cano y Leonor Ludlow (coords.), Historia del pensamiento económico: del mercantilismo al liberalismo, México, IIH-UNAM/Instituto Mora, 2007. *América Latina en la Historia Económica, 30*, 191–202.
Del Rey-Reguillo, F. (2003). La historia empresarial y la historia política en la España contemporánea. *Ayer, 50*, 333–353.
Fernández-Paradas, M., & Larrinaga Rodríguez, C. (2021). *Business History in Spain (19th and 20th centuries)*. Peter Lang. https://doi.org/10.3726/b17988
Fontana, J. (2002). *La quiebra de la monarquía absoluta (1814–1820)*. Crítica.
García-Tabuenca, A., Crespo, J. L., Pablo, F., & Crecente, F. (2012). *Empresas y empresarios en España en la primera década del siglo XXI*. Marcial Pons.
Hernández-Barahona, J., Gil-López, Á., & San Román, E. (2025). Entrepreneurship capital in Spain and its impact on modern economic growth (1886–2000). *Revista de Historia Económica—Journal of Iberian and Latin American Economic History, 43*(1), 1–26. https://doi.org/10.1017/S0212610925100670
Maluquer de Motes, J. (2016). *España en la economía mundial: Series largas para la economía española (1850–2015)*. Instituto de Estudios Económicos.
Martín Aceña, P., & Comín, F. (1991). INI. 50 años de Industrialización en España. *Revista de Economía*, 11.
Matés-Barco, J. M. (2023). La economía en la etapa de la dictadura (1939–1975). In L. Garrido González & M. Castro-Valdivia (Eds.), *España (1923–2023): un siglo de economía* (pp. 85–158). Marcial Pons. https://doi.org/10.2307/jj.4908201.4
Matés-Barco, J. M., & Caruana de las Cagigas, L. (2021). *Entrepreneurship in Spain: A History*. Routledge. https://doi.org/10.4324/9781003126973
Prados de la Escosura, L. (2017). *Spanish Economic Growth, 1850–2015*. Palgrave Studies in Economic History. https://doi.org/10.1007/978-3-319-58042-5
Toboso-Sánchez, P. (2007). Empresarios y política en la dictadura de Franco. *Ayer, 66*(2), 143–173.
Tortella, G., & García Ruiz, J. L. (2013). *Spanish Money and Banking: A History*. Palgrave Macmillan. https://doi.org/10.1057/9781137317131
Tortella, G., & Núñez, C. E. (2021). *El desarrollo de la España contemporánea: historia económica de los siglos XIX y XX*. Alianza.
Valdaliso, J. M. (2005). El espíritu emprendedor en España: un análisis histórico. En Cuervo y Sastre (Coord.), *La empresa y el espíritu emprendedor de los jóvenes* (pp. 115–148). Ministerio de Educación Cultura y Deporte, Secretaría General Técnica.
Valdaliso, J. M., & García, J. L. (2013). El espíritu empresarial en la Historia Económica española. *Revista de Historia Industrial, 51*, 15–18.
Vázquez-Fariñas, M. (2023). La economía española en los inicios de la democracia (1976–1996). In L. Garrido González & M. Castro-Valdivia (Eds.), *España (1923–2023): un siglo de economía* (pp. 159–200). Marcial Pons. https://doi.org/10.2307/jj.4908201.5
Vázquez-Fariñas, M., Ortúñez-Goicolea, P. P., & Castro-Valdivia, M. (2021). Preface. In M. Vázquez-Fariñas, P. P. Ortúñez-Goicolea, & M. Castro-Valdivia (Eds.), *Companies and Entrepreneurs in the History of Spain: Centuries Long Evolution in Business since the 15th century* (pp. V–VIII). Palgrave Macmillan. https://doi.org/10.1007/978-3-030-61318-1

María Vázquez-Fariñas is a Lecturer in History and Economic Institutions at the University of Málaga, having previously taught at the universities of Jaén and Cádiz. She holds a degree in Business Administration and a PhD in Social and Legal Sciences from the University of Cádiz. Her research focuses on contemporary public services and networked companies in Spain, and in the nineteenth-century Cádiz, including the wine industry, trade, the port, and slavery. She has published extensively in national and international journals and with prestigious publishers such as Brill, Routledge, Palgrave, and Springer. She has participated in numerous international projects, conferences, research initiatives, and editorial and scientific committees.

Francisco Cabrera-Gallardo is an Interim Assistant Professor of History and Economic Institutions in the Department of Economics at the University of Jaén (Spain). He holds a degree in Business Administration and Management, having been awarded the Platinum Curriculum Prize by the University of Jaén. He holds a Master's Degree in Business Administration (MBA). For one year, he was a fellow at the Spanish National Research Council (CSIC). He is currently working on his doctoral thesis in the field of Economic History, in the Doctoral Program in Economics and Business at the University of Málaga.

The Spanish System of Grain Banks (Sixteenth–Nineteenth Centuries)

Rafael Barquín Gil and Pablo A. Martín-Grande

> *Do you suppose it is the same thing whether you are occupied in seeing that the corn is transferred to the granaries intact, neither injured by the dishonesty nor by the negligence of those who bring it, so that it be not harmed by moisture or heated, that the weight and measure be guaranteed; or whether you apply yourself to those sacred and elevated studies?*
>
> *Seneca, De Brevitate Vitae (On the Shortness of Life)*

Abstract This chapter analyses the functioning and evolution of the *pósitos*, the system of grain banks in Spain from the sixteenth to the nineteenth centuries. It examines the economic logic of storage and cereal speculation, distinguishing between short- and long-term operations, and assessing their profitability through econometric models and price data. The study explores the development of *pósitos* as municipal public institutions, designed both to support farmers in years of poor harvests and to guarantee affordable urban food supplies. Although they expanded significantly during the eighteenth century, their profitability was constrained by state regulation, price ceilings, and restrictions on private trade. Their final decline, accelerated by agricultural crises and wars, transformed the *pósitos* into primarily charitable rather than economic entities, revealing the limited success of the system.

R. Barquín Gil
Applied Economics and Economic History, National University of Distance Education (UNED), Madrid, Spain
e-mail: rbarquin@cee.uned.es

P. A. Martín-Grande (✉)
Applied Economics I and History and Economic Institutions, King Juan Carlos University (URJC), Madrid, Spain
e-mail: pablo.martin.grande@urjc.es

M. Vázquez-Fariñas, F. Cabrera-Gallardo (eds.), *Business Trajectories in the History of Spain*, Frontiers in Economic History,
https://doi.org/10.1007/978-3-032-16214-4_2

1 Background

One of the main reasons why cereals such as wheat, barley, corn, and rice have served as staples of the human diet is their storability. These grains can be preserved for a certain period in silos and granaries, whose construction and maintenance involve relatively low costs. In the past, farmers themselves stored their harvests in handmade pits dug into the ground (Valls et al., 2015), or in stone, brick, or wooden structures that offered some protection from rain, as well as from insects, birds, and rodents (Kaplan, 1996, pp. 356 and 562). There were simple techniques for keeping the grain in good condition, but nothing particularly sophisticated. In the short term (less than a year), if basic precautions were taken, losses were minimal (Kaplan, 1984, pp. 67–79).

Wheat must be processed into flour to be consumed, but flour deteriorates much more quickly than grain. This fact influences the location of certain economic activities. A granary can be built almost anywhere, whereas a bakery should be located close to a mill. Although flour takes up less space than the wheat it comes from, it suffers considerable losses during transport. For that reason, transporting grain was more economical than transporting flour, at least until the development of the railroad.

As in any economic activity, there are basic principles that cannot be ignored. The most important of these is that prices in free markets serve as useful signals for producers and consumers (Hayek, 1945). However, governments have often felt a moral obligation to protect the supply chains of cereals and other essential goods. As a result, grain markets were never entirely free and were consistently subject to regulation and oversight by doctrinal authorities, especially during times of scarcity, which tended to affect poor families most severely.

Since the Middle Ages, Europe has developed an extensive body of interventionist legislation, whose effectiveness has often been questionable. In Spain, a network of public grain storage facilities known as *Sistema de Pósitos* was also established. This study describes how that system operated and analyses its evolution from the mid-eighteenth to the mid-nineteenth century.

2 Speculation in the Long Run

Grain spoilage does not follow a linear pattern. In general, wheat can be stored between harvests with minimal losses. Under favourable climatic conditions, particularly in dry environments, where humidity is the main cause of deterioration, losses in both quantity and quality typically remain below 5% over a period of less than 1 year (Manandhar et al., 2018). However, when storage conditions are inadequate, these losses can increase significantly, reaching as high as 20% or even 30% during the period studied in this chapter.

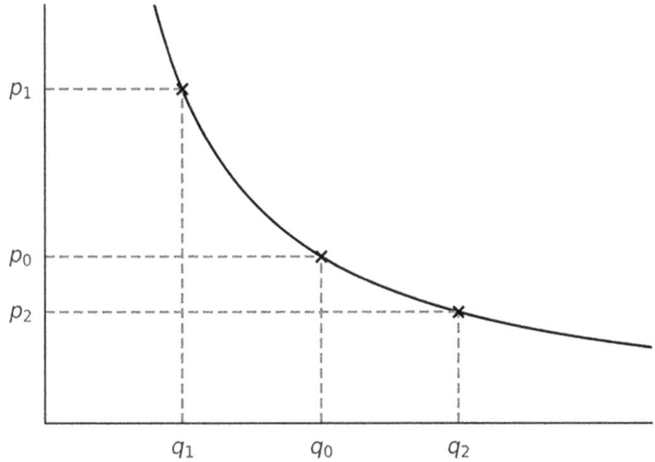

Fig. 1 Demand curve for the wheat market. Source: author's own elaboration

This reality sets clear limits on the feasibility of long-term speculation in grain markets. Although some portions of stored grain may carry over into the following year, such volumes are generally small. As will be discussed in the following section, business activities aimed at long-term grain speculation involve high levels of risk and, in practice, prove unviable.

Any speculative activity must operate on a demand function with inelastic price elasticity, so that in bad years the speculator's gain outweighs the loss incurred in good years. Several studies on cereal markets in Europe (Barquín, 2005; Parenti, 1942; Persson, 1993) and with a specific focus on Spain (Barquín, 2011) estimate the price elasticity of demand for grain in the pre-industrial period at approximately −0.65. Based on this evidence, it is reasonable to assume a demand curve for wheat with constant price elasticity of less than 1, as follows:

$$Q = AP^{\varepsilon}$$

where Q is quantity, P is price, A is a constant, and $\mathcal{E}$ represents the price elasticity of demand (less than 1 and negative, given the inverse relationship between price and quantity). Figure 1 provides a graphical representation of a function with these characteristics.

In this scenario, it can be assumed that a wheat speculator's storage facility can only hold a small fraction of the total production in the municipality. The speculator acts as a price taker and does not influence market prices.

During years of poor harvests, the price of wheat would rise to p_1, while in years of good harvests, it would fall to p_2. The speculator's profit would depend on whether the gains made during years of scarcity (when prices are high) exceed the losses incurred during years of abundance (when prices are low). That is:

$$p_1 - p_0 > p_0 - p_2$$

However, operating costs and losses due to grain shrinkage or spoilage must also be considered. Therefore, the profit (or loss) from the speculator's activity would be given by:

$$B = q_0\left[\left(p_1 - p_0\right) - \left(p_0 - p_2\right) - G\right] - q_0^{dt}$$

$$B = q_0\left[p_1 + p_2 - 2p_0 - G\right] - q_0^{dt}$$

In this expression, B represents the profit from the business, q_0 is the quantity of wheat stored, G stands for operating costs, d is the deterioration coefficient, and t is the time elapsed between storage and sale. It is assumed that both operating costs and shrinkage losses are proportional to the amount stored. However, storage loss also increases over time and follows an exponential function: $m = q_0^{dt}$.

While poor harvest years may require the speculator to invest more in grain protection, such additional costs are relatively minor within the overall operating expenses and can be disregarded. In contrast, shrinkage cannot be ignored, as it is primarily time-dependent and grows exponentially.

Taking a hypothetical example of a locality where the wheat harvest fluctuates by 10% up or down in alternating years, and assuming a price elasticity of demand of −0.65, the gross return on long-term speculation would be around 4%. However, once storage shrinkage, which increases sharply after 1 year, and custody costs are taken into account, it becomes virtually impossible for such an operation to yield a net profit.

In smaller regional markets, especially in southern Spain where harvests tend to be more irregular, speculative gains might be possible, although they would rarely be substantial. In any case, short-term speculative operations would offer higher returns with significantly lower risk. For this reason, a grain speculator would be compelled to act in the short term, given both the high risks associated with long-term storage and the comparative advantages of short-term strategies.

3 Speculation in the Short Run

Unlike long-term speculation, short-term speculation in the grain market could be considered relatively safe. Each year, the arrival of the new harvest in July and August caused a noticeable drop in grain prices. However, from September or October onwards, prices would start to rise again, reaching their peak between May and June of the following year.

This seasonal pattern made it possible to engage in low-risk speculative activity over a short period (of roughly 10 months). The strategy was simple: purchase grain after the harvest; when prices were low, and sell it before the next harvest, when prices were at their highest.

In principle, if the wheat market met even basic conditions of competition, the price difference between June and September would roughly correspond to the costs involved in speculative activity. Under those conditions, there would be no extraordinary profit; instead, the return earned by the grain trader-speculator would be similar to that of any standard economic activity.

Of course, such ideal market conditions did not always exist. Nevertheless, the more developed the market, the greater the opportunities for arbitrage and the lower the likelihood of extraordinary gains. In such cases, speculators would lack market power and would not benefit from advantages related to geographic location or other specific circumstances.

This approach forms the basis of the work by McCloskey and Nash (1984), who aimed to estimate what the basic interest rate might have been in mediaeval England. At that time, short-term speculation with wheat was likely the most common commercial activity, as the majority of the population depended on agriculture, particularly peasants who cultivated cereals. Throughout Europe, there were thousands of retail grain markets and numerous intermediaries, both private and institutional. Therefore, speculation took place in a broad, diverse, and deep market.

This activity was not without risk. Beyond potential physical damage to the grain or storage facilities, there was uncertainty over whether prices would follow seasonal expectations. No business is free from risk, and the essence of grain storage and speculation lies precisely in managing that risk. The peasant selling the grain transferred part of this risk to the trader in exchange for a lower price than could have been obtained by selling directly. This assumed risk constitutes what is commonly understood as entrepreneurial profit.

For McCloskey and Nash (1984), the profit derived from wheat storage and speculation can be seen as an estimate of the general or basic interest rate in a mediaeval agrarian economy. In modern terms, this would be the expected return on a very safe investment, and thus one with low profitability, such as government bonds.

Indeed, no other commercial activity could match wheat speculation in volume, scope, or number of participants, as wheat was the main product traded. The cost of this activity was the capital invested, including the purchase, maintenance, and custody of the grain, as well as the depreciation of the storage facility. From another perspective, this investment was safer than any other industrial or commercial project.

One of the central points in McCloskey & Nash's argument is the assumption of a reasonably free market. For a speculator's profit not to be considered "extraordinary" and to approximate a basic rate of return, it is essential that the speculator lacks market power. While certain circumstances might allow for such power, this seems unlikely.

The wheat market had structural features that made it difficult for any single actor to dominate. First, the homogeneity of the product—a classic condition of a free market—was a key factor. Despite the many local varieties of wheat, their prices remained in a relatively stable proportion to those of higher-quality wheat.

Farmers could also easily switch from one variety to another, which meant that no product monopoly existed, nor was one conceivable.

Second, wheat production operated in highly atomized markets. In Western Europe, large estates were rare due to their high management costs, and most producers were smallholders with no capacity to influence even local prices. Large landholdings were more common in Eastern and Southern Europe (regions that were less populated and more recently settled) but even there, it is unclear whether those producers operated under monopoly conditions.

Moreover, although most peasants were subject to various obligations, such as tithes and feudal rents, which diverted part of their output to privileged classes, there is no evidence that these elites acted in a coordinated or collusive way to control prices.

In general, aside from the darkest periods of the Middle Ages, economic activity was not restricted by significant entry barriers. In practice, the only factor capable of sustaining a monopoly was the high cost of transportation (Madrazo, 1984), which limited the geographical scope of markets and enabled local dominance.

Even so, this local power was vulnerable during periods of scarcity. Rising prices expanded the effective reach of the market. High-value goods such as Baltic amber could be transported as far as Rome because their high price per unit of weight made shipping costs negligible. In contrast, cheaper staples such as maize were rarely sold outside their immediate production area. Wheat occupied a middle and variable position between these extremes. In normal years, its relatively low value limited its trade to local markets, but in years of crisis, it could travel long distances. Thus, under high-price conditions, the market expanded, and the arrival of unexpected competitors could easily disrupt any local monopoly.

Lower maritime transport costs allowed coastal cities to import wheat from distant regions. This reduced costs and enabled a more consistent supply, resulting in greater price stability over time. As a result, subsistence crises were generally less severe in coastal areas than in the interior. This improved access to grain had a positive effect on both demographic growth and economic development.

This dynamic helps explain one of the apparent paradoxes of the mediaeval and early modern grain markets: the countries with the highest wheat prices (England and the Netherlands) were also those least affected by subsistence crises (Abel, 1973; Martínez González, 2016; Persson, 1999). By contrast, Spain may represent the opposite case, as will be explored below.

4 Calculating the Profitability of a Storage and Speculation Business

Assuming a homogeneous and fragmented structure of wheat production and trade, along with a degree of spatial market integration, it is possible to analyse the profitability of a business dedicated to storage and speculation. McCloskey and Nash (1984) propose a model in which the value of stored grain changes over time according to the interest rate and storage costs. The price evolution follows this equation:

$$P_t = P_0 e^{(r+m+G)t}$$

P_t represents the price of grain at a later time t, P_0 is the initial purchase price, r is the annual interest rate (that is, the opportunity cost of capital), m is the rate of physical depreciation (losses due to spoilage or shrinkage), and G refers to the physical storage costs, including infrastructure, labour, and security.

This model shows that speculative profit depends on the difference between the selling price after storage and the initial purchase price, minus the associated costs. To estimate the implicit interest rate, we apply the natural logarithm to both sides and isolate r:

$$\ln P_t = \ln P_0 + (r+m+G) \bullet t$$

$$r+m+G = \frac{(\ln P_t - \ln P_0)}{t}$$

$$r = \frac{\ln P_t - \ln P_0}{t} - (m+G)$$

Alternatively, using the relative change in price instead of the logarithmic form, the general profitability equation can be written as:

$$R = \frac{P_t - P_0}{P_0} - (m+G)$$

Here, $(P_t - P_0)/P_0$ measures the percentage change in the price of wheat from the time of purchase to the time of sale. This reflects the potential gain from price appreciation, while $m + G$ accounts for the reduction in profit due to storage-related losses and costs.

It is important to note that the depreciation rate m is substantially lower in short-term speculation, since spoilage increases exponentially over time, and the storage period here is relatively brief.

In a market where grain traders are price-takers, speculation is only viable if the interest rate is high enough to offset both the physical deterioration of the grain and the storage costs. According to McCloskey and Nash (1984), the high-price volatility in mediaeval England and the evidence of low interannual carryover (which, as addressed earlier in this text, seems plausible) suggest that grain storage involved annual costs ranging from 27% to 43%. This points to an economy highly dependent on immediate consumption and characterised by high interest rates.

Under such conditions, mediaeval grain markets would have been relatively inefficient due to the limited capacity to store surpluses and the resulting inability to smooth out price fluctuations.

However, this thesis has been challenged by several scholars, with Brunt and Cannon (1999) providing an alternative econometric analysis that lowered the estimated mediaeval interest rate to around 12% per year. Their findings suggest that grain storage was not as costly as McCloskey & Nash had proposed, and that cereal markets were more stable than previously assumed.

Gregory Clark (2015) expanded on this critique, arguing that mediaeval grain markets were far more efficient than traditionally believed. Using an expanded dataset of wheat prices from 227 English towns, he claimed that markets were both spatially and temporally integrated. According to Clark, within-year price variations reflected combined storage costs and interest rates ranging from 10% to 15%.

In the case of pre-industrial Spain, the profitability of speculative operations in the wheat market can be estimated using available historical price data (Barquín, 2001). Following the logic outlined above, a suitable approach is to measure the difference between the prices in May/June and those in August/September, relative to the initial purchase price. This can be expressed mathematically as follows:

$$R = \frac{P_{May/June} - P_{August/September}}{P_{August/September}} - (m + G)$$

Given that only short-term speculation is considered viable, the average prices in May and June (typically the annual peak before the new harvest) are taken as reference for the selling point, while the average prices in August and September (following the previous harvest) represent the purchase point. This approach models a hypothetical speculative cycle lasting approximately ten months.

In this context, $P_{May/June}$ is the average of the May and June prices (the seasonal peak), while $P_{August/September}$ represents the average of August and September prices (the post-harvest dip). The result of this first calculation, the Theoretical Maximum Return (TMR), is then adjusted by subtracting grain losses and operating costs.

$$R = TMR - m - G$$

Applying the previously described model to the available data for late eighteenth-century Spain yields the following results (Table 1):

At first glance, the Theoretical Maximum Return (*TMR*) in these cities ranged from 10% to 14%, except in Pamplona, where it exceeded 20%. The overall average was approximately 13.7%. To estimate the net return (*R*), this percentage must be adjusted by subtracting the estimated costs of operation (*G*) and spoilage (*m*). In any case, these figures differ significantly from those reported by McCloskey and Nash (1984) and are more consistent with the scenarios proposed by Brunt and Cannon

Table 1 Rates of return and average prices in Spain (1765–1793)

	Barcelona	Gerona	Pamplona	Rioseco	Tárrega	Tolosa	Average
TMR	13.64%	10.80%	20.86%	12.45%	11.94%	12.36%	13.68%
Price (ptas/hl)	22.30	20.94	13.97	12.04	19.37	20.29	18.15

Source: prepared internally based on data from Barquín (2001)

(1999) and Clark (2015). They also suggest a competitive performance in local grain markets.

5 A Historical Analysis of Public Grain Banks in Spain

The previous four sections provide the conceptual framework for examining one of the most remarkable institutions in European history: the public grain banks, or *pósitos*. These were municipal grain storehouses operated by local officials and designed to fulfil a dual purpose. On the one hand, they provided grain loans to farmers facing hardship, whether due to a poor harvest or the loss of seed. On the other, they served as a safeguard for the community by offering grain at affordable prices during times of scarcity. In this sense, the *pósitos* functioned both as banks and as instruments of market regulation: public institutions that aimed to offer relief in times of need while also generating enough revenue to sustain their operations.

Although they were particularly prevalent in Spain, *pósitos* were not unique to this country. Similar institutions emerged across Europe, especially during the late Middle Ages and the early modern period. Public grain storage played an important role in certain centralised and militarised states such as Sweden and Prussia, as well as in Portugal and some parts of southern Italy. However, from the sixteenth century onwards, the liberalisation of grain markets in England led to their gradual decline. Later, as mercantilist policies gave way to more liberal economic doctrines, grain banks fell into disuse in much of Europe.

In Spain, public grain banks eventually followed the same path of decline as elsewhere in Europe, albeit under very different circumstances (Escrivá & Llopis, 1987, p. 112). Far from being a time of crisis, the second half of the eighteenth century marked a period of significant growth for Spanish grain banks. In 1751, the creation of the *Superintendencia General de Pósitos* (General Superintendency of Grain Banks) sparked a major expansion in both the number of banks and the volume of grain they held. The previous system of local management had left too much room for corruption, and the new oversight brought greater administrative order, which was welcomed by local authorities.

It is important to note that the *pósitos* remained independent institutions under municipal control. While historians often refer to them as a "system", this term mainly reflects the shared administrative guidelines that shaped their operations. It does not imply centralised ownership or coordination. In practice, there was never anything resembling a unified, interconnected network of grain banks.

Table 2 presents figures from various surveys and audits carried out between the mid-eighteenth and mid-nineteenth centuries. The term "funds" refers to two main components: grain or cash physically held in the grain banks, and outstanding loans. These figures have no equivalent elsewhere in Europe. At their peak, around 1790–1800, Spanish grain banks may have handled as much as a quarter of the country's total wheat harvest (Anes Álvarez, 1970, pp. 149–151; Moral Ruiz, 1975, p. 48). Given that at least half of agricultural production was reserved for peasant

Table 2 Evolution of royal granaries and their funds (1751–1850)

Year	Number	Funds in wheat	Funds in money	Wheat/*Pósito*	Money/*Pósito*
1751	3751	1,994,000		531.59	
1773	5225	3,667,000	10,584,000	701.82	2026
1793	5521	4,886,000		884.98	
1800	5151	5,166,000	13,600,000	1002.91	2640
1803	5208				
1850	3410	2,288,000	6,947,000	670.97	2037
1863	3308	1,288,000	6,847,000	389.36	2070

Source: prepared internally based on data from Anes Álvarez (1969) and Carasa Soto (1983)
Note: Neither *pósitos píos* (grain reserves) nor funds for "minor grains" (barley, corn, rye, etc.) are included. Wheat funds are in hl and money funds are in pesetas

self-consumption, this suggests that *pósitos* may have managed most of the wheat sold in Spain. However, since each grain bank operated independently, this cannot be considered a monopoly.

Between 1753 and 1800, the expansion of public grain banks in Spain can be divided into two phases. Until 1773, both the number of grain banks and the size of their funds grew significantly; however, the growth in funds was even greater (Giménez López & Martínez Gomis, 1993). Afterwards, the number of grain banks stabilised and even slightly declined by 1800, while their funds continued to grow. Consequently, by 1800, each granary stored twice as much grain as it had 50 years earlier. This suggests that the initial momentum driven by improved administrative practices faded quickly. Nevertheless, the accumulation of funds continued for two main reasons: first, Spain experienced steady economic growth from the mid-eighteenth century onwards; second, legal restrictions on private grain speculation gave the grain banks a key role. While the buying and selling of grain were permitted, storing it for profit (known at the time as "reserve trade") was strictly prohibited. Although enforcement was likely inconsistent, the ban limited private storage and reinforced the importance of public grain banks as the main institutional channel for such activity.

In 1765, the Spanish government attempted to liberalise grain markets through a royal decree that allowed limited speculative grain trading. The aim was to stabilise prices by fostering a new class of grain merchants. However, the measure faced strong opposition from local officials, who often viewed grain traders as harmful to the public interest (Anes Álvarez, 1970, p. 351). This resistance, rooted in long-standing moral and religious prejudices, led to the repeal of the law following the agricultural crisis of 1789 (Llombart Rosa, 1992, pp. 174–176). Ironically, this was only the first of a series of increasingly severe crises, including those of 1803–1805 and 1810–1812, which were the worst in Spanish (Gómez Urdáñez & Lorenzo Cadarso, 2008, pp. 580–589) and even European history. These events revealed the structural weaknesses of a distribution system based solely on local public granaries, which highlighted the need for private interregional trade to balance market shortages.

Unlike private grain merchants, who could buy low in one region and sell high in another, *pósitos* were limited to serving their local communities, mainly by lending grain to farmers and supplying local mills and bakeries. Their restricted geographical scope prevented them from offsetting regional crop failures. Furthermore, state regulation capped their income, which derived from interest on loans ("*creces*") and grain sales. Official interest rates ranged from 4.2% to 8.3%, but actual returns were lower due to widespread defaults during poor harvests. Local authorities often forgave debts out of compassion, further reducing profitability. Sales were also constrained by state-imposed price ceilings during crises, forcing granaries to sell below market value and absorb losses. Even when controlled prices were temporarily profitable, they undermined the long-term financial sustainability of the institution.

Another source of income for the grain banks was the sale of wheat to mills, bakeries, and other local producers. As previously noted, the main difference between a *pósito* and a grain wholesaler was that the former could only benefit from seasonal price fluctuations within the local market, not from interregional price differences. Yet even within that limited scope, additional constraints applied.

In years of scarcity, the municipal council or *corregidor* could impose a legally binding *tasa*: a price ceiling on wheat, flour, or bread. As a public institution, the *pósito* was compelled to sell its reserves at that fixed price, often incurring losses. Even when the fixed price was relatively high and yielded short-term profits, it undermined long-term sustainability. Profits from crisis years were essential to offset losses incurred in more stable periods.

Figure 2 illustrates this dynamic. The price level p_1 is never reached because a *tasa* is imposed before that point, likely depleting the *pósito*'s stock. In the long term, a *pósito* might have reached break-even results or minimal profits under a scenario of inelastic demand. However, price controls eliminated access to the most

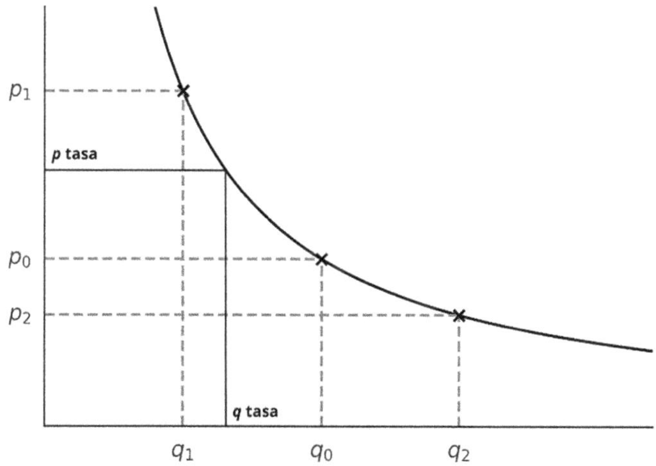

Fig. 2 Effect of *Tasa* on the wheat market demand curve. Source: author's own elaboration

favourable segments of the demand curve, ensuring that long-term profitability became negative.

Some *pósitos* specialised in lending grain, while others focused on buying and selling it. Based on limited existing research (Agüero Díez, 1997; Caro Puro et al., 2014), lending *pósitos* appear to have been typically located in agricultural areas (such as the town of Osuna), whereas those involved in grain trade operated in urban centres far from major farming zones (such as Alicante). This distinction is possible, but intermediate cases were likely more common.

In the eighteenth century, wheat was cultivated throughout most of Spain, except for the far northwest, though even there, some production remained. As a result, nearly every town or region could have needed both services: credit for farmers and supply stabilisation for consumers. This suggests an inherent trade-off in how grain reserves were used.

From the perspective of a *pósito* administrator, grain could either be lent to farmers for sowing or held for later sale during the high-price months. The return on lending ranged from approximately 4.2% to 8.3%, minus the risk of default. Based on estimates in Sect. 2.4, returns from speculative sales averaged around 13.7%, though this figure would need to be reduced to account for spoilage losses and the imposition of price ceilings during crisis years.

There were also other distorting factors. For example, in the case of Ávila: the significant growth experienced by Madrid in the eighteenth century occasionally necessitated the hoarding of grain from a wide production area. This forced local councils to seek various strategies to mitigate local shortages, including ruinous direct investments of municipal funds (Martín García, 1995, pp. 112–114).

Ultimately, it is difficult to imagine a *pósito* as a profitable enterprise. It seems more likely that only extraordinary contributions from local councils allowed them to remain operational in the long term. In years of average or good harvests, the modest returns from lending and grain sales may have been sufficient to preserve capital and prepare for the occasional bad year. Overall, the period from 1751 to 1787 could be considered favourable, or at least not adverse. However, successive poor harvests could prove catastrophic, particularly due to unpaid loans and the imposition of official price ceilings. This is precisely what happened in Spain from 1788 onwards, in repeated waves. While the number of grain banks continued to grow (mainly due to the absence of private alternatives), reports of their fragile financial situation also became increasingly frequent.

The final blow came when both the Bourbon and Napoleonic regimes failed to support the *pósitos* in their time of need. Instead, they confiscated their funds to finance the growing costs of the war with (and later under) Napoleon. On the eve of the Peninsular War, Spanish grain banks were essentially giants with feet of clay (Ruiz Martín, 1970).

What followed was, predictably, the mirror image of the earlier trajectory. During the reign of Fernando VII, reserve grain trading remained officially banned. Yet there is ample reason to believe that, after the disruption of the war and amid rising liberal sentiment among political and administrative elites, the law was more often ignored than enforced (Castro, 1987). After all, the boundary between speculation and trade is inherently blurred: all commerce involves speculation to some degree. In any case, following the death of the so-called Felon King in 1833 (or perhaps even earlier), Spain entered a period of economic liberalisation that included the legalisation of grain and flour merchants.

Although there are no precise figures for the number or volume of *pósitos* during this transitional period, it is known that by 1850, despite an agricultural output possibly twice that of 1800, only two-thirds of the *pósitos* remained, and their grain stocks had fallen to less than half their previous levels. Unsurprisingly, the demise of the *pósitos* system led to subsistence crises becoming far less severe (García Sanz, 1985). This improvement would have occurred much earlier if the trade policies of the Spanish Liberal Party governments had been truly free market (which they were not).

In any case, the *pósitos* were unable to overcome their structural decline. By the time of the next national count in 1863, both their number and grain reserves had further diminished. Faced with genuine market competition, they were increasingly reduced to functioning as charitable institutions, while still serving a minor role as local grain exchanges. Ultimately, they lost all relevance as instruments of economic regulation to the benefit of ordinary people.

6 Conclusions

Storing grain is an economic activity inseparable from its cultivation. After harvest, most cereals are stored for a significant (though not indefinite) period, as both time and climate gradually degrade their quality. In a society where agricultural production is organised through private property and free markets, it would be expected that the storage and distribution of grain follow the same principles. Given the technical constraints of the time and the seasonal nature of production and consumption cycles, grain storage would likely remain a short-term endeavour (typically within a year) and yield moderate, even modest, returns, comparable to those of any other commercial enterprise. Such activity should also contribute to greater price stability in grain markets. Under these conditions, the role of the state would be minimal or entirely absent.

This is all logical, coherent, and economically sound. But it is not history. History tells us that economic life is often structured not by markets but by power, the ultimate foundation of which is coercion in its many forms. In the eighteenth-century Spain (and much of Europe), the ideal of a fully liberalised agricultural system grounded in private property and market exchange was largely aspirational. While many peasants operated under long-term leases and sold their harvests at local markets (conditions approaching a market economy) this was far from a general rule. Non-market mechanisms for the storage and distribution of grain were common, although not always dominant. What makes the Spanish case exceptional is not the existence of these mechanisms but their sheer scale. By the end of the eighteenth century, Spain arguably had the largest public grain distribution system in Europe and one of the weakest private ones. The consequences were dire: the catastrophic famines of the early nineteenth century. As always, the poorest suffered most.

Just as predictably, low social returns coincided with low private returns. Viewed as economic enterprises, the *pósitos* were unsustainable. Part of the problem was structural: their operations were legally confined to the boundaries of the municipality, often preventing grain from reaching areas where it was most needed. Furthermore, fixed lending rates and price ceilings (the *tasa*) severely limited profit margins. But the fundamental flaw lay in a deeper contradiction: the irreconcilable tension between welfare goals and economic viability. In this context, the eventual redefinition of the *pósitos* as purely charitable institutions in the nineteenth century was not a failure, but a step in the right direction.

Competing Interests The authors have no conflicts of interest to declare that are relevant to the content of this chapter.

References

Abel, W. (1973). *Crisis agraires en Europe (XIIIe-XXe siècle)*. Flammarion.

Agüero Díez, M. T. (1997). Evolución del pósito alicantino durante el reinado de Carlos III (1759–1788). Los conflictos generados en torno al pan. *Revista De Historia Moderna, 16*, 331–352. https://doi.org/10.14198/RHM1997.16.15

Anes Álvarez, G. (1969). *Economía e Ilustración en la España del siglo XVIII*. Ariel.

Anes Álvarez, G. (1970). *Las crisis agrarias en la España moderna*. Taurus.

Barquín, R. (2001). *Precios del trigo e índices de consumo en España (1765–1883)*. Universidad de Burgos.

Barquín, R. (2005). The demand elasticity for wheat in the 14th to 18th centuries. *Revista de Historia Económica / Journal of Iberian and Latin American Economic History, 23*(2), 241–267. https://doi.org/10.1017/S0212610900011976

Barquín, R. (2011). Analysis of Spanish regional wheat prices (1765–1855). *Histoire & Mesure, 26*(2), 77–104. https://doi.org/10.4000/histoiremesure.4236

Brunt, L., & Cannon, E. (1999). *A grain of truth in medieval interest rates? Re-examining the McCloskey-Nash hypothesis*. University of Bristol.

Carasa Soto, P. (1983). Los pósitos en España en el siglo XIX. *Investigaciones Históricas, 4*, 249–304. http://uvadoc.uva.es/handle/10324/21226

Caro Puro, R., Hernández Borreguero, J., & Donoso Anes, A. (2014). Estudio normativo sobre la administración y contabilidad de los Pósitos y su aplicación al Pósito de la Villa de Osuna (1753–1763). *De computis: Revista Española de Historia de la Contabilidad, 11*(20), 116–143. https://hdl.handle.net/11441/81280

Castro, C. (1987). *El pan de Madrid*. Alianza.

Clark, G. (2015). Markets before economic growth: The grain market of medieval England. *Cliometrica. Journal of Historical Economics and Econometric History, 9*(3), 265–287. https://doi.org/10.1007/s11698-014-0117-7

Escrivá, J. L., & Llopis, E. (1987). La integración del mercado triguero en la Castilla la Vieja-León del Antiguo Régimen: avance y estancamiento. *Hacienda Pública Española, 108–109*, 117–131.

García Sanz, A. (1985). Crisis de la agricultura tradicional y revolución liberal. *Historia Agraria de la España contemporánea, 1*, 7–99.

Giménez López, E. & Martínez Gomis, M. (1993). La revitalización de los pósitos a mediados del siglo XVIII. En J. I. Fortea López & C. M. Cremades Griñán (Eds.), Política y Hacienda (pp. 285–299). Universidad de Murcia. https://doi.org/10.20350/digitalCSIC/10970
Gómez Urdáñez, J. L. & Lorenzo Cadarso, P. L. (2008). Castilla en la Edad Moderna. En J. J. García González (Dir.), *Historia de Castilla: De Atapuerca a Fuensaldaña*. La Esfera de los Libros.
Hayek, F. A. (1945). The use of knowledge in society. *The American Economic Review, 35*(4), 519–530. http://www.jstor.org/stable/1809376
Kaplan, S. L. (1984). *Provisioning Paris: Merchants and millers in the grain and flour trade during the eighteenth century*. Cornell University Press.
Kaplan, S. L. (1996). *The bakers of Paris and the bread question, 1700–1775*. Duke University Press. https://doi.org/10.1215/9780822381983
Llombart Rosa, V. (1992). *Campomanes, economista y político de Carlos III*. Alianza Universidad.
Madrazo, S. (1984). *El sistema de transportes en España*. Turner.
Manandhar, A., Milindi, P., & Shah, A. (2018). An overview of the post-harvest grain storage practices of smallholder farmers in developing countries. *Agriculture, 8*(4), 57. https://doi.org/10.3390/agriculture8040057
Martín García, G. (1995). *El Ayuntamiento de Ávila en el Siglo XVIII: La elección de los Regidores Trienales*. Diputación Provincial de Ávila.
Martínez González, J. L. (2016). Construyendo una serie física anual de trigo en Inglaterra (1645–1761): Metodología, retos y oportunidades. *Documentos de trabajo de la Asociación Española de Historia Económica, 16*.
McCloskey, D. N., & Nash, J. (1984). Corn at interest: The extent and cost of grain storage in medieval England. *American Economic Review, 74*(1), 174–187. https://www.jstor.org/stable/1803317
Moral Ruiz, J. (1975). *Hacienda y sociedad en el Trienio Constitucional 1820–1823*. Instituto de Estudios Fiscales.
Parenti, G. (1942). *Prezzi e mercato del grano a Siena 1546–1765*. C. Cya.
Persson, K. G. (1993). *Integration and deregulation of European grain markets, 1500–1900*. University of Copenhagen.
Persson, K. G. (1999). *Grain Markets in Europe, 1500–1900*. Cambridge University Press. https://doi.org/10.1017/CBO9780511527692.003
Ruiz Martín, F. (1970). La Banca en España hasta 1782. In *El Banco de España. Una historia económica* (pp. 1–196). Urgoiti Editores.
Valls, A., García, F., Ramírez, M., & Benlloch, J. (2015). Understanding subterranean grain storage heritage in the Mediterranean region: The Valencian silos (Spain). *Tunnelling and Underground Space Technology, 50*, 178–188. https://doi.org/10.1016/j.tust.2015.07.003

Rafael Barquín Gil is a Professor of Economic History at the National University of Distance Education (UNED). His research focuses on three main areas: global history, Spanish railways, and wheat markets in the early modern and modern periods. He has published widely on grain trade, speculation, and price dynamics, including studies on competition and monopoly in grain routes, the role of speculation in wheat and flour markets, and analyses of Spanish wheat prices and demand elasticity between the fourteenth and nineteenth centuries in leading international journals and academic volumes.

Pablo A. Martín-Grande is an Associate Professor of Economic History and History of Economic Thought at King Juan Carlos University, Madrid. He is a PhD candidate in the Interuniversity Doctoral Program in Economics DEcIDE, focusing on usury and the doctrines of interest. He holds a Bachelor's degree in Food Engineering and a Master's in Agricultural Economics from the Technical University of Madrid (UPM), and a Master's in Economic Research from UNED. He has published articles in peer-reviewed journals and chapters in academic books.

Entrepreneurship and Spanish Bourgeoisie at the Start of the Liberal Revolution: Study of Antequera (Málaga), 1835–1836

Antonio J. Pinto-Tortosa

Abstract This chapter analyses the emerging role of the local bourgeoisie of Antequera (Málaga) during the early stages of the liberal revolution in Spain, focusing on the years 1835–1836. It explores how certain sectors of this class began to develop entrepreneurial activities in a context of significant political and economic change, following the death of Fernando VII and the start of the confiscation process (1836–1837). I study the connections between this bourgeoisie and the new forms of property, investment, and business management. I also examine how the conflict between the *Ancien Régime* and the new liberal order affected local social and economic dynamics, having an impact on political decisions, and contributing to the emergence of power networks among businesspeople, politicians, and landowners. In the introduction, I describe the start of Isabel II's liberal monarchy in Antequera. After that, I identify the main socioeconomic actors who led the transition. Thirdly, I underline the political repercussions of the aforementioned changes. I conclude with a summary of the major achievements of the period studied. Taken together, this chapter offers a microhistory approach to the Spanish liberal revolution, which allows us to understand the processes of economic modernisation from a regional/local perspective.

A. J. Pinto-Tortosa (✉)
Department of Modern and Contemporary History, University of Málaga, Málaga, Spain
e-mail: antoniojesus.pinto@uma.es

M. Vázquez-Fariñas, F. Cabrera-Gallardo (eds.), *Business Trajectories in the History of Spain*, Frontiers in Economic History,
https://doi.org/10.1007/978-3-032-16214-4_3

1 Introduction

The end of Fernando VII's reign took 1 year to materialise, from September 1832 to October 1833. The Spanish King is not well remembered by later generations, who have used different terms to call him, all of them in a negative sense. Maybe, the most famous is «the felon king», which refers to Fernando's treason to his own people in 1823, when he called for a French invasion to finish the three-year liberal government (1820–1823) and restore his absolute, uncontrolled power over the kingdom. The last 10 years of his reign, between 1823 and 1833, have been defined by Spanish historiography in a pejorative sense: «the ominous decade», referring to his acts to extinguish any attempt to favour the installation of liberalism in the country. In the process, such disgraceful episodes as the execution of Mariana Pineda, and of General José María Torrijos, both in 1831, have been used as examples of the King's intentions to guarantee the prolongation of absolutism after he was gone (Castells, 2000, pp. 73–98; Serrano, 2000, pp. 99–126).

Despite his severe attitude towards liberalism, Fernando VII knew that changes were necessary in Spain, and he surrounded himself with advisors who helped him modernise the country, up to certain limits. The latter persuaded him that he needed to guarantee the succession of his daughter, Princess Isabel, born in March 1830: as the Salic law ruled the country, the alternative was the succession by the King's brother, Prince Carlos María Isidro, ultra-catholic and defender of the *Ancien Régime*. That is why Fernando approved the Pragmática Sanción in April 1830, derogating the aforementioned Salic law, and proclaiming Isabel his rightful heiress. The decision angered «the apostolic» band, that is, the members of the court who distrusted the King's advisors, and who advocated for Prince Carlos' becoming new sovereign. In September 1832, when the court was at La Granja de San Ildefonso palace, the King's health deteriorated and everyone feared, or wished, that he might die. Taking advantage of the context, the so-called «apostolic» politicians, namely the Secretary of Justice, Tadeo Calomarde, pressured the Queen, María Cristina, to persuade an agonising Fernando VII to annul the Pragmática Sanción, making his brother Carlos heir to the throne.

However, the mediation of the Queen's sister, Luisa Carlota, and the King's recovery frustrated the plot: Fernando rejected the documents he had signed in the deathbed, and ratified his daughter's condition as future Queen (Burdiel, 2010, pp. 25–32).[1] In June 1833, Isabel, aged 3, was sworn as Princess of Asturias (the title that the heir to the Spanish throne traditionally holds)[2]; in October, Fernando VII died, and Isabel II became the new Queen. During the Queen's childhood, her mother, María Cristina, would act as Queen Regent. Prince Carlos had already left for Portugal, and the new Government, led by Francisco Cea Bermúdez, approved a

---

[1] *Gaceta de Madrid*, n° 1, 1 January 1833. The appointment of the new cabinet had occurred on 1 October 1832; Antequera Municipal Historical Archive (AMHA), Actas Capitulares (AACC), 15 January 1833, box 1825.

[2] AMHA, AACC, 27 June 1833, box 1825.

general amnesty to sympathisers of liberalism, downgrading and expelling the so-called «Carlist» elements from the army. Carlos' supporters rebelled against the Queen and started the First Carlist War (1833–1839) (Fontana, 2007, pp. 137–146; Burdiel, 2010, pp. 26–33). By late October 1833, Spanish municipalities received the copy of the Pragmática Sanción, made law, plus a decree announcing the coronation of Isabel II. Following the dispositions by Cea Bermúdez's cabinet, political prisoners benefitted from the general amnesty, and municipal administrations underwent a deep transformation. The latter was inspired by the need to erase any trace of absolutism, and to facilitate the implantation of liberalism, which irradiated from Madrid to all towns, cities, and villages of the Spanish territory.

When these changes were happening, Antequera, 50 km to the North of Málaga, had just begun to recover from a demographic recession during the eighteenth century, which was not over until the 1820s. In 1825, there were 15,000 people in the village, but by 1838 population figures had gone up to 19,386 inhabitants (Parejo, 1987, p. 295). Birth rate was 77.5‰, and death rate was 39.8‰, during the whole nineteenth century (quoted in Pinto, 2009, p. 24); hence, the population grew at a 3.7% yearly rate (Parejo, 1987, p. 295). In economic terms, the place went through a depression, too, especially between 1833 and 1835. Poor harvests led to an increase in grain prices: in the summer of 1834, wheat was sold at 58 *reales*/bushels, which provoked bread scarcity (average wages of a Spanish peasant were 1 peseta a day, that is, 4 *reales* a day) (quoted in García, 1978). In order to calm the people down, the town hall rejected an increase in the price of the loaf of bread, which the bakers demanded. The reason for this situation lays partially in the underdevelopment of the Spanish countryside: there was almost no mechanisation of rural tasks, and latifundia dominated the structure of Spanish rural property; farming played a very irrelevant role in the whole system (Parejo, 1987, pp. 296–298, 315–320).

The sole exception was a rising industrial hub, focused on wool textiles, which would only take off in the 1830s, showing a positive progress until the 1870s. Antequera was the only middle-sized Andalusian enclave to transit from textile craftwork to industry, thanks to a small technological infrastructure, skilled labour force, and a very specific, highly demanded product: cloth (Pinto, 2009, p. 25). The sector took off in 1833, and I will mention its main characteristics, presenting the major investors, in the next section (Parejo, 1995, pp. 209–250). Once I have described the historical context at the beginning of the liberal regime, the first goal of my research is to depict the actors that led the transition from absolutism to liberalism, in political, economic, and social terms. The second goal is to determine whether their acts differed that much from those of traditional elites, and how their economic mentality had an impact in the first relevant initiatives that the liberal monarchy undertook. Mine is a research of political, social, and economic history, based on primary sources, namely the book of minutes by Antequera's town council between 1833 and 1836, and notarial protocols, all of them at the Antequera Municipal Historical Archive (AMHA).

2 Economic Transition: Main and «Secondary» Characters

The socioeconomic transformation occurred at municipal level in Spain in 1833 can be assessed evaluating the differences in the composition of the last city council under Fernando VII, and the first one under Isabel II. In January 1833, the members of the city council in Antequera were:

The organigram is the result of the reform by King Carlos III (1759–1788), in the eighteenth century, aimed at increasing municipal representation, in favour of the wealthier members of the municipality. The latter could even elect their representatives, though via indirect suffrage (Marina, 1984–1985, pp. 249–292). As I have pointed out in Table 1, the Mayor represented the Crown, so the King directly appointed him. Councillors could be either elected or perpetual, that is, members of influential families, who exercised the position generation after generation. Juries were supposed to represent the interests of common people, but in time their position also ended up in the hands of local oligarchies. Deputies of Common and Legal trustees were positions specifically created by Carlos III: the former were elected every year, and participated in debates about food supply; the latter defended the demands and proposals of the people (Castro, 1979, pp. 34–44).

Table 1 Antequera's city council under Fernando VII. January 1833

Position	Name
Mayor (appointed by the king)	Manuel Doñamayor
Councillors	Francisco de Paula Muñoz
	José Delgado
Deputies of common	Joaquín Alveza
	Antonio Llamas
Juries	José Castañeda
	Joaquín Muñoz
	Pedro Moscoso
	Francisco Delgado
	Diego Jiménez
	Pedro del Pino
	Manuel Jiménez
	Miguel Quirós
Legal trustee	José Antonio Aguilar

Source: AMHA, AA.CC., box 1825, January 1833

2.1 Liberalism, and the Socioeconomic Structure of the City Council (1833–1834)

As the end of Fernando VII's reign approached, the newly appointed Ministry of Development, Javier de Burgos, carried out certain reforms to foster liberal participation in municipal governments, since early 1833. He even approved the election of all municipal representatives, via qualified, property suffrage (Nieto, 1996, p. 215). After the King's death, a Royal Decree of 10 November 1833 made all municipalities adapt to the requirements and needs of the new liberal regime. Following the orders, Antequera prepared to celebrate local elections, according to the February census of property holders (Pinto, 2021, pp. 14.15). The elections happened in December, and the result, shown in Table 2, evidences not only a change in the names of the new members of the town council, but also in its structure:

From a socio-political scope, there is a clear transformation in the content, and in the spirit of the new municipality. At first glance, it might surprise the observer that the number of members of the city council went from 14 to 12. Nevertheless, what counts is not the quantitative side of the changes, but the qualitative impact: the number of deputies went down, and they were not called «of the common» anymore, as everyone understood that they were supposed to represent the interests of their voters. The absence of juries, monopolised by elite families, generation after generation, also implied that new liberal governors aimed at constituting truly representative corporations (Pinto, 2009, p. 32).

The reach of social transformations at the start of Spanish liberalism is interesting, in order to determine whether we must talk about a «liberal revolution», or rather of a «social transition» that happened smoothly. The latter option seems more likely: on the one hand, traditional families still occupied relevant positions in the government of the city; on the other hand, aware of the decay of old values, as well as of conventional ways of exercising power, they opted for linking their blood to

Table 2 Antequera's first liberal municipal council. December 1833

Position	Name
First councillor	Francisco de Rojas Díez de Tejada
Second councillor	Juan Casasola Fonseca
Third councillor	Vicente Robledo Castilla
Fourth councillor	Pedro Herrera Capitán
Fifth councillor	Agustín Carrasquilla
Sixth councillor	Francisco Cañizares
Municipal attorney general	Joaquín Narváez
First deputy	José Pérez Valiente
Second deputy	Andrés Romero casas
Third deputy	Miguel Gómez Quintero
Fourth deputy	Antonio de Gálvez (indirectly [sic])
Legal trustee	Francisco Rodríguez Contreras

Source: AMHA, AA.CC., box 1825, December 1833

that of the ascending bourgeoisie. Thus, aristocrats and oligarchs gained liquidity, and liberal bourgeois benefited from titles that provided them with the social relevance they lacked otherwise. Both social groups participated in a kind of symbiotic relation, concentrating their efforts on keeping the changes linked to the new regime within restricted boundaries (Castells, 1995, pp. 127–161; Cruz, 2000; Pinto, 2021, p. 16).

In the first city council of Isabel II's reign, not all the sectors of the Spanish liberal bourgeoisie were present: we can only find the agrarian bourgeoisie, alongside the urban bourgeoisie. The former diversified capital investments, to not depend only on income from the countryside, but also from urban properties. The way it connected with traditional aristocracy can be seen in the example of Francisco de Rojas Díez de Tejada, first councillor in the first liberal city council. An urban bourgeois by nature and family tradition, he had invested money in rural and urban properties alike,[3] and he also built relations with one of the most relevant aristocratic families: his sister, María del Carmen, married Joaquín de Rojas González Aguilar, Marquis of La Peña de los Enamorados. As can be seen, in spite of Rojas Díez de Tejada being liberal in the political scenario, he was conservative in a social and economic sense. In fact, though during the confiscation process in 1836–1837, he bought the Belén convent, which belonged to a community of Barefoot Carmelite nuns; he rented it to the Saint Claire order, and in his testament, he annulled the rent the nuns had to pay.[4]

Vicente Robledo Castilla was another significant example of the changes happening in Antequera's socioeconomic universe. Third councillor, he was the head of an influential family: father to Vicente Robledo Checa, secretary-to-be of the city council, and grandfather to future minister of Home Affairs under Alfonso XII's reign (1875–1885), Francisco Romero Robledo. At first, he had bought rural properties, but during the confiscation process he acquired some urban buildings, becoming one of the first owners in the city, with an estimated patrimony of 554,232 hectares. He invested part of his wealth in shares, and in the acquisition of a textile factory at the Henchidero place, at the outskirts of Antequera, by the Río de la Villa; his son-in-law, Juan Casero, was a temporary associate of it. When he left the society, they settled benefits, which rose up to 259,649.10 *reales*. Casero's departure, plus the assassination of his son Antonio Robledo Checa in 1840 (Pinto, 2021, pp. 68–73), persuaded Vicente Robledo Castilla to sell one sixth of the textile society to his son Vicente. Since then, the company was called *Robledo e hijo*.[5] When he died, he had an estimated fortune of 2.5 million *reales*, which he donated to his grandson Francisco Romero Robledo, so he could study Law at the Universidad Central, in Madrid.[6]

---

[3] AMHA, Notarial Protocols (NNPP), box 2885, 521 front (f)–536 back (b).

[4] Ibid., 525f-b.

[5] *Robledo and Son.*

[6] AMHA, NNPP, box 2439, 1274f–1280b. Universidad Central was how the Universidad Complutense was called at the time.

2.2 *Changes? The Revolutionary Process (1835–1836)*

The 1833–1837 period was shaken by instability in the whole country: while Carlist troops threatened Isabel II's reign in the North, gathering supporters, and a significant Carlist fifth column acted in the rest of the Spanish territories, the people felt disappointed by the reach of the so-called «liberal revolution». To begin, in the summer of 1834, rumours of the friars in Madrid, opponents to liberal legislation, poisoning public fountains to provoke the spread of a cholera epidemy, encouraged the uncontrolled mob to carry out the slaughter of friars and the burning of certain convents in the capital of the Kingdom (Vidal, 1989, pp. 271–279).[7] Francisco Cea Bermúdez's cabinet had already fallen 1 year before, but the new Prime Minister, Francisco Martínez de la Rosa, was not capable of calming the people down, either. So, in late-May 1834, he resigned, leaving his position to José María Queipo de Llano, Count of Toreno (Pinto, 2009, pp. 38–39).

The new cabinet included Juan Álvarez Mendizábal as minister of Internal Revenue. Hopes were focused on him, as everyone thought Mendizábal was the person who would contribute to restore Spanish finances, deeply harmed by a prolongated economic crisis, added to the war effort (Fontana, 2007, p. 152). Yet, the Spanish people seemed impatient about a liberal regime whose initiatives were limited: a revolution exploded in the summer of 1835. Workers at the Bonaplata Factory, in Barcelona, burned their job site (Nadal, 1983, pp. 79–95), and *juntas* spread all over the country, following a tradition that had started during the Peninsular War (1808–1814) (Moliner, 2007, pp. 65–83; Artola, 1973, pp. 188–189). Wishing to extinguish the revolutionary flame at once, Toreno's government tried to make the *juntas* surrender, but the popular negative reaction to his initiative persuaded Queen Regent Maria Cristina to dismiss him, asking Juan A. Mendizábal to form a new cabinet.

At municipal level, Antequera reproduced the events in Madrid. Members of the city council did not attend the meetings during the summer, distrusting the national turn of events, and evidencing how little they paid tribute to their voters (Nieto, 1996, pp. 401–404). According to the so-called *Arreglo Provisional*, the new municipal legislation approved by the former cabinet, municipal elections needed to be held in the summer of 1835, while the popular uprising was happening. The *Arreglo* provided for all municipal positions to be democratically elected, and for centralisation of state administration, via the *gobernador civil*, the Crown's representative in every province (Nieto, 1996, pp. 310–311). The city of Málaga joined the revolution on 25 August, and Antequera followed suit the day after. The whole town council was dismissed, and the authorities of the local *junta* called for new elections. Meanwhile, the 1823 corporation was restored, as its members were supposed to

[7] *Eco del Comercio*, n° 79, 18 July 1834.

Table 3 Antequera's 1823 town council, restored in August 1835

Position	Name
First mayor	Luis María Pareja Rojas, Count of La Camorra
Second mayor	Francisco Rodríguez Contreras
First councillor	Joaquín Machuca
Second councillor	Antonio María Fernández
Third councillor	José de Burgos
Fourth councillor	Rafael Chacón y Romero de Cisneros, Marquis of Cela
Fifth councillor	Antonio de Gálvez Paraíso
Sixth councillor	Manuel de Juano
Seventh councillor	Juan Mantilla Jiménez, Marquis of Casa-Saavedra

Source: AMHA, AA.CC., box 1827, 28 August 1835

have been loyal defenders of liberalism (Pinto, 2009, p. 45).[8] Table 3 shows the members of the 1823 municipality, restored in August 1835:

The socioeconomic composition of the city council reflected that of Spain in the 1820s, and all the important sectors of local elites were present: aristocracy, agrarian bourgeoisie, business and trade bourgeoisie, and low/modest bourgeoisie (Pinto, 2009, p. 46). For the purpose of this research, I have studied four testaments, belonging to four members of the municipality. Luis M. Pareja y Rojas, Count of La Camorra, represented the local aristocracy.[9] For example, in terms of social symbiosis, his wife was the sister of the Countess of Castillo del Tajo. However, he was a «modern, open-minded» noble, as he accepted the suppression of entailed states in 1820. He invested in urban and rural properties, and he always expressed his sympathies for liberalism, demanding even that he be buried without luxury, at all.

Joaquín Machuca was a member of the agrarian bourgeoisie, as owner of lands, cattle, and farming devices. Together with some urban properties, and some loans on his favour, those were his sources of income. Though he had invested most his wealth in farms, he diversified his investments, and he also participated in financial enterprises.[10] Business and trade bourgeoisie was represented by Antonio María Fernández. In his testament, he only mentions some loans for and against him, as well as income from trade, without further detail.[11] The fact that the executor of his testament was Juan Rubio Torres, a merchant from Málaga, reveals his socioeconomic connections. Finally, the humble, low bourgeoisie found a representative in Antonio de la Cámara Tejada, in whose testament there is only a slight mention of goods, titles, rights, and shares (Pinto, 2009, pp. 46–47).

Head of the municipality, and one of the most relevant leaders of the progress faction in Antequera, the Count of La Camorra demanded food supplies to a city that was starving, as well as investments to face the critical situation of the

[8] AMHA, AACC, box 1827, 25–28 August 1835.

[9] AMHA, NNPP, box 224, 230f–238b.

[10] Ibid., box 2439, 982f–987b.

[11] Ibid., box 2401, 197f–200b.

municipality's finances.[12] Once popular unrest had almost quieted down, the Crown and Mendizábal's cabinet contributed to the demobilisation of the *juntas*, while preparations were made for municipal elections all over the country (Burdiel, 2010, pp. 40–41). According to the census of property owners, out of 16,604 people in Antequera, only 1,087 (6.51%) had the right to vote, and 212 had the right to be elected (1.27%).[13] Table 4 illustrates the result of the election:

More interestingly, the book of minutes of the city council's meetings included a list of the same personalities, mentioning not only the position for which they were proposed, but also their social class, plus their economic activity (Table 5).

Complying with the *Arreglo Provisional*, the Crown elected the Mayor, as happened in all towns and villages over 2000 people: in Antequera, the Count of La Camorra was the chosen one. Hence, the final composition of the new municipal council, installed on 20 December 1835, is shown in Table 6.

Table 4 1835 municipal elections in Antequera: results

Candidate	Votes	
Count of La Camorra	497	Absolute majority
Diego Lumpie	425	
Francisco Rodríguez Contreras	416	
José Argüétar	384	
Joaquín Machuca	366	
Juan Casasola Fonseca	356	
Antonio de la Cámara	339	
José Casasola Cuéllar	331	
Juan de Rivera y Aren	314	
Fracisco Hernández	311	
Pedro Herrera Capitán	303	
José de Burgos	249	
Rafael Chacón, Marquis of Cela	240	
Diego Moreno Burgos	229	
José de Bores	206	
José González Gálvez	203	
Juan Auroux	193	
Gaspar Moreno y Mancha, Marquis of El Vado de las Carretas	192	
José Guerrero Gáinza	179	
Legal trustee of the common: José Díez de Tejada y Urbina	416	

Source: AMHA, AA.CC., box 1827, 23 November 1835

[12] AMHA, AACC, box 1827, 10 September 1835.

[13] Ibid., 17–22 October 1835.

Table 5 Elected members of the municipality, social position, and economic activity

Position	Candidate	Social class	Economic activity
Mayor	Luis María Pareja Rojas, Count of La Camorra	Aristocracy	Knight of the real Maestranza de Sevilla, National Guard (knight)
Id.	Diego Lumpie	n/d	Trade
Id.	Francisco Rodríguez Contreras	n/d	Owner and farmer
Councillor (absolute majority)	José María Aguilar	n/d	Owner
Id.	Joaquín Machuca	n/d	Owner and farmer
Id.	Juan de Casasola Fonseca	n/d	Owner
Id.	Antonio de la Cámara	Agrarian bourgeoisie	Owner and farmer
Id.	Juan dc Rivcra y Arcn	n/d	Owner
Councillor (simple majority)	Francisco Hernández	Industrial and trade bourgeoisie	Trade
Id.	Pedro Herrera Capitán	Agrarian, industrial, and trade bourgeoisie	Owner; trade
Id.	José de Burgos	Low bourgeoisie; liberal professions	Owner and pharmacist
Id.	Rafael Chacón, Marquis of Cela	Aristocracy	
Id.	Diego Moreno Burgos	Agrarian, industrial, and trade bourgeoisie	Owner and farmer
Id.	José de Bores	n/d	Physician, owner, and farmer
Id.	José González Gálvez	Agrarian bourgeoisie	Owner and farmer
Id.	Juan Auroux	Industrial and trade bourgeoisie	Trade
Id.	Gaspar Moreno y Mancha, Marquis of El Vado de las Carretas	Aristocracy	n/d
Id.	José Guerrero Gaínza	n/d	Owner and farmer
Legal trustee of the common (absolute majority)	José Díez de Tejada y Urbina	n/d	Owner and farmer

Source: AMHA, AA.CC., box 1827, 7 December 1835. *n/d* no data

The socioeconomic composition of the latter city council is very similar to that of the 1823 municipality, restored in August 1835. The bourgeois-like aristocracy had in the Marquis of Fuente Piedra, El Vado de las Carretas, and Cela its main representatives. The first one based his wealth on rural properties; besides, in a

Table 6 Antequera's town council after the November 1835 elections

Position	Name
Mayor	Luis María Pareja Rojas, Count of La Camorra
First lieutenant mayor	José María Casasola y Cuéllar, Marquis of Fuente Piedra
Second lieutenant mayor	José de Argüétar
Third lieutenant mayor	Joaquín Machuca
First councillor	Juan Casasola Fonseca
Second councillor	Antonio de la Cámara
Third councillor	Francisco Hernández
Fourth councillor	Pedro Herrera Capitán
Fifth councillor	José de Burgos
Sixth councillor	Rafael Chacón y Romero de Cisneros, Marquis of Cela
Seventh councillor	Diego Moreno Burgos
Eighth councillor	José González y Gálvez
Ninth councillor	Juan Auroux
Tenth councillor	Marquis of El Vado de las Carretas
First legal solicitor of the common	Manuel de Moya

Source: AMHA, AA.CC., box 1827, 17 December 1835

typical behaviour within traditional aristocracy, he had served as an army officer, as second-born son of his father, but the death of his brother Francisco, first-born and meant to be heir to the title, made him new Marquis by accident.[14] In a similar way, Gaspar Moreno Mancha, Marquis of El Vado de las Carretas, received his income from urban and rural properties. In addition, the title came to him through his mother, after the death of his uncle Joaquín.[15]

Manuel de Moya, Antonio de la Cámara, Pedro Herrera, José de Burgos, Diego Moreno Burgos, and José González y Gálvez represented the agrarian bourgeoisie. In the case of Manuel de Moya, his wealth was based on urban and rural properties, though he had some links with dynamic bourgeois elements at the time: he was the executor of the will of Ramón Garrido, a trader from Gibraltar.[16] Pedro Herrera, Francisco Hernández, Diego Moreno Burgos, and Juan Aroux belonged to the industrial bourgeoisie. According to Antonio Parejo Barranco (1987, p. 346), Diego Moreno Burgos incarnated the ascending industrial bourgeoisie that threatened the status of traditional oligarchs. Apart from investing in rural properties, Moreno Burgos was basically a leading figure in the local textile industry, whose patrimony rose up to eight million *reales* when he died. He distributed 25% of his society

[14] AMHA, NNPP, box 2337, 284f–289b.

[15] Ibid., box 2381, 275f–281b.

[16] Ibid., box 2442, 449f–451b.

among his children.[17] Alongside his brother José, he was the major representative of Antequera's industrious class.

Juan Auroux was a French migrant who arrived in Antequera in 1820. He and his brother Francisco devoted their efforts to producing cloth, and their family soon became the second most important industrial saga in Antequera, at the shadow of the Moreno Burgos brothers. Their nephew, Pedro Bordenave, owned a trading house together with another French associate: Vicente Sarrailler y Poey. When Juan Auroux died, Sarrailler substituted him as administrator of the cloth factory.[18] Their socioeconomic attitudes reflect national solidarity between foreigners, but the most interesting aspect of Juan Auroux's role was his involvement in local politics, too, as he was elected ninth councillor in the November 1835 elections. Though he asked Málaga's civil governor for an allowance to refuse the appointment, he was ordered to accept it, as he had already shown a major involvement in the affairs of Antequera. Finally, José de Burgos represented the low bourgeoisie, linked to liberal professions.

3 Political Impact of the Liberal (R)Evolution

The first weeks of Mendizábal's rule were positive: the revolution expired, and the cabinet implemented initiatives to improve the country's finances. In this sense, the Prime Minister had asked for a vote of confidence at Parliament, so he could carry out the secret operations he thought necessary to get funds for the state. Nevertheless, a bigger effort was required: not only did the Government need to regulate the state's budget, but it also had to finance the army fighting the Carlist rebels in the northern front, where governmental troops had not had any relevant triumph so far. To achieve both goals, that is, financial recovery and military success, Mendizábal conceived his star project: the ecclesiastical confiscation, approved by Royal Decree on 19 February 1836 (Tomás, 1971).

Manuel Gómez Becerra, minister of Internal Revenue, designed and implemented it: male religious orders were suppressed, together with their monasteries, and their properties were nationalised. The reasons behind such initiatives were two: first, by attacking regular clergy, the Government took power off the hands of one of the main actors who had resisted liberalism, and had even supported the Carlist cause; second, the confiscated properties were regarded as lands in «dead hands», say, unproductive lands. Once the state took them, it sold them in public auction, where middle and grand landowners bought them, and the money paid went to the public treasury. Thus, the liberal regime contributed to the economic promotion of the same bourgeois class that was supporting it, in the hope that the

[17] Ibid., box 2865, 629f–633b.

[18] Ibid.

Table 7 Report by the confiscating commission in Antequera. February 1836

Building/property	Future use
Los Remedios convent	Internal revenue see; post office; clerks' office; first instance court house
San Agustín church	Ruinous; rented to private owners while the commission decides on its use
San Juan de Dios	Hospital and foundlings' house (the place was already being used as such)
Capuchinos convent	Leper colony, given its situation, at the outskirts of the city
Barefoot Trinitarian convent	Ruinous. No decision was made on its future use
Barefoot Carmelite convent	Correction house
Victoria convent	Next to the La villa river, might be turned into see of a factory or engine
Chocked Carmelite convent	Infantry headquarters
Jesus basilic	Totally destroyed. Of no use
Santo Domingo basilic	Deformed and in a bad state. Of no use
Magdalena convent	In the outskirts of the city. Leper colony
San Francisco convent	Downton, but ruinous. Rented to private owners

Source: AMHA, Secretaría (S), box 950, 9 February 1836

new owners of the confiscated lands would do their best to make them productive (Marichal, 1980, pp. 99–100).

Antequera's city council was loyal to that same class, and to liberal principles. Likewise, it was devoted to the defence of individual liberties and private property. Hence, in early February 1836, the municipality appointed a commission to make a list of the religious buildings and properties to be confiscated in the following weeks. The list is interesting, as together with the name of the building and/or property, it mentioned its potential use, considering its preservation state, and its situation within the city (Table 7):

4 Conclusions

The elements that I have presented in this research lead me to conclude that, instead of a liberal revolution, it is more appropriate to talk about a transition from an old regime to a new one, at least in terms of economic and social transformations. The major social change was the increasing participation of Spanish bourgeoisie in national politics, but that class had already been performing a relevant social and economic role in the country for the past half century. At local level, my assertion can be tested in the presence of such characters as Vicente Robledo Castilla, or the Moreno Burgos brothers, in the first municipal governments after Fernando VII's death. The patrimony they had at the time, they had been building for decades, in a process that did not happen violently, neither did it occur suddenly.

Therefore, their participation in national politics seemed only a question of time, and it just had to wait for the Fernando VII's death to benefit from the political circumstances that favoured the official end of the old regime, and the enabling of a new, liberal way of making politics. Only the Spanish people had some hope on the new regime to approve initiatives to benefit the poor, which were never in the minds of the new liberal elites. In fact, when the latter started making decisions to consolidate the political change, what they actually did was to favour their own class, as happened in the confiscation process. That attitude could also be observed in their symbiosis with the aristocrats who did not wish to lose their influential role in Spanish society. That is why, among other reasons, disappointment with liberal politics made many poor peasants and workers repent their support to liberalism, turning even to Carlism in many cases.

Antequera, and the city's elites, were a small-scale manifestation of events that happened all around the country, and in all other nations where a similar liberal transition occurred. It is true that Spain lived some violent episodes in the path towards liberal consolidation, as the 1835 revolution, and its echo in the summer of 1836. But they were more likely resistance movements against reactionary forces, and cannot be seen as dramatic episodes aiming at transforming the Spanish scenario once and for all, as had previously happened in France.

Competing Interests The author has no conflicts of interest to declare that are relevant to the content of this chapter.

Sources Antequera Municipal Historical Archive. Actas Capitulares, 1833–1835.
Antequera Municipal Historical Archive. Notarial Protocols.

References

Artola, M. (1973). *La burguesía revolucionaria (1808–1874)*. Alfaguara.

Burdiel, I. (2010). *Isabel II: una biografía*. Taurus.

Castells, I. (1995). La rivoluzione liberale Spagnola nel recente dibattito storiografico. *Studi Storici, 1*, 127–161.

Castells, I. (2000). José María Torrijos (1791–1831). Conspirador romántico. In I. Burdiel & M. Pérez Ledesma (Eds.), *Liberales, agitadores y conspiradores. Biografías heterodoxas del siglo XIX* (pp. 73–98). Espasa Calpe.

Castro, C. (1979). *La Revolución Liberal y los municipios españoles*. Alianza Editorial.

Cruz, J. (2000). *Los notables de Madrid: las bases sociales de la revolución liberal española*. Biblioteca Nueva.

Fontana, J. (2007). *La época del liberalismo*. Crítica—Marcial Pons.

García Montoro, C. (1978). *Málaga en los comienzos de la industrialización: Manuel Agustín de Heredia (1786–1846)*. Universidad de Córdoba.

Marichal, C. (1980). *La revolución liberal y los primeros partidos políticos en España, 1834–1844*. Cátedra.

Marina Barba, J. (1984–1985). La reforma municipal de Carlos III en Ciudad Real (1766–1780). *Chronica Nova: Revista de Historia Moderna de la Universidad de Granada*, 14, 249–292.
Moliner i Prada, A. (2007). El juntismo en la primera mitad del siglo XIX como instrumento de socialización política. In C. Demange, P. Géal & R. Hocquellet (Coords.), *Sombras de mayo: mitos y memorias de la Guerra de la Independencia en España (1808-1908)* (pp. 65-83). Casa de Velázquez. https://doi.org/10.4000/books.cvz.14152
Nadal, J. (1983). Los Bonaplata, tres generaciones de industriales catalanes en la España del siglo XIX. *Revista de Historia Económica - Journal of Iberian and Latin American Economic History, 1*(1), 79–95. https://doi.org/10.1017/S021261090001243X
Nieto, A. (1996). *Los primeros pasos del régimen constitucional en España. Historia administrativa de la regencia de María Cristina de Borbón*. Ariel.
Parejo Barranco, A. (1987). *Historia de Antequera*. Biblioteca Antequerana de la Caja de Ahorros.
Parejo Barranco, A. (1995). Los viajes europeos de un burgués antequerano: José Moreno Burgos en Francia, Bélgica e Inglaterra, 1842–1851. *Revista de Estudios Antequeranos, 1*, 209–250.
Pinto Tortosa, A. J. (2009). *El medio agrario andaluz ante la llegada del liberalismo: las revoluciones de 1835 y 1836 en Antequera*. Ayuntamiento de Antequera.
Pinto Tortosa, A. J. (2021). «La población más temible»: Antequera durante el reinado de Isabel II y el Sexenio Democrático (1833–1874). Comares.
Serrano, C. (2000). Mariana Pineda (1804-1831): mujer, sexo y heroísmo. In I. Burdiel & M. Pérez Ledesma (Eds.), *Liberales, agitadores y conspiradores. Biografías heterodoxas del siglo XIX* (pp. 99–126). Espasa Calpe.
Tomás y Valiente, F. (1971). *El marco político de la desamortización en España*. Ariel.
Vidal Galache, F. (1989). La epidemia de cólera de 1834 en Madrid. Asistencia y represión a las clases populares. *Espacio, Tiempo y Forma. Serie V, Historia Contemporánea, 2*, 271–279. https://doi.org/10.5944/etfv.2.1989.2670

Antonio J. Pinto-Tortosa is a Senior Lecturer at the Department of Modern and Contemporary History, University of Málaga (2022–present). His research is focused on five different topics: Spanish liberalism in the nineteenth and early twentieth centuries; transatlantic slavery and the Haitian Revolution, paying attention and current relation between Haiti and the Dominican Republic; urban history and the history of energy, with a special attention to gas; global geopolitics; and educational innovation. He has previously worked as lecturer in International Relations at the Universidad Europea (Madrid). He currently teaches at the BSC Degree in History, at the University of Málaga.

Foreign Capital in the Gas Industry in Spain, *Lebon et Cie* (1841–1925)

Mercedes Fernández-Paradas and José Joaquín Luque-García

Abstract This chapter analyses the influence of foreign capital on the development of the gas industry in Spain through the case of the French company *Lebon et Cie*, which was active between 1841 and 1925. It examines how this company introduced and consolidated public and private gas lighting in various Spanish cities, especially during the second half of the nineteenth century. The study shows how *Lebon et Cie* established a dominant position thanks to municipal concessions and its investment capacity. This chapter also describes the progressive nationalisation of urban services in the twentieth century, which marked the decline of the concession model in the hands of foreign companies such as Lebon.

1 Introduction

During the nineteenth century, globalisation advanced progressively, intensifying from the early decades of the Second Technological Revolution in the 1860s and the 1870s. This acceleration was driven by the revolutions in transport and

This research forms part of the outcomes of the R + D + I Project *"Gas in Latin Europe: A Comparative and Global Perspective (1818–1945)"* (PID2020-112844GB-I00), funded by the Ministry of Science and Innovation of the Government of Spain and the European Regional Development Fund (ERDF). It also constitutes part of the doctoral research project of José Joaquín Luque-García and the results of a research stay at the Department of Contemporary History, UMR Sirice, Sorbonne University (France). The stay was carried out under the theme *"Un réseau international: la presse spécialisée dans le gaz à Paris comme un nœud fondamental dans la circulation des connaissances entrepreneuriales, scientifiques et techniques"*, in collaboration with the Committee for the History of Electricity and Energy and with the support of the EDF Group Foundation.

M. Fernández-Paradas · J. J. Luque-García (✉)
Department of Modern and Contemporary History, University of Málaga, Málaga, Spain
e-mail: paradas@uma.es; joseluque@uma.es

M. Vázquez-Fariñas, F. Cabrera-Gallardo (eds.), *Business Trajectories in the History of Spain*, Frontiers in Economic History,
https://doi.org/10.1007/978-3-032-16214-4_4

communications, scientific and technical progress, and financial resources, particularly through foreign investment. During the First Technological Revolution, which began in Britain in the late eighteenth century and was subsequently followed by France, an unprecedented accumulation of capital took place in these countries. The integration of these factors, together with the establishment of the gold standard, enabled the expansion in both the number and the scope of enterprises operating across national borders. These enterprises were able to do so because they possessed qualified personnel, superior technology, access to capital, and/or more efficient organisational structures. In their investment decisions, it was common to take into account existing opportunities, relationships of trust, and cultural ties. In the nineteenth-century Spain, there was a notable shortage of capital necessary for the development of capitalism. This limitation was partly mitigated through foreign investment, particularly French, which played a major role in sectors such as mining, banking, railways, and urban services, among them the gas industry (Anes, 1970; Broder, 1981; Costa, 1981; Castro, 2018). Spain shared with France a similar cultural background and linguistic and legal proximity (Cameron, 1971).

With regard to the gas industry in Spain, during its early phase between 1842 and 1861, investment was dominated—in this order—by capital from France, the United Kingdom, and Belgium (Fernández-Paradas et al., 2022, p. 76; Vázquez-Fariñas et al., 2023, pp. 19–20). The predominance of French and British investment is consistent with the fact that coal gas technology first emerged in those countries at the end of the eighteenth century.

The emergence of the gas industry in Spain coincided with the end of British hegemony in the European gas sector, which had lasted until around 1840. From that point onwards, French gas technology, together with French capital, became increasingly prominent. French investment in this sector was concentrated in the southern Europe and North Africa (Williot, 2006). France had accumulated substantial capital during its process of industrialisation and possessed abundant coal reserves—the raw material used in gas production. The establishment of the gas industry required a number of factors that were largely lacking in Spain. As noted above, there was a shortage of capital, and particularly an absence of a modern banking system. The industry depended on a new form of infrastructure and technology that did not yet exist in Spain, demanded significant financial investment, and relied on skilled personnel—especially engineers—who were scarce both in private enterprises and within public administration. Spanish municipal councils suffered from chronic financial difficulties and lacked the technical staff necessary to manage such a complex activity. Consequently, almost all of them opted to entrust this service to private companies. All these factors help to explain why, between 1842 and 1861, 71.4% of gas plants in Spain were foreign-owned, and why, in the second half of that century, 82.6% of the capital invested in the sector was French (Costa, 1981).

Lebon et Cie played a pivotal role in the prominent position that French investment held in the introduction of gas in Spain. This chapter is based on existing literature, as well as on primary and secondary sources, including specialised press covering the gas sector and related economic activities. Unfortunately, it has not been possible to consult the company's own archive. This chapter is structured as follows: this introduction outlines the research focus and its significance, followed by three main sections. The first examines where and how the company's principal founder, Charles Lebon, introduced gas to Spain, why he was compelled to relinquish his initial undertakings, and how he later returned, establishing a managerial model that, in part, endured after 1872, when control of the company passed exclusively to his son, Eugène. The second section covers the period between approximately 1872 and 1874 and the end of the nineteenth century. In 1870–1871, the Franco-Prussian War took place; in 1872, Charles Lebon stepped down from the management of the multinational company; and in 1874, the Bourbon Restoration was established in Spain. Following these political events, both countries entered a period of relative political stability, which facilitated the expansion of the company's operations within Spanish territory. To this end, *Lebon et Cie* implemented various strategies, including diversification into the emerging electricity business. This section concludes at the end of the nineteenth century, when both the Spanish economy and electrical technology entered a new phase. The third section covers the period from that point until 1925, the year in which the multinational completed the sale of its assets in Spain. This chapter concludes with a summary of the most significant findings.

2 Early Years, Disillusionment, and Return

Charles (1799–1877) was born in the French town of Dieppe, where he established his first gasworks in 1838, became a pioneer in the introduction of gas lighting in France, Spain, Algeria, and Egypt (Lebon et Cie, 1947, pp. 14–15). Shortly thereafter, Charles Lebon directed his attention towards several Spanish municipalities that shared certain characteristics: all were potentially significant markets for gas consumption owing to their economic strength and demographic weight. In Madrid, the capital of Spain (around 157,397 inhabitants), he failed in his 1843 attempt to obtain the gas concession, together with Pedro Gil y Serra (1814–1867), the son of Pedro Gil y Babot (1773–1853). By contrast, in economically dynamic maritime cities with easy access to coal, he succeeded—jointly with other partners—in securing gas concessions in Barcelona (1841; 121,815 inhabitants), Valencia (1843; 112,800 inhabitants), and Cádiz (1845; 58,922 inhabitants), where gas lighting was inaugurated in 1842, 1844, and 1845, respectively. It is also worth considering the possible role of these coastal cities as strategic points of connection between France and North Africa. Furthermore, Charles became acquainted with Ferdinand de Lesseps, who had served as the French consul in Barcelona and could therefore inform him of the city's economic potential. In addition, Pedro Gil y Serra was established as a banker in Paris, where he acted as correspondent for the banker Léon Adolphe Laffitte, who was involved in the gas industry in the French capital and held business interests in Madrid. While in Paris, Pedro Gil y Serra could observe that gas supply was a highly profitable business and/or that Laffitte may have drawn his attention to this opportunity (Arroyo, 1996, p. 24).

In Barcelona and Valencia, the companies responsible for implementing the gas supply contracts were the *Sociedad Catalana para el Alumbrado por Gas* (*La Catalana*), founded in 1843, and the *Sociedad Valenciana para el Alumbrado de Valencia*, established in 1844. In both cases, Charles Lebon relied on local capitalists who possessed connections with municipal and central authorities, as well as wealth and business experience. Charles held the concession contract and provided the necessary technology, while local investors supplied the capital (García, 1984, pp. 79–80, 84). In Cádiz, in 1845, Charles Lebon successfully competed for the public gas lighting concession on behalf of *La Catalana*. However, it is known that he subsequently reached an agreement with John Grafton and Goldsmidt, since by 1846, the three of them jointly held the concession. This change may be linked to the difficult relations that Lebon maintained with his local partners in Spain (Fernández-Paradas, 2015, pp. 38–39). His usual practice consisted of obtaining the concession and then moving on to other cities to secure new ones, leaving the construction of the gasworks in the hands of engineers he trusted, and often making decisions without consulting the local investors (Arroyo, 1996, p. 34).

From 1844 onwards, a conflict arose between Lebon and the Gil family over control of *La Catalana*, which soon resulted in Lebon's departure from the company. In 1846, his partners in Valencia negotiated the sale of the gas operation to the *Empresa General Peninsular para el Alumbrado de Gas*, which had been established that same year with the participation of both British and *Spanish* investors. Two years later, Lebon transferred his remaining shares to the *Sociedad Valenciana*. Between 1845 and 1846, the Cádiz concession was likewise transferred to *Waterton & Cie* (Fernández-Paradas, 2015, pp. 49–50).

Lebon's withdrawal from Spain should be understood in relation to his strained relations with local partners and an unfavourable short-term context within Spain, marked by the creation of other companies—such as the aforementioned *Empresa General Peninsular*—which possessed greater financial resources. Added to this was the economic crisis that erupted in France in 1848 in the form of a revolutionary movement, which severely affected his business interests (Fernández-Paradas, 2015, p. 50; Fàbregas, 2018, pp. 66–67).

Once Charles had begun developing gas operations in various cities, he founded, in 1847, together with engineers Léger Marchesaux and Émile Leborge, the *Compagnie Centrale d'Éclairage pour le Gaz, Lebon et Cie*, with a capital of 1.2 million francs. The partners were linked by family or friendship ties, a characteristic that remained a defining feature of the company throughout its existence in the gas business until 1947, the year in which the gas and electricity sectors were nationalised in France. The multinational changed its name several times: in 1853 to *Lebon Père et Fils & Cie*, when his son Eugène became co-manager; in 1872 to *Eugène Lebon & Cie*; and in 1907 to *Lebon et Cie*. Another notable feature of the company's operations in Spain was its employment of both Spanish and foreign engineers who often worked for extended periods, and in some cases across two generations—brothers and/or fathers and sons—such as the Santomá and Martínez families, among others. During the second half of the nineteenth century, most of the engineers came from France and Spain, with smaller numbers from Poland and Belgium. In the first two decades of the twentieth century, the number of Spanish engineers increased, although a significant French presence persisted (Fernández-Paradas et al., 2021).

In 1860, Charles Lebon, representing *Lebon et Cie*, began managing the company's return to Spain, specifically to Granada, where he obtained authorisation to supply gas in 1863. That same year, Joseph Manby transferred to him the gas contract for Santander, and he also secured the concession for private gas supply in Barcelona. In 1867, a gasworks was inaugurated in Almería. Both this plant and the one in Granada were leased to the brothers José, Juan, and Isidoro Boixader until 1878. In 1868, the company built a gasworks in Valencia, near Villanueva del Grao, intended to supply gas to Pueblo Nuevo del Grao and Valencia itself. However, opposition from José Campo, the holder of the gas concession in the capital, prevented the multinational from distributing gas in that territory. In 1869, *Lebon et Cie* obtained the concession for public gas lighting in Villanueva del Grao and Pueblo Nuevo del Mar, which were incorporated into Valencia in 1897. In 1873, the gas plant in El Puerto de Santa María began operations. Between 1868 and 1871, the company also leased its gasworks in Cartagena and Alicante to the Dutch group Stockman (*Le Gaz*, 15-04-1870; García, 1984, pp. 99, 119, 332). The decision to lease some of its plants can be linked to the difficult circumstances of the *Sexenio Revolucionario*.

In February 1872, Charles Lebon was compelled to resign as co-manager of *Lebon et Cie* following a ruling by the Tribunal de Commerce of the Seine, initiated by fifty shareholders (*Le Gaz*, 15-01-1872). The decision was based on his alleged failure to meet his obligations during the severe economic crisis that affected Spain between 1866 and 1868, as well as the major political and social upheavals of the *Sexenio Revolucionario* (September 1868–December 1874) and the Franco-Prussian War (July 1870–May 1871) in France (Fernández-Paradas, 2015, p. 70).

3 *Lebon et Cie* between 1872 and 1898

In February 1872, Charles Lebon resigned from his position as co-manager of *Lebon et Cie*, marking the beginning of a new stage in the company's development. The managerial post was assumed by his son, Eugène Lebon (1824–1907), who held the position until his death, after which he was succeeded by his son Alfred, thus ensuring that the firm remained under the control of the Lebon family. Eugène was among the founders of the *Société Technique de l'Industrie du Gaz en France*, established in 1874 (Martínez-López & Mirás-Araujo, 2024). He pursued his engineering studies at the École Centrale des Arts et Manufactures (École), the Parisian institution where most gas engineers in France during the period under consideration received their training. The school provided a strong theoretical and practical education in engineering, complemented by an economic component that enabled its graduates to combine technical and managerial responsibilities within gas companies. From 1853, he served as co-manager alongside his father, becoming the sole manager in 1872. He was the principal figure responsible for steering the multinational company towards the electricity sector (Journal des Usines à Gaz, 04-04-1907).

During his long tenure at the head of the company, he also oversaw the factories in Spain. Until 1890, ultimate authority rested with the general manager, whose headquarters were located in Paris. Each factory was likewise directed by an engineer who held overall responsibility for both the technical and managerial. These directors were almost always graduates of the École or of the Barcelona School of Engineers, established in 1851 (Fernández-Paradas et al., 2021). In 1890, Eugène appointed Raveau—a friend of Alfred Lebon, Eugène Lebon's son—as general director in Spain, with Alfred Toussaint as his deputy. They held these positions until 1904, when Toussaint succeeded Raveau upon the latter's death. Toussaint continued in this role for 20 years.

In Spain, during the period under consideration in this section, *Lebon et Cie* expanded its operations to other localities and brought an end to the leasing of gasworks, opting instead for the direct management of all its enterprises. At the same time, the company had to confront three major challenges: competition from other gas companies and from the emerging electricity sector, as well as the debts incurred by municipal councils, which frequently delayed payment for public gas lighting. This problem became particularly acute during the *Sexenio Revolucionario* and worsened thereafter.

About the expansion of the gas business to additional municipalities, *Lebon et Cie*, besides resuming the direct management of its previously leased operations, acquired in 1886 from *La Propagadora* the gasworks supplying San Gervasi, Gràcia, and Les Corts de Sarrià, in 1888 obtained the city's exclusive gas concession. In 1895, using a high-pressure pipeline from Valencia, it began supplying gas to Godella (Lebon et Cie, 1947, p. 132; García, 1984, p. 100).

With regard to municipal debts, this was a widespread issue. In Spain, the amounts owed to the multinational amounted to 261,614 francs at the beginning of 1876 (*Le Journal des finances*, 01-04-1876). Through the persistence of the factories' directors and lawyers, *Lebon et Cie* won the legal proceedings and compelled the council to sign pledge contracts, according to which, if it failed to pay gas bills, the company could recover payments directly from municipal revenues (Lebon et Cie, 1947, pp. 99–100).

Regarding competition in the energy market, the Municipal Law of 1877 prohibited local councils from granting monopolies over public lighting, which enabled local electricity companies to obtain permission to build power stations. There was also competition from other gas companies. For instance, at the end of 1884, when the Cádiz City Council authorised the renewal of *Lebon et Cie*'s gas concession, a group of residents promoted the *Sociedad Cooperativa Gaditana para la Fabricación*

Table 1 Number of gas subscribers of *Lebon et Cie* (1884–1922). 1884 = 100

Territories/years	1884	1890	1900	1910	1920
France	3500 (100)	4000 (114.3)	6500 (185.7)	10,000 (285.7)	15,000 (428.6)
% France of total	15.7	12.6	8.1	8.1	9.3
Argelia	2000 (100)	2800 (140.0)	8500 (425.0)	29,500 (1475.0)	31,000 (1550.0)
% Argelia of total	9.0	8.8	10.6	23.9	19.2
Egypt	800 (100)	1000 (125.0)	7000 (875.0)	12,000 (1500.0)	13,000 (1625.0)
% Egypt of total	3.6	3.1	8.7	9.7	8.1
Spain	16,000 (100)	24,000 (150.0)	58,000 (362.5)	72,000 (450.0)	102,000 (637.5)
% Spain of total	71.7	75.5	72.5	58.3	63.3
Total	22,300 (100)	31,800 (142.6)	80,000 (358.7)	123,500 (553.8)	161,000 (722.0)

Source: author's own elaboration based on Lebon et Cie (1947, p. 84)

de Gas (1885). The influence of some of the Cooperative's promoters prevailed in the city council, which granted the company the contract for public gas lighting.[1]

Competition from electric companies posed a far greater challenge for *Lebon et Cie*, which the firm addressed primarily by introducing technological improvements, entering the electricity business, and engaging in marketing. Among the technological innovations, the Auer burner was particularly noteworthy, as it reduced the cost of gas lighting and enabled it to compete with electric lighting until approximately the First World War. Moreover, the company built new gasworks.

Lebon et Cie acquired and integrated an electricity plant into each gas factory. By 1896, it operated in Cádiz, Santander, Murcia, El Puerto de Santa María, and Almería. In the same year, the multinational and *La Catalana* entered into an agreement to establish the *Central Catalana de Electricidad* (García, 1984).

The French company's strategy produced positive results, as by the end of the nineteenth century, it had succeeded in acquiring local electricity companies and, in the lighting market, gas was able to compete effectively in both price and quality. This explains the considerable growth in the number of its subscribers across all the territories in which it operated, including Spain (Table 1). In 1880, the company had 16,000 gas subscribers, representing 71.7% of the total; by 1900, the figure had risen to 58,000—an increase of 362.5% compared with 1880—and accounted for 72.5% of the total. By 1920, the number of subscribers had reached 102,000, an increase of 637.5%, representing 63.3% of the total. Despite this notable growth in the number of subscribers in Spain, during the first two decades of the twentieth century, the country's relative weight within the company declined.

[1] Municipal Archive of Cádiz, Boxes 159, 3740 and 4058.

4 The Withdrawal of *Lebon et Cie* from Spain

In 1907, as previously mentioned, Alfred Lebon became the company's manager, a responsibility he shared with his son-in-law, Léon Bergès (1850–1934). Alfred's sons, Pierre Lebon and Marcel Lebon, later joined the management of *Lebon et Cie*. Marcel served as co-manager from 1914, but injuries sustained during military service in the First World War forced him to relinquish the position. The Lebon family headed the business for five generations—founder, son, grandson, great-grandsons, and great-great-grandson—all of them engineers trained at the École, except for the founder. The great-great-grandson, Bernard, son of Pierre, joined the company after the sale of its assets in Spain (Lebon et Cie, 1947). It should be recalled that, from 1904 onwards, Toussaint succeeded Raveau as general director in Spain.

From the beginning of the twentieth century, Spanish capitalism experienced significant growth, largely fuelled by the repatriation of capital belonging to Spaniards or their descendants returning from Cuba—following its loss after the Disaster of 1898—as well as from other parts of the Americas. Part of this capital was invested in major electricity companies that harnessed large hydroelectric plants, which reduced the cost of electricity and made it possible to distribute power over long distances. To these domestic investments were added the resources of powerful foreign financial groups. In part, this may explain the multinational's decision to dissolve the *Central Catalana de Electricidad* in 1912 (García, 1984, pp. 108–110).

In this context of growing competition from electricity companies, *Lebon et Cie*—like most gas firms—chose to withdraw from Spain. Among them, *Lebon et Cie* was the most significant, holding in 1911 no less than 82% of the declared capital in Spain's gas sector, amounting to 35.1 million pesetas. This figure reached its peak in 1915 (40 million) before declining to 29.8 million by 1920 (Vázquez-Fariñas et al., 2025, pp. 79–82). Meanwhile, the company opted to enter into various agreements in different localities, often with satisfactory results (García, 1984, p. 128).

In this context, both international and domestic developments further worsened the situation for *Lebon et Cie* from the late nineteenth century onwards: fluctuations in the exchange rate, the introduction of new taxes, and—linked to these—a body of legislation intended to hinder the activities of foreign capital in Spain. Added to this were the growing strength of the labour movement, increasing disagreements with municipal authorities that ceased to offer advantages to foreign gas companies and refused to renew their contracts, and finally, the impact of the First World War.

Regarding the exchange rate, from 1896 and at least until the early twentieth century, the rate between the peseta and the franc declined to the detriment of the latter, while the cost of coal—and consequently overall expenses—increased, leading to a significant fall in the multinational's profits. For instance, in 1897, the company recorded profits of seven million in Spain; however, because of the exchange rate, it incurred a loss of 1.5 million (La Cote de la Bourse de la banque, 12-05-1898; L'Information financière, économique et politique, 27-08-1903).

As for the new taxes, in 1898—a year marked by crisis in Spain, exacerbated by the outbreak of war with the United States—the Spanish government introduced a tax on the consumption of gas, electricity, and calcium carbide, which increased the cost of these products. Furthermore, a 1920 law established a tax on the profits of foreign companies, calculated on the basis of their total earnings in proportion to the capital invested in Spain. In addition, the Spanish government, in its drive to "nationalise" the economy, sought to prevent foreign companies and individuals from obtaining or managing public service concessions. This was enacted through the decrees of 1900 and 1907, a law in 1917, and further provisions adopted at the end of 1918, which stipulated that concessions for hydroelectric plants producing more than 1000 kW could only be granted to Spanish firms. From 1921 onwards, foreign engineers were also prohibited from overseeing their construction and operation.

A hostile environment was also shared by municipal authorities, which were unwilling to renew or establish new gas and electricity supply contracts with *Lebon et Cie*, as many of these were due to expire around 1920. Some city councils even proposed the municipalisation of public lighting services (Castro-Valdivia et al., 2019, pp. 58–59, 72).

Regarding the labour movement, the company's policy was not to make concessions under the threat of strike action, though it was willing to grant them (such as medical benefits) if workers, in return, signed the so-called employment contract committing themselves not to strike. In 1903, a strike took place at the Arenal gasworks, which was repeated in 1904. In Barcelona itself, during the *Semana Trágica* (26-07-1909 to 02-08-1909), the workers of *Lebon et Cie* were forced to abandon their duties (Lebon et Cie, 1947, pp. 97, 108 and 130).

The First World War proved particularly damaging to the for *Lebon et Cie* in Spain, as coal became scarce and its price soared, while hydroelectric companies were able to exploit water resources. This rise in costs, together with increased wages, led to higher company expenditures. The shortage of coal forced the multinational to interrupt gas supply and, in some cases, to suspend operations altogether. The management of *Lebon et Cie* in Spain became problematic, as Toussaint, mentioned earlier, remained largely isolated from the company's headquarters in France, and the border between the two countries was frequently closed. Moreover, several of *Lebon et Cie*'s employees in Spain were mobilised to the front.[2] During the war and in the years that followed, compared with the early twentieth century, revenues from gas lighting fell sharply, while those from electric lighting increased only marginally. Moreover, the gas company had to contend with major strikes in 1919 and 1920 in Barcelona and Valencia (García, 1984, pp. 263–264; Fernández-Paradas, 2015).

Lastly, as shown in Table 1, although the number of gas subscribers of *Lebon et Cie* in Spain increased considerably in both quantitative and qualitative terms, its contribution to the company as a whole declined—from 71.7% in 1880 to 58.3% in

[2] Le Journal des chemins de fer, 10-05-1915, 26-03-1918 and 05-04-1919.

1900 and 63.3% in 1920. By contrast, the growth in subscribers in Algeria and Egypt was proportionally much greater, as there were no restrictions on the expansion of gas and electricity operations. The multinational had made substantial investments in these two territories, which resulted in a reduced share of its investments in Spain, falling from one-half in 1906 to 41% in 1920. For this year, data are available on capital and production in gas and electricity: on the one hand, for Spain, and on the other, for France and Algeria combined. Across these three territories, total capital amounted to 139.5 million francs, of which 45% corresponded to Spain. The total capital invested in gas operations was 99.1 million francs, while that in electricity amounted to 40.3 million. The gas operations in Spain, valued at 47 million francs, represented 47.4% of the total capital invested in that sector and accounted for 60.2% of total gas sales. Meanwhile, the electricity operations in Spain, valued at 3.8 million francs, represented 37.3% of the capital invested in that activity. This indicates that the gas business in Spain generated a higher proportion of income for the company than would be expected based on its share of capital value—a situation that entailed risk given the adverse context already discussed. By contrast, in the electricity sector, the construction of power stations in Spain was almost proportionally balanced between capital investment and the revenue generated, at around 38%. These figures also show that in France and Algeria, the company had invested more heavily in electricity than in Spain, for the reasons previously noted. Together, France and Algeria accounted for 60.6% of the company's total capital in the electricity business and 62.7% of its revenues (Lebon et Cie, 1947, p. 95).

To continue producing electricity in Spain, the company would have had to invest substantial capital, since its power stations, as previously noted, were smaller than those of the major hydroelectric firms. At the end of the war, the devaluation of the franc against the peseta—at a rate of more than three francs to one peseta—made such an investment even more onerous. It should also be recalled that *Lebon et Cie*'s gas and electricity operations in Spain were located far apart, which made interconnection difficult and greatly increased the associated costs. Moreover, these operations were at risk, given the imminent expiry of their concessions and the decisions of several municipalities to replace public gas lighting with electricity. By contrast, the proceeds from the sale of the company's gas and electricity plants in Spain could be invested in refurbishing its facilities in France, which had been damaged by the war, and in strengthening its operations in Algeria—then a French territory—and in Egypt, where conditions appeared more stable. Furthermore, due to the exchange rate, the operation was financially advantageous, as when the company sold its Spanish assets, one peseta was worth more than three francs (Lebon et Cie, 1947, pp. 63, 65; Broder, 1981, pp. 1677–1678). These funds were essential after several years of continuous decline in profits between 1913 and 1920, during which they fell from 8.3 million francs to 926,000 francs.[3]

[3] L'Information financière, économique et politique, 06-09-1921.

For all the reasons analysed above, from 1912 onwards, *Lebon et Cie* began to divest its assets in Spain. It should be recalled that in that year the company sold half of *Catalana de Electricidad* to *La Catalana* for eight million pesetas. The remaining assets were sold between 1921 and 1925. In 1921, the electricity and gas plants in Almería were sold to *Fuerzas Motrices del Valle del Lecrín*, and the Valencia power station to *Hidroeléctrica Española* and *Electra Valenciana*, for 7.2 million francs. Unfortunately, the amounts received for the other assets are unknown.[4] The *Compañía General de Electricidad* purchased the Granada power station. The multinational intended to transfer its remaining assets to *La Catalana*, but they were ultimately acquired by the *Arnus-Garí Bank*. On 31-12-1923, this bank established the *Compañía Española de Electricidad y Gas Lebon* with a capital of 24 million pesetas, which enabled it to acquire the gas plants in Valencia, Granada, and El Puerto de Santa María, as well as the gas and electricity plants in Murcia, Santander, and Cádiz in 1924. In addition, in 1925, it purchased *Lebon et Cie*'s shares in the *Sociedad Cooperativa Gaditana de Fabricación del Gas* (García, 1984, p. 41; Castro-Valdivia et al., 2019, p. 73).

5 Conclusions

Lebon et Cie played a key role in the early development and establishment of piped gas in Spain. Initially, this was a personal endeavour of Charles Lebon, although he was surrounded by trusted relatives and friends. He was forced to leave the country when other gas companies with greater financial resources emerged, coupled with disagreements with local partners and the economic crisis that affected France around 1848. The company returned to Spain in the early 1860s, and, by the beginning of the twentieth century, it was supplying gas to the largest number of Spanish municipalities. The departure of Charles Lebon as company manager in 1872 marked a turning point, after which the firm was led by his son Eugène, who played a decisive role in establishing its presence in the electricity sector in Spain. However, its gas and electricity plants were located far apart, making interconnection extremely difficult in a country with particularly mountainous terrain. The fact that the multinational did not invest in hydroelectric power at the dawn of the electricity industry, and failed to secure large water concessions once the Spanish government began implementing its policy of economic nationalisation—combined with the intensification of labour unrest, increasing hostility from municipalities, the unfavourable exchange rate between the franc and the peseta, and the difficulties brought about by the First World War— led the company to decide to sell its assets, a process carried out between 1912 and 1925.

[4] La vie financière, 03-04-1922.

Competing Interests The authors have no conflicts of interest to declare that are relevant to the content of this chapter.

References

Anes, R. (1970). Las inversiones extranjeras en España, 1855–1880. In P. Schwatz. (Coord.), Ensayos sobre la economía española a mediados del siglo XIX (pp. 187–203). Banco de España.

Arroyo, M. (1996). *La industria del gas en Barcelona (1841–1933)*. Ediciones del Serbal.

Broder, A. (1981). *Le rôle des intérêts étrangers dans la croissance économique de l'Espagne, 1815–1913*. University of Paris.

Cameron, R. E. (1971). *Francia y el desarrollo económico de Europa, 1800–1914*. Tecnos.

Castro, R. (2018). Historia de una reconversión silenciosa. El capital francés en España, c.1800–1936. *Revista de Historia Industrial, 33*, 81–118.

Castro-Valdivia, M., Fernández-Paradas, M., & Matés-Barco, J. M. (2019). Las empresas extranjeras de agua y gas en España (circa 1900–1923). In J. M. Matés-Barco & A. Torres-Rodríguez (Eds.), *Los Servicios Públicos en España y México (siglos XIX–XX)* (pp. 51–74). Sílex.

Costa, M. T. (1981). *Financiación exterior del capitalismo español del siglo XIX*. Universidad de Barcelona.

de la Fuente, D. G. (1984). *La Compañía Española de Gas, S. A, "CEGAS" "Más de cien años de historia"*. Artes Gráficas Vicent S.A..

Fàbregas, P.-A. (2018). *Naturgy. 175 años de compromiso con la energía y la sociedad*. Naturgy Energy Group, S. A..

Fernández-Paradas, M. (2015). *La industria del gas en Cádiz (1845–2012)*. Fundación Gas Natural Fenosa.

Fernández-Paradas, M., Larrinaga Rodríguez, C., & Matés Barco, J. M. (2021). Los ingenieros y el suministro de gas en la España del siglo XIX. *Revista De Historia Industrial, 83*, 43–72. https://doi.org/10.1344/rhiihr.v30i83.31307

Fernández-Paradas, M., Martínez-López, A., & Mirás Araujo, J. (2022). The gas companies in Spain, a long-run approach (1842–2018). *Business History, 64*(1), 75–97. https://doi.org/10.1080/00076791.2019.1683162

Lebon et Cie. (1947). *Lebon & Cie. Un Centenaire 1847–1947*. Lebon et Cie.

Martínez-López, A., & Mirás-Araujo, J. (2024). La transferencia de tecnología en la Europa Latina: el papel de la Société Technique de l'industrie du Gaz en France, 1895–1938. *Asclepio, 73*(2). https://doi.org/10.3989/asclepio.2021.21

Vázquez-Fariñas, M., Castro-Valdivia, M., & Matés-Barco, J. M. (2023). The internationalisation of the British gas industry in Latin Europe in the nineteenth century. In A. Cardoso de Matos, A. Fernandez, & A. J. Pinto (Eds.), *The gas sector in Latin Europe's industrial history. Lighting and heating the* world (pp. 13–24). Springer. https://doi.org/10.1007/978-3-031-36674-1_3

Vázquez-Fariñas, M., Castro-Valdivia, M., & Matés-Barco, J. M. (2025). The withdrawal of foreign capital from the gas industry in Spain in the first third of the twentieth century. In A. Martínez-López, J. Mirás-Araujo, & N. Rodríguez-Martín (Eds.), *Economic history of the European energy industry. Lighting up Western Europe, 19th to 21st centuries* (pp. 73–86). Routledge. https://doi.org/10.4324/9781003428695-6

Williot, J.-P. (2006). La diffusion de la technologie gazière française dans le bassin méditerranéen: de la construction des usines à gaz à la mise en place des réseaux de gaz natural (1840–1890). In M. Merger. (Dir.), Transferts de technologies en Méditerranée (pp. 207–220). PUPS.

Mercedes Fernández-Paradas is a Full Professor of Contemporary History at the University of Málaga (Spain). Her research fields are utilities (gas, electricity, water) and business history, on which she is the author of several articles and books, such as, recently, *Bajo la cálida luz del gas: los mercados regionales de la industria gasista en España (siglos XIX y XX)* (Sílex, 2022, with I. Bartolomé Rodríguez & J. Mirás Araujo), *Business History in* Spain *(nineteenth and twentieth centuries)* (Peter Lang, 2021, with C. Larrinaga). She has been a visiting fellow in The London School of Economics and Political Science.

José Joaquín Luque-García is a PhD candidate in Contemporary History at the University of Málaga (Spain). His research focuses on the analysis and cataloguing of the specialist gas press in Western Europe. He has undertaken research stays at the University of Barcelona, the Sorbonne, and the London School of Economics and Political Science.

A Century-Old Coal Company: *Hullera Vasco-Leonesa*

Leonardo Caruana de las Cagigas and Julio Tascón Fernández

Abstract This chapter traces the history of *Hullera Vasco-Leonesa*, one of the longest-standing mining companies in Spain's coal sector, from its foundation in the late nineteenth century to well into the twentieth century. It analyses how the company established itself in the León mining basin, contributing to the economic and industrial development of the region. The text addresses its corporate structure, the working conditions of miners, and its relations with the state within the framework of a strategic and heavily subsidized industry. It also examines its ability to adapt to technological, energy, and political changes, as well as its resilience in the face of recurring coal crises. Through the case of *Hullera Vasco-Leonesa*, this chapter offers a representative view of the rise, transformation, and progressive decline of coal mining in Spain.

1 Introduction

Coal has played a central role in powering modern economies since the Industrial Revolution. Despite its historical relevance, coal use has declined steadily in many parts of the world. The global shift away from coal results from a combination of environmental, economic, and social forces. Coal is the most carbon-intensive fossil fuel. Burning coal releases large quantities of carbon dioxide (CO_2), thus contributing to global warming and climate change. In addition, coal combustion emits harmful air pollutants such as sulphur dioxide (SO_2), nitrogen oxides (NO_x), and particulate matter, which have been linked to respiratory illnesses, acid rain, and

L. Caruana de las Cagigas (✉)
Department of Economic Theory and History, University of Granada, Granada, Spain
e-mail: lcaruana_1@ugr.es

J. Tascón Fernández
Department of Economics, University of Oviedo, Oviedo, Spain
e-mail: juliotf@uniovi.es

M. Vázquez-Fariñas, F. Cabrera-Gallardo (eds.), *Business Trajectories in the History of Spain*, Frontiers in Economic History,
https://doi.org/10.1007/978-3-032-16214-4_5

environmental degradation (World Health Organization, 2018). Increasing public awareness and scientific consensus about these impacts have led to widespread environmental advocacy and international agreements aimed at reducing coal dependence. The rise of renewable energy technologies—including solar, wind, hydroelectric, and geothermal power—has provided viable alternatives to coal. These sources produce electricity with little or no greenhouse gas emissions and are increasingly cost-competitive thanks to rapid technological advancements and economies of scale. Natural gas, though still a fossil fuel, emits roughly half the CO_2 of coal per unit of energy and has often replaced coal in power generation in Spain. Economic changes have played a crucial role in the decline of coal. In many regions, coal-fired power plants can no longer compete with renewable energies and natural gas. Additionally, many coal plants require costly upgrades to meet modern environmental standards. Financial institutions are also divesting from coal-related assets due to growing concerns over "stranded assets" and long-term financial risks. Government policies have accelerated the transition away from coal. Several countries have introduced carbon pricing, emissions trading systems and regulations that penalize or phase out coal use. Nations have announced timelines for closing coal power plants. Subsidies and incentives have been granted to renewable energy technologies, encouraging investment in cleaner sources. Advances in energy storage technologies, particularly batteries, have mitigated the intermittency issues associated with solar and wind power. Additionally, the development of smart grid systems and energy efficiency measures have enhanced the reliability and sustainability of electricity systems, reducing the need for coal as a backup energy source. Finally, public opinion has shifted significantly in favour of environmental protection, leading to increased activism against coal projects. Environmental groups and citizens have pressured governments and corporations to divest from coal and adopt sustainable energy practices. Many corporations have set net-zero targets, aligning with investors' and consumers' expectations to reduce carbon footprints.

This trend is also evident in Spain, where the main coal mining regions were Asturias and León. In Asturias, the industry was largely dominated by the state-owned company HUNOSA, set up in 1967. From its inception, HUNOSA consistently operated at a financial loss. In contrast, coal mining in León was driven by the private sector. *Hullera Vasco-Leonesa* stood out for its ambitious New Mine Project, approved by the Commission of the European Communities in 1989. Although cessations of mining operations were scheduled for 2030, HUNOSA and *Hullera Vasco-Leonesa* closed before (Sudrià, 1993). In December 2010, the European Union (EU) issued a directive mandating the closure of all unprofitable coal mines by 2018. As a result, HUNOSA was closed in December 2024, marking the end of the coal era in Asturias. *Hullera Vasco-Leonesa* had already ceased operations in January 2019.

The rise and fall of *Hullera Vasco-Leonesa, S.A.* is a clear example of the evolution of coal mining in Europe. With a 124-year history—from its foundation 1893 to its closure in 2019—it was the subject of the first history of a private coal mining company in Spain (Anes & Tascón, 1993).

2 The History of *Hullera Vasco-Leonesa*

Hullera Vasco-Leonesa's history stands out within the Spanish coal sector. The company was founded on October 19, 1893, when twenty-nine shareholders met in Bilbao under the supervision of a notary of the Illustrious College of the Territory of Burgos to set up the company with a capital of 1,350,000 pesetas. This capital was divided into 2750 shares. The company aimed to exploit the founders' coal mines and any other mines—whether coal or other minerals—that might be acquired, leased, or registered in the future. The first Board of Directors was chaired by José Amézola y Viriga, representing *Amézola and Company*, a firm established in Bilbao in 1889 to operate part of the mines later managed by *Hullera Vasco-Leonesa*.

In 1988, *Hullera Vasco-Leonesa* ranked second in productivity among major national underground mining companies such as HUNOSA, ENCASUR, *Antracitas de Gaiztarro*, *Gillón*, MSP, *Lieres*, *Figaredo*, and *Hullas Coto Cortés* with an output of 608.8 metric tons per worker per year. *Hullas Coto Cortés* ranked first, although *Hullera Vasco-Leonesa*'s workforce was three times larger (Sudrià, 1993). Productivity cycles—measured in annual metric tons of marketable coal extracted per worker—revealed a consistent upward trend, which was only reversed during the economic crisis of the 1970s and the miners' strike of 1991.

The company's history can be divided into four stages, which reflect its adaptation to shifting market demands as a coal supplier. The first phase began with its foundation and the construction of the La Robla–Valmaseda railway, aimed to transport the coal for the steel industry in Biscay. The second stage focused on providing coal to RENFE (*Red Nacional de los Ferrocarriles Españoles*), Spain's national railway company. The third stage began in 1958, when *Hullera Vasco-Leonesa* started to deliver coal to a cement factory and, from 1971 onwards, to a thermal power plant—both located in La Robla. In the last stage, the company has promoted social welfare initiatives as a component of its strategic development.

3 Coal Supplied to Meet the Energy Demands of the Steel Industry in Vizcaya

In the early 1890s, coal mining in the province of León was largely managed by *Hullera Vasco-Leonesa*. In April 1890, the *Compañía del Ferrocarril Hullero de La Robla* was set up to build a railway connecting La Robla (León) with Valmaseda (Biscay). Its primary aim was to facilitate the transport of coal from León to the industrial hubs of the Basque Country.

The motivation underlying the construction of the La Robla–Valmaseda railway was the rising cost of British coal used by the steelworks in Biscay. Under the law of 31 December 1891, coal tariffs rose from 1.25 to 2.50 gold pesetas, and to 3.50 pesetas by 30 June 1895. Fluctuating tariffs also affected the final cost of imported coal. Throughout the 1890s, the price of imported coal stood at around 30 pesetas per ton and went up to 44 pesetas by 1900.

The sharp increase in coal prices in 1890 prompted Biscayan steelmakers to acquire coal mines—a trend known as the "coal fever"—leading to investments in mining operations in Asturias, León, and Palencia. These acquisitions allowed companies to install coking ovens, which did not only reduce production costs but also made it possible to recover of by-products such as tar, oils, and benzoles. Given the expansion of the European steel industry and the inevitable rise in coal prices, acquiring coal mines became a strategic tool for competing in international iron markets. This explains the foundation of various coal companies and the construction of the La Robla–Valmaseda railway to transport León coal to Biscay.

It is clear that *Hullera Vasco-Leonesa* was established with a view to supplying coal to the Biscayan steel industry (see Table 1). Even before mining operations had begun, the company's board offered coal to Altos Hornos de Bilbao at a very low price. However, reaching an agreement depended on lowering transport costs, although the coal from León was cheaper than the coal from Asturias. The type of coal was a major issue, because León coal was short-flame, whereas Biscayan blast furnaces required long-flame coal.

Hullera Vasco-Leonesa changed its strategy when it was found that León coal could not be used in Biscayan ironworks. The company entered negotiations with the *Compañía de los Caminos de Hierro del Norte de España* (*Northern Spanish Railway Company*) to find alternative outlets for its coal. Negotiations went smoothly because the *Northern Company* operated the Madrid–Gijón railway, which passed through Santa Lucía; and José Antonio de Ibarra, a member of the *Hullera Vasco-Leonesa* board, was also a member of the *Northern Railway Company*'s board.

Table 1 Founding members of *Hullera Vasco-Leonesa*

Esteban de Amézola y Viriga	Ramón de Ibarra y Arregui
José de Amézola y Viriga	Julián llamas Gusano
Julián Arregui y Erdoiza	Calixto López Sáez
Manuel Barrenechea Irunciaga	Pedro mac-Mahón Aguirre
Julián Basarte e Ibarra	Carolina Noval Montes
Pedro Pablo Benoist Hipp	Elvira Noval Montes
Francisco José Brevers y Marichal	Félix Noval Montes
Vicente Dotzaner y Hamm	Perfecta Noval Montes
Julio Eraso y Ángel	José María Olábarri y Massino
Laureano Fernández Bayón	Santiago Olábarri y Azaola
Víctor Fernández Bayón	Melitón Rodrigo y Abadía
Francisco González Ibarra	Ignacio Ureola e Ibarra
María Nicolasa Iturriaga e Iraragorri	José Vilallonga y Cipuló
José Antonio Ibarra y Arregui	Luis de Zubiría e Ibarra
Juan Luis Ibarra y Arregui	

Source: Anes and Tascón (1993, p. 32)

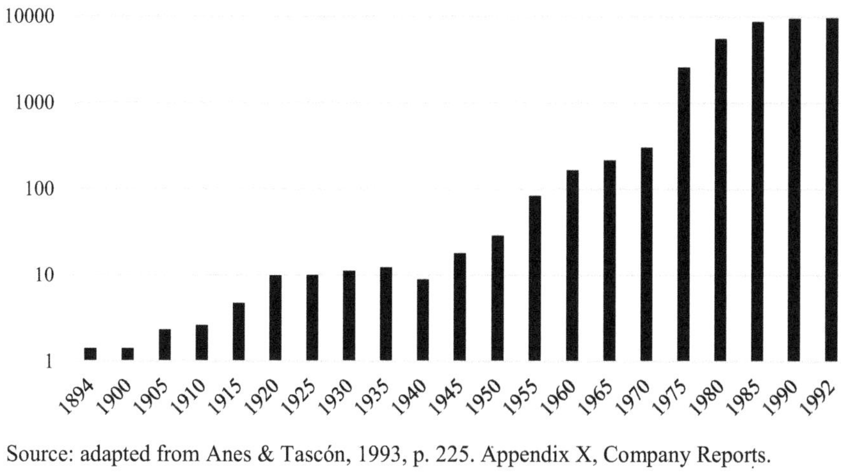

Fig. 1 Equity capital of *Hullera Vasco-Leonesa*, 1894–1992 (in millions of pesetas). *Source*: adapted from Anes and Tascón (1993, p. 225). Appendix X, Company Reports

In 1898, the *Hullera Vasco-Leonesa* board reported that sales to the *Northern Railway Company* had secured the annual production of briquettes, allowing for the efficient use of fine coal. On December 29, 1902, the board approved the sale of 28,000 tons of briquettes to the Northern Company—the company's most significant contract to date. Though this target was ambitious (the previous year's briquette production being 22,777 tons and saleable coal 18,149 tons), it stimulated expansion. The company purchased the Ciñera mines, although this led to disputes over property boundaries. The *Hulleras de Ciñera* company, established in Brussels in 1900, wound up in 1909 after *Hullera Vasco-Leonesa* offered 1,200,000 pesetas for its assets. The acquisition was completed on February 1, 1910. In 1912, doubled (134,788 tons of marketable coal). The Northern Railway Company purchased nearly all the coal.

Economic indicators show the company's expansion. Equity capital increased from 1.4 million pesetas in 1894 to 12.3 million pesetas in 1935 (Fig. 1). Commercial coal production rose from 9.9 thousand metric tons in 1896 to 105.8 thousand metric tons in 1935 (Table 2). Briquette production grew from 4.8 thousand metric tons in 1896 to 103.4 thousand metric tons in 1913 and dropped to 61.7 thousand metric tons in 1935 (Table 3).

Immediately after the Civil War, the civilian deaths that occurred in those valleys affected part of the know-how surely.

Table 2 Coal production, 1896–1993 (in metric tons)

1896	9914
1900	21,724
1905	42,168
1910	55,561
1915	143,836
1920	127,216
1925	99,830
1930	128,417
1935	105,821
1940	126,504
1945	269,350
1950	282,311
1955	288,229
1960	504,161
1965	531,618
1970	662,249
1975	657,623
1980	878,603
1985	1,045,792
1990	1,108,279
1993	1,177,075

Source: *Sociedad Hullera Vasco-Leonesa,* Annual Reports. Note: Until 1951, the data refer to bituminous coal production. From 1952 onwards, they include both bituminous coal and anthracite production

Table 3 Briquette production, 1896–1980 (in metric tons)

1896	4818
1900	12,740
1905	29,154
1910	55,333
1915	93,334
1920	84,533
1925	64,280
1930	72,700
1935	61,650
1940	47,500
1945	107,300
1950	143,020
1955	205,505
1960	346,530
1965	354,168
1970	144,398
1975	95,920
1980	24,560

Source: *Sociedad Hullera Vasco-Leonesa,* Annual Reports

4 Company Restructuring and Expansion (1940s–1950s)

In 1940, Emilio del Valle Egocheaga entered into an agreement to purchase all coal produced at the Santa Lucía and Ciñera mines. The duration of the contract was prolonged in 1942 for the 1943–1947 period. Alos, investors from León associated with the firm *Valle y Díez, S.R.C.* acquired a significant stake in *Hullera Vasco-Leonesa*. As a result, the original members of the Board of Directors only owned the 20 shares required by the company's statutes to hold their position.

During this transitional period, the Board approved amendments to the company's statutes to relocate its headquarters from Bilbao to León. An Extraordinary General Meeting was held on September 28, 1943 to formalize these changes. At this meeting, the Board—previously chaired by Francisco de Ibarra y González—was replaced by a new team of directors: Francisco Díez Rodríguez, Leonardo Manzanares Serrano, José and María Luz del Valle Menéndez, and Eloy Rojo Melero, who became the President. Despite being the company's largest shareholder, Emilio del Valle Egocheaga rejected a management position. However, he joined the Board in 1946 and was appointed CEO in 1948.

With the involvement of new shareholders and a focus on optimizing production, the integration of the Matallana coalfield became a strategic priority. This site was a natural extension of the Santa Lucía and Ciñera operations and was also owned by Emilio del Valle Egocheaga. The last hurdle was to obtain authorization from the Ministry of Finance for a capital increase, which was approved and fully subscribed in 1946, raising the company's capital to 25 million pesetas.

The integration of the Matallana coalfield in 1944 enhanced the company's position. According to the company's annual report, the mining complex had become one of the most important ones in Spain in terms of size and volume of coal reserves. The report further noted that if exploratory drilling confirmed initial findings, *Hullera Vasco-Leonesa* would "clearly be positioned at the forefront of coal mining operations in our country".

5 RENFE as a Principal Client and the Shift to Industrial Expansion (1950s–1960s)

A new development in *Hullera Vasco-Leonesa* took place in the 1950s, marked by the leadership of Antonio del Valle Menéndez. Appointed chief engineer in 1951, he became general director in 1953, deputy managing director in 1959, and eventually CEO in 1972 and president in 1977 (Tascón, 2000). He ran a company that played a crucial role in consolidating the shift from an agrarian economy to a coal-centred economy mining, a transformation that had begun in the nineteenth century but accelerated in the postwar period. His work facilitated the economic and social transition of the workforce in the mountainous regions of northeastern León, where traditional livestock farming gave way to employment in the mining sector (Tascón, 2000, p. 498).

RENFE, the national railway company, was established in January 1941 and began acquiring standard-gauge railway lines that same year. However, under the law of 8 May 1939, the supply of coal briquettes from *Hullera Vasco-Leonesa* required formal agreements with RENFE. Once this agreement was reached in 1951, plans were developed to build a new briquette plant with a capacity of 1000 tons per day.

These industrial developments demanded substantial investment, leading to successive capital increases: 100 million pesetas in 1956 and 200 million by 1963. Briquette production became the company's priority, as confirmed in its 1955 Annual Report. Negotiations with RENFE culminated in a contract to build a new plant in La Robla. RENFE was fully aware of the advantages of using briquettes, which provided more structural integrity and reduced moisture content. In 1956, RENFE placed an order for 250,000 tons of briquettes.

Despite this significant demand, the company faced long-term challenges due to the gradual electrification of Spanish railways. Although the transition was slow, it signalled the eventual decline of coal as the primary fuel for trains, prompting *Hullera Vasco-Leonesa* to seek alternative markets.

One such diversification effort was the company's bid to build a cement plant in northwestern Spain; a project approved in 1957. A plant was built in La Robla, with an annual production capacity of 100,000 tons. In 1958, *Cementos La Robla, S.A.* was set up. It was a new development in the company's industrial strategy (Tascón, 2000).

6 An Inevitable Shift in Coal Demand

The cement factory could not accommodate the total amount of coal produced by *Hullera Vasco-Leonesa*. The company's management, in their search for alternative uses to channel the coal output, hoped to distribute the coal to the coal chemical and the thermal power industries. A thermal power plant was seemingly the most advisable option. In 1965, a plant construction project was submitted, in partnership with *Unión Eléctrica Madrileña* and *Hidroeléctrica de Moncabril*. The La Robla thermal power plant was included in the National Energy Plan, and in 1968 the regulations for the new partnership were signed. The plant was due to be operational by the spring of 1971, with further expansions planned.

In line with this, in 1988, supply contracts were approved to deliver coal to *Unión Eléctrica Fenosa*, *Hidroeléctrica del Cantábrico*, and TERMINOR. Consequently, there was a change in the demand for coal produced by *Vasco-Leonesa*: initially destined for railways, it was now intended to supply thermal power stations.

In 1956, the expansion of *Vasco-Leonesa*'s mining operations became a matter of national interest. In 1976, the company signed the coordinated action agreement, and it was evident that the company had grown significantly since its registered office was moved from Bilbao to León. Several capital increases were carried out, and equity rose from nine million pesetas in 1943 to 9401 million pesetas in 1990. Commercial coal production reached 115,560 tonnes in 1943 and rose to 1,108,279 metric tonnes in 1990. This growth was accompanied by major technical improvements, and the workforce, which was 1844 employees in 1951, decreased to 1661 in 1990. The maximum size of the "*Vasco*" workforce was reached in 1963, when it peaked at 2599 workers.

In line with the evolution of the workforce and the technology, average production per worker was 150 tonnes in 1951, 197 tonnes in 1963, and 667 tonnes annually per worker in 1990. There are no available data for the second half of the twentieth century. Thus, the discussion on productivity focuses on this period, when coal, particularly in Europe, existed in a competitive energy market in which productivity gains became increasingly important. During the industrial crisis, highly productive coal companies across Europe—despite operating under the shadow of a foretold demise—struggled to offset inefficient cost structures and remain competitive in modern markets (Tascón, 1996, p. 4).

In the case of *Vasco-Leonesa*, both production and productivity increased in the second half of the twentieth century (Fig. 2).

The increase in the company's return on assets (Fig. 3) reveals an upward trend until the 1920s, which was more evident during the Great War. The growth in returns was much more moderate in the 1940s and the 1950s. There was a sharp rise in the 1970s and the 1990s, which encouraged further investment in the mines. The sector became particularly attractive in the 1990s, when the company began receiving financial assistance from the European Union.

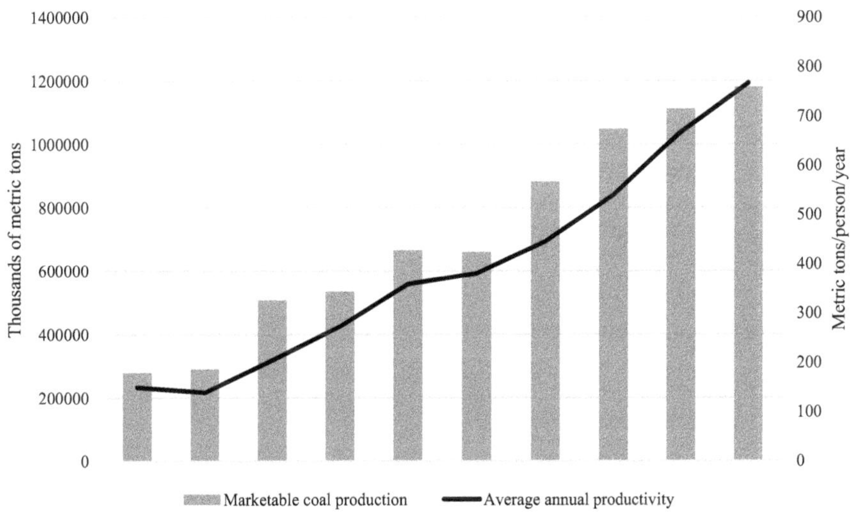

Fig. 2 Production and productivity at *Hullera Vasco-Leonesa*, 1951–1993. *Source*: adapted from Tascón (1996, p. 14)

Fig. 3 Return on assets of *Hullera Vasco-Leonesa*, 1895–1992 (in percentage). *Source*: adapted from Anes and Tascón (1993, pp. 223 and 226); and the company's Annual Reports. Company profits and assets deflated using the GDP deflator (Prados-de-la-Escosura, 2025)

The income statement of *Vasco-Leonesa* reflects a positive trend for shareholders' interests from the end of the Spanish Civil War to the 1990s (Fig. 4). Annual productivity data per worker back the evolution of the company's profit and loss accounts. However, it is difficult to compare the information on return on assets with the information of other firms. It should be noted that national and European Community subsidies need to be explained to determine the true investment appeal, as illustrated by the Nueva Mina, which was expected to be the mine of the twenty-first century. This mine was meant to exploit the deep synclines of Matallana and Llombera and, despite achieving high and even excellent productivity levels, when compared to the mining operations of HUNOSA, it did not yield competitive profitability within the European mining sector.

In the company's last stage, lack of interest and inadequate implementation of safety measures have been considered factors contributing to the fall in *Vasco-Leonesa*'s production. For instance, the inability to foresee the "instantaneous methane outburst" that occurred in October 2013 resulted in a devastating accident.

The progression of the company's return on assets (Fig. 3) reveals an initial period up to the 1920s marked by high percentages, particularly pronounced during the years of the Great War. The growth in returns was much more moderate during the 1940s and the 1950s. A renewed upswing began in the 1970s and continued through the 1990s, encouraging further investment in the mines. The sector became especially attractive in the 1990s, when the company began receiving financial support from the European Union.

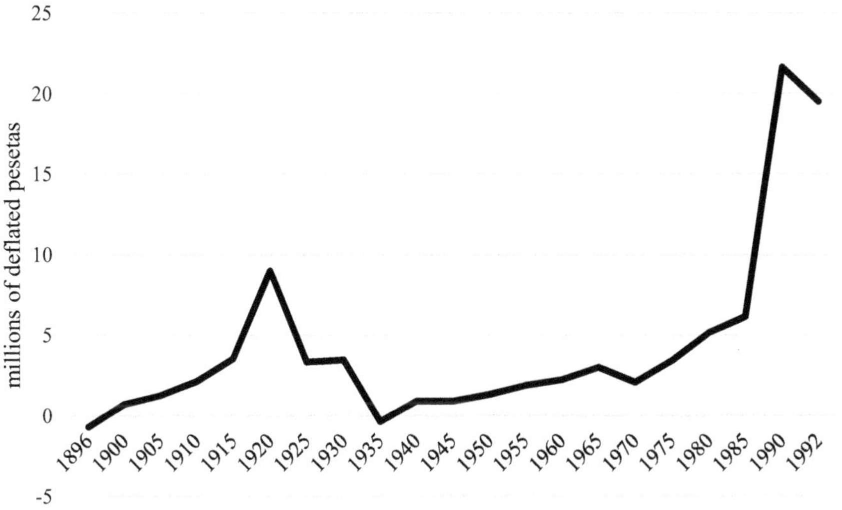

Source: adapted from Anes & Tascón, 1993, pp. 191-208. GDP deflator according to Prados-de-la-Escosura (2025).

Fig. 4 Evolution of the profit and loss account, 1896–1992. *Source*: adapted from Anes and Tascón (1993, pp. 191–208). GDP deflator according to Prados-de-la-Escosura (2025)

The income statement of the *Vasco-Leonesa* company reflects a favourable trend for shareholders' interests from the end of the Spanish Civil War through to the 1990s (Fig. 4). Annual productivity data per worker also support the trajectory observed in the company's profit and loss accounts. However, the information on return on assets—which is often used to measure the company's pull to investors—is difficult to compare with that of other firms. It should be noted that the complex aid of national and European Community subsidies needs to be explained to determine the true investment appeal, as was the case with the Nueva Mina, which was expected to be the mine of the twenty-first century. This mine was projected to exploit the deep synclines of Matallana and Llombera and, despite achieving high or even excellent productivity levels, when compared to the mining operations of HUNOSA, it did not yield competitive profitability within the European mining sector.

In the company's final phase, a lack of interest and inadequate implementation of safety measures have been cited as contributing factors to the decline of *Vasco-Leonesa*'s productive activities. For instance, the inability to foresee the "instantaneous methane outburst" that occurred in October 2013 resulted in a devastating accident.

7 Social Welfare: From a "Relief Fund" to the "Labour Foundation"

Vasco-Leonesa had been concerned about its staff since it was founded. At the beginning, the management could not implement effective measures quickly; however, they were committed to ensuring that workers were covered in case of accident or illness. They even considered setting up a pension scheme. On 23 September 1901, the company's Board of Directors met to agree on the first step towards social assistance. The Board decided that the remaining balance of 719.14 pesetas, left after the distribution of profits for the 1900–1901 fiscal year, would be spent on opening an account called the Workers' Relief Fund. The company's management intended the funds in this account to help workers who, though not covered by industrial accidents law, deserved financial assistance (Sierra, 1990).

On 24 May 1910, the Board member Pablo Benoist brought up the initiative to open a company store (*economato*), an idea submitted to him during a visit to the mines. The purpose was "to create a company store in Santa Lucía that would protect workers against potential abuse from local retailers". In addition, "there was a real need for housing" and the Board of Directors decided to undertake "the construction of new houses for workers" at the meeting held on 18 June 1913.

Although the pension scheme was not set up, the company store did come to fruition, as evidenced by a letter sent to the company's president by Santa Lucía's managing director on 28 June. The director's report said that a workers' committee, demonstrating little inclination to strike, requested that the company open a store where they could purchase groceries at lower prices than those charged by local retailers. On 30 June 1923, the Board decided to open a store.

In 1930, coinciding with the inauguration of the Ibarra shaft, the company developed a plan to build housing for workers and employees, as well as a hospital and barracks for the Civil Guard. The Board justified the plan on 29 November 1930, deeming it particularly "necessary due to the deplorable conditions in which these people currently live". During that session, the Board reviewed the building plans and instructed the mine manager to:

> The mine manager was urged to acquire land so that the construction of a housing development consisting of 96 rooms could start; chalets to accommodate 15 employees' families; a hospital with a capacity of 7 beds, including living quarters for the doctor and nurse; and Civil Guard barracks to house 10 guards. The estimated total cost was 1000,000 pesetas.

At the Extraordinary General Meeting held on 10 April 1931, the company authorized a loan application, and on April 29, the Board granted Mario Zapatero the authority to manage the financial arrangements and undertake "the construction of the workers' housing development, employee residences, a first aid hospital, and the Civil Guard barracks in Santa Lucía".

In May 1910, during a visit to Santa Lucía, Pablo Benoist received the first request for educational assistance from workers. As a result, a girls' school was built to improve both education and moral instruction, which was considered "quite difficult when in contact with boys". Three years later, at a meeting held on 18 June, the Board agreed to build.

> a new higher-level school, run by a female teacher, on the company's premises, aiming to teach domestic skills (ironing, sewing, cooking, washing, etc.) to the daughters and sisters of the company's staff.

The Ciñera mine group, which had been acquired by the company, was the first to ask for assistance in starting a school in 1910. *Vasco-Leonesa* also supported education in Santa Lucía and was willing to collaborate with nearby villages, as evidenced by the request for financial aid made by the town of La Vid. In 1918, Huergas de Gordón sought help to repair its school. La Vid and Huergas de Gordón received 500 pesetas and 2000 pesetas, respectively. Similarly, in 1920, two villages, Valle and Villar, requested assistance to complete their school buildings and improve water supply (Muñiz, 2024, p. 4; Crespo, 2025). The Board approved these requests on April 26, 1920, given the "good behaviour of the workers from these villages employed at Ciñera during the 1914 strike".

The next request to *Vasco-Leonesa* came from the residents of Llombera, near Santa Lucía, who wanted to build a boarding school. The company agreed and, on 22 January, covered approximately 50% of the costs. In 1932, company workers living in Ciñera requested that their 53 children be admitted to the Santa Lucía nursery school. The company agreed that one of the teachers from Santa Lucía would travel to Ciñera to teach in the place chosen as a school.[1]

Medical and hospital care was always provided by the company. Religious education and practices were also closely overseen by *Vasco-Leonesa*.

The postwar period was characterized by the expansion of the company and an increase in the number of workers. Housing was thus a major concern. In June 1947, the Board approved that the manager executes and signs before a notary public the transfer made by the National Delegation of Trade Unions of a property in the Ciñera area to build 194 protected housing units. On 10 April 1948, the company approved the construction of a barracks-house in Ciñera, with a capacity of 80–100 workers. Likewise, the construction of a "foremen's house in Santa Lucía" was approved. In 1949, the Board authorized the transfer of the Peña Utrera property to the municipality of Matallana del Torío to build social housing, granting preferential rights to *Vasco-Leonesa*'s workers. The construction of housing in Matallana faced various challenges, which were solved at the Board meeting on 26 September 1950.

In addition to housing, the company also took responsibility for the sports and recreational activities of workers and their families. In April 1948, the Board agreed to build sports facilities in Ciñera, including a soccer pitch, swimming pools, a fronton court, and bowling alleys. In May 1949, it also approved the allocation of one million pesetas to a sports centre for the Santa Lucía's workers, in cooperation with

[1] Support from mining companies to build schools is peculiar to the Asturian mining region (Muñiz, 2024, p. 4). However, not all coal mining areas appear to have benefited from such assistance. In the Bierzo region in León, the Tremor and Boeza valleys share similar concerns about miners' housing but do not seem to take interest in providing educational facilities (Crespo, 2025).

the Education and Rest programme. At the 1949 Annual s' meeting, it was noted that a church and a school were being built in Ciñera, the project being funded by the Devastated Regions programme, as well as improvements in water supply. At the Board meeting held on 4 November 1950, the managing director Emilio del Valle Egocheaga emphasized the need to create in Santa Lucía:

> a nursery to take care of the young children of women working for the company while they are at work.

It was agreed to contact the parish priest of Santa Lucía to discuss how to build such a charitable institution. Finally the Employees' Club of the *Hullera Vasco-Leonesa* was officially inaugurated on 4 December. On 10 April 1951, the Board tackled the issue of bringing in water to ensure regular supply to Santa Lucía, Ciñera, and La Vid.

Between the national interest statement made on 18 December 1955 and the concerted action agreement signed by the company in 1976, the company launched further social welfare initiatives. The housing shortage worsened as the workforce increased, and staffing needs required better conditions to recruit new workers. At the Board meeting held in December 1956, the aid granted to workers to build their own homes was discussed. The Board also approved arrangements to build 30 houses in La Robla for employees of the new agglomerates factory.

In 1960, the company decided to take the necessary steps to build 50 houses in collaboration with *Cementos La Robla, S.A.* (Board of Directors, 11/10/1960). The schooling of the workers' children remained a major issue for the company. When the La Robla facilities were built, *Vasco-Leonesa* and *Cementos La Robla* committed to build schools and housing for teachers. The need for specialized staff led the company to organize intensive training courses, which also promoted the creation of a Vocational Training School in La Robla. The *Virgen del Buen Suceso School* was inaugurated on 15 August 1965. The municipality of Pola de Gordón received (deed dated September 3, 1971) land from *Vasco-Leonesa*, which expanded the area designed for an elementary school under resolution of the Board at a meeting held on 17 October 1975.

Social welfare initiatives in the 1960s include: *Colegio Nuestra Señora del Camino* (500 female students in primary and secondary education); the *School Board Patronage* (500 students in primary education); *Colegio Santa Bárbara* (600 male students in secondary education); *Virgen del Buen Suceso Vocational Training School* (200 male students); a female *Vocational Training School* (75 students); four cooperative stores; 590 houses; a cinema; a children's summer camp; the *Emilio del Valle Egocheaga Labor Foundation*; a monthly magazine; and three recreational centres, a sports centre, a hunting club, a shooting range, and houses in the village of Perlora.

The Labor Foundation aimed to "encourage the relationship between workers and the Board of Directors and to foster human relations between both parties" (Anes & Tascón, 1993, pp. 184–186). The Foundation was established on 4 May 1963, and its statutes were revised on 7 June 1965, and on 3 November 1983. Loans were granted for acquisition and improvement purposes, the total amount being

324,780,300 pesetas as of 31 December 1992, of which 286,235,164 pesetas had already been repaid by that date. The Foundation built houses chalets in Perlora, on the Asturian coast, but also rented apartments in Mediterranean coastal towns such as Xeraco and Tavernes (Valencia), and Torremolinos (Málaga) in July and August 1992. Besides financing youth camps, it provided grants to schools, old age homes, parents' associations, athletics groups, and financed competitions held at the *Vasco-Leonesa* Sports Facilities.

8 Conclusion

Vasco-Leonesa developed different strategies to keep its position in the market. It first supplied coal to the Basque steel industry, RENFE being its main client. Then, when the demand for coal from the railway sector declined as a result of electrification, the company focused on the thermal power plant at La Robla.

Thus, the stages covered include the foundational years and their expansion until the years prior to the Civil War; the Bilbao to León phase, spanning from the post-war reorganization to the declaration of national interest (1955); the subsequent period leading up to the concerted actions (1965–1975); and finally, the phase of "company consolidation" (1976–1993).

Hullera Vasco-Leonesa undeniably shaped the economy of the Northeastern León Mountain region and contributed to economic growth and well-being in the area. Despite the European industrial decline, it managed to be operational until 2000 thanks to its great market adaptability. Indeed, after supplying coal to RENFE, its main customer, it succeeded in building a cement factory and a thermal power plant to supply its products, in the 1990s, it carried out the "New Mine" project, equipped with cutting-edge technology. In the 1950s and the 1960s, the company achieved the best national performance levels, comparable to those of the Ruhr coalfields, and overtook the public company HUNOSA in the 1980s (see Table 4). The company's good performance was only hindered by negative factors such as the loss of 106 of the 248 working days in 1991.

Sources: adapted from Anes and Tascón (1993), Vázquez (1994, p. 782), Tascón (2000, p. 503).

By 2010, the European Union had set the closure of unprofitable mining operations for 2018. In this study, we have left aside the period from 1994 to 2019, during which the *Sociedad Hullera Vasco-Leonesa* declined and ultimately ceased operations. The concern for workplace safety observed in the preceding years appeared to wane during certain years of the twenty-first century. The contradictions between

Table 4 Average annual productivity (tons per worker/year), 1983–1990

Year	1983	1984	1985	1986	1987	1988	1989	1990
HUNOSA	188.6	179.5	174.5	176.0	145.9	166.7	173.2	174.1
Hullera Vasco-Leonesa	502.0	511.2	539.6	541.0	627.1	608.8	629.0	667.2

the notably high average productivity figures—such as those presented in Table 4—and an inefficient cost structure may shed light on the company's decline. Additionally, consideration should be given to the impact of the decision made during Rodríguez Zapatero's second term to remove the production premium for electricity generated from national coal (1 peseta per kWh produced) granted to electric utilities. Given the global importance of coal, it is reasonable to suppose that different corporate trajectories might have accompanied *Vasco-Leonesa* if Spain had followed certain European examples regarding coal production and the supply of thermal power plants.

Competing Interests The authors have no conflicts of interest to declare that are relevant to the content of this chapter.

References

Anes Álvarez, R., & Tascón Fernández, L. J. (1993). *Hullera Vasco-Leonesa. Los cien primeros años de su historia, 1893–1993*. Gráfica Spainfo S. A., Sociedad Anónima Hullera Vasco-Leonesa.

Crespo Martínez, V. (2025). *Minas, negocios y riqueza en los valles de Tremor y del Boeza*. Image y Print Services S. L.

Muñiz Sánchez, J. (2024). «Faltan muchos porque les quedó mal cuerpo del día anterior». Antialcoholismo patronal en un contexto de paternalismo industrial. El caso de la Sociedad Hullera Española (Asturias), 1892-1936. *Hispania, 84*(278), 1092. https://doi.org/10.3989/hispania.2024.1092

Prados-de-la-Escosura, L. (2025). What was Spain's GDP then? *Measuring Worth, 2025*. Retrieved September 12, 2025, from https://measuringworth.com/datasets/spaingdp/result.php

Sierra Álvarez, J. (1990). *El obrero soñado. Ensayo sobre el paternalismo industrial (Asturias, 1860–1917)*. Siglo Veintiuno de España.

Sudrià y Triay, C. (1993). El sector energético: condicionamiento y posibilidades. In J. L. García Delgado. (Dir.), España. Economía (pp. 267–295). Espasa-Calpe.

Tascón Fernández, J. (1996). Productividad del trabajo durante el declive de la minería del carbón europea. El modelo de la Hullera Vasco-Leonesa, 1933–1993. *EUI working paper HEC* 96/2, 77 pp.

Tascón Fernández, J. (2000). Antonio del Valle Menéndez (1923). In E. Torres Villanueva & G. Tortella Casares (Eds.), (Coords.) *Los 100 empresarios españoles del siglo XX* (pp. 498–503). LID Editorial Empresarial.

Vázquez, J. (1994). La economía asturiana (1985–1992). Los nuevos ajustes. In G. Ojeda Gutiérrez, & J. A. Vázquez García (Coords.), *Historia de la Economía Asturiana*, vol. 3 (pp. 770–784). La Nueva España.

Leonardo Caruana de las Cagigas is a Professor of Economic History at the University of Granada. His research focuses on economic development, bilateral relations during WWII, and entrepreneurship. He Coordinated *Cambio y crecimiento económico* (Pirámide) and edited *Entrepreneurship in Spain: A History (Routledge), among others*. Key articles include "*An elephant in the garden*" (*European Review of Economic History*, 2007) and studies on Spanish insurance and SMEs. He teaches in bilingual economics programmes and supervises graduate research. With a PhD from Universidad Complutense de Madrid, he is active in historical economic analysis, contributing to books, journals, and academic debates on Spain's economic transformation.

Julio Tascón Fernández , Full Professor at the University of Oviedo, Department of Economics, Dean (Nov. 2014–Dec. 2018); Vice-Dean of International Relations and ECTS Coordinated, School of Economics and Business (2010–2011). He is the author of several renowned works, including "European capital movements (FDI) 1958–2018 dataset", *EUI Research Data* (2020, Robert Schuman Centre for Advanced Studies, https://hdl.handle.net/1814/68416); "The Spanish miracle and the American FDI: a new interpretation" (2023), co-authored with Leonardo Caruana in *Araucaria. Revista Iberoamericana de Filosofía, Política, Humanidades y Relaciones Internacionales* (54, 703–737, https://doi.org/10.12795/araucaria.2023.i54.32); and "Mejora de competitividad turística en España con democracia, 1975–1995" (2025), in *Hispania Nova* (23, 99–127, https://doi.org/10.20318/hn.2025.7969).

The Business History of the Málaga Steel Industry

Víctor M. Heredia-Flores

Abstract This chapter analyses the evolution of the steel industry in Málaga through the business legacy of the Heredia family, one of the most influential families in the nineteenth-century Andalusian capitalism. It studies how Manuel Agustín Heredia founded one of the first major Spanish steel industries, taking advantage of local resources, international trade networks, and the momentum of economic protectionism. Over three generations, the Heredia family consolidated a business complex that encompassed mining, metallurgy, transport, and finance. The chapter examines both the initial boom of this industrial initiative and the internal and external factors that led to its decline, such as competition from the north, lack of modernisation, and changes in economic policies. Through this case, it illustrates the role of family elites in Spanish industrialisation and the fragility of their long-term projects.

1 Introduction

The exploitation of iron ore from the Marbella area gave rise, starting in 1826, to a long business venture that marked the beginning of the civil steel industry in Spain. Initial difficulties in achieving results discouraged the partners of the first companies established for its exploitation, with the exception of businessman Manuel Agustín Heredia, who opted for technological innovation with the help of the military officer Francisco Elorza. The success of his initiative led to Málaga's dominance of the Spanish steel industry during the middle decades of the nineteenth century, now under the management of the second generation of the family, until the problem of coal costs led to a near-final crisis with its closure in 1893. A few years later, there was a brief revival with the contribution of Belgian capital that lasted

V. M. Heredia-Flores (✉)
Department of Economic Theory and Economic History,
University of Málaga, Málaga, Spain
e-mail: vmheredia@uma.es

M. Vázquez-Fariñas, F. Cabrera-Gallardo (eds.), *Business Trajectories in the History of Spain*, Frontiers in Economic History,
https://doi.org/10.1007/978-3-032-16214-4_6

until 1906. The Great War created a favourable opportunity for a third and final phase that lasted until 1924.

Between the last decades of the eighteenth century and the beginning of the nineteenth century, the economy of the Málaga region, on the Mediterranean coast of Andalusia, experienced successive periods of prosperity and crisis. The expansion of an agricultural sector focused on production for foreign markets through the export of local fruits (raisins, wine, almonds, olive oil, etc.) had been reinforced by the increase in trade with the American colonies beginning in 1765, when the port of Málaga was authorised to trade directly with overseas territories. The opening of the colonial market was accompanied by a revitalisation of commercial relations with northern Europe. In particular, the city of Málaga itself and Vélez-Málaga, in the neighbouring region of Axarquía, channelled this trade based on the establishment of commercial, financial, and service networks essential for the maintenance of growing trade, as indicated by Antonio Parejo (2009).

Agricultural and commercial expansion came to an abrupt halt with the crisis of the early nineteenth century. Rising international conflict affected trade networks, epidemics—most notably the yellow fever epidemic of 1804—decimated the population, and poor harvests reduced agricultural production, creating a bleak picture that worsened with the effects of the Napoleonic invasion and the loss of the American colonies. This critical period largely liquidated the network of foreign trading houses that had been consolidated throughout the eighteenth century (Gámez Amián, 1994; Villar García, 1997). However, at the same time, it was a period of opportunity for national merchants who took advantage of the situation to maintain operational commercial links with northern European markets and who were also closely following the industrialisation process initiated by Great Britain. As a result, by 1820 the Málaga commercial register had changed substantially, and the name of Manuel Agustín Heredia stood out with particular brilliance.

2 Manuel Agustín Heredia: A Nineteenth-Century Spanish Businessman

Manuel Agustín Heredia moved to Málaga in the early years of the nineteenth century. His activity far exceeded local boundaries; his business ventures extended to the Americas and other continents, leading him to lead the development of several industrial sectors in Spain, while maintaining close relations with Great Britain and other European countries.

Manuel Agustín Heredia was born in Rabanera de Cameros (La Rioja, northern Spain) in 1786, to a family of modest noblemen. The Sierra de Cameros had traditionally based its economy on transhumant livestock farming and the scattered wool-based textile industry, which in turn had generated a certain commercial prosperity. The crisis at the end of the eighteenth century gradually dragged its towns into a state of decline that prompted emigration to lands with better prospects (Moreno, 2001).

Heredia emigrated south to work as a clerk in a trading house in Vélez-Málaga. This city was then an important commercial centre, located in the heart of an agricultural region that produced figs, almonds, raisins, wine, and oil. From the outset, Heredia displayed his two main qualities: intelligence and a great capacity for work. García Montoro (1978) points out that Heredia's fortune arose during the Peninsular War. In 1808, he formed a trading company in Vélez with two other partners, Ramón de Córdoba and Manuel María Fernández. Four years later, he created a new company with Fernández, based in Gibraltar, which was dissolved in 1813.

His contacts in Gibraltar allowed him to conduct his first business ventures, collaborating with the supplies to maintain the resistance against the French invaders. As a reward, general Francisco Ballesteros, who commanded the Spanish troops in the Serranía de Ronda, granted him the right to exploit the graphite mines of Marbella area in 1810. The engineer Álvarez de Linera (1857) said years later that Heredia himself "naively confessed that this speculation had been so lucrative that he could consider the Marbella graphite mines to be the source of his great fortune".

In less than ten years, Heredia amassed a considerable fortune that allowed him to become independent in business. Thanks to his wealth, he was able to join the Málaga oligarchy, marrying Isabel Livermore (1795–1849) in 1813, the daughter of Thomas Livermore, a tannery merchant of English origin. The couple had fourteen children, of whom only seven survived: Isabel, Manuel, Tomás, Enrique, Amalia, Ricardo, and María. One of her sisters-in-law, Petronila, married the banker José de Salamanca, and another, Josefa, married Martín Heredia Escolar, half-brother of Manuel Agustín and his closest collaborator in the management of the family businesses.

Heredia permanently established his residence in Málaga. His businesses expanded into different sectors, responding to a business strategy based on risk diversification and the exploitation of opportunities.

Trade with the Americas brought him significant profits. Heredia was the first Spanish merchant to resume commercial trade with the former colonies, initially using ships of other nationalities (especially British and American) and later creating his own merchant fleet (García Montoro, 1978). His ships sailed to northern Europe, the Americas, and Asia, engaging in intense commercial activity. Pascual Madoz (1848) confirmed that Heredia was "the first Spaniard who, with his direct expeditions to the new States of South America, re-established the relations interrupted since the declaration of their independence". Since 1812, when he operated from Gibraltar, Manuel Agustín Heredia traded in tobacco from the Americas, supplying it to the State, which held a monopoly on the distribution and sale of this product. He also continued to exploit the graphite mines in Marbella and export his production.

Heredia was admitted to the Consulate, a commercial institution created in 1785 by order of Charles III. As prior of the Consulate, from 1824 he promoted the repair of roads, the cleaning of the seabed of the port of Málaga, and a project to promote the study of industrial chemistry (Bejarano, 1947).

Manuel Agustín Heredia's business activities encompassed virtually all branches of production. Of course, real estate development was not outside his interest, although it was not the sector to which he devoted the most attention. In 1816, he acquired land in the Alameda district on which he built four houses, including his residence. The Alameda district had become the most representative urban space and was the location of the main merchant families (Ordóñez Vergara, 1991).

Heredia also delved into soap making, an industry that Frenchmen such as Maury and Reboul had successfully launched in Málaga at the end of the eighteenth century. The promising prospects of the soap business attracted the attention of the entrepreneurial Heredia, who entered the business beginning in 1830 and eventually owned three soap factories and became the largest soap manufacturer in Spain (García Montoro, 1978). Heredia expanded his industrial business with lead, extending his scope of operations to the province of Almería. In 1837, he acquired the San Andrés lead smelter in Adra and introduced technological and production improvements (Pérez de Perceval Verde, 2018; García Montoro, 1978).

Shortly before his death, Heredia promoted two other industrial projects. The first was the creation of a large chemical factory next to his forge, intended for the production of sulphuric acid for use in soap and candle making and in the treatment of fabrics. The second project consisted of launching a cotton, linen, and hemp spinning and weaving factory, a pioneer in Spain. Once again applying his entrepreneurial spirit and direct knowledge of the British industrialisation process, he partnered with the Larios family for this project. The negotiations began in 1845, and the factory was completed the following year. Heredia's death postponed the formalisation of the founding deed until April of the following year. The capital was divided into three lots of twenty shares each between the heirs of Manuel Agustín Heredia and the companies *Larios Hermanos y Compañía* of Málaga and *Larios Hermanos* of Gibraltar. In subsequent years, Heredia's heirs withdrew from the company, and management remained in the hands of the Larios family (Parejo Barranco, 1990).

Heredia was a modern businessman who paid special attention to the new business opportunities arising from industrialisation. As an owner of merchant ships and urban properties, he participated in the creation of insurance companies. He was the main shareholder of the *Sociedad Anónima de Seguros Marítimos y Terrestres* (Maritime and Land Insurance Company) called *Unión Malagueña* (1838) and was also among the promoters of the *Sociedad de Seguros Mutuos contra incendios de edificios en Málaga* (Mutual Insurance Society against building fires in Málaga), established in 1840. The appearance of the first steamships also did not escape his interest. Heredia managed to mobilise other Málaga capitalists around the project of a company established in 1845 with the aim of establishing a regular steamship line between Cádiz and Marseille (García Montoro, 1978).

From the beginning, Manuel Agustín Heredia's activities included lending to farmers, as was common among Málaga merchants. Furthermore, his relationship with his brother-in-law, José de Salamanca, led Heredia to participate in financial transactions in which he provided his relative with the guarantee of a solid financial position. In 1841, both men signed a contract with the government for the capitalisation of the interest on debt placed abroad. Under this agreement, Heredia and

Salamanca agreed to place ten million *reales* in London and another five million in Paris, the amount of six months' worth of the capitalisation of the interest (Tedde de Lorca, 1999).

Heredia also participated in the creation of the *Banco de Isabel II* in 1844 (Tortella Casares, 1975). Heredia also attempted to open a joint-stock deposit bank with issuing capacity in Málaga, but his initiative met with government opposition (Tedde de Lorca, 1999). Despite this setback, Heredia took over the representation of the *Banco de San Fernando* in Málaga. During those years, Salamanca obtained a salt lease from the state, in a transaction that also included Heredia and Gaspar Remisa, another of the great financiers of the time (Tedde de Lorca, 1999).

By 1840, Heredia was the largest Spanish businessman. He himself boasted of "employing the greatest number of workers ever fed by a private individual in these provinces" (Heredia, 1841). Shortly before his death, he employed almost three thousand people, including all his industries and businesses.

Manuel Agustín Heredia was, above all, a man of his time and a businessman. An admirer of the British political and economic model, he always acted as a pragmatic businessman in a time of profound political change. He maintained good relations with liberals and absolutists, and after the death of Ferdinand VII, he supported the liberal cause by providing donations for the Carlist War (García de Cortázar, 2006).

He was made a Knight of the Order of Charles III for his contribution to boosting national wealth. In his later years, Heredia served as a senator twice, in 1843 and 1845. During those years, he actively participated in the debates over the establishment of tariffs, calling for protection for national steel production while also requesting the reduction of restrictions on the import of British coal until the productive conditions of the mining areas in the northern Spain improved (Heredia, 1841). He died at his home in Málaga in 1846 (García Montoro, 1978). Ramón de la Sagra, who met him personally in 1845, stated that he possessed "a rare combination of talents", because he knew how to combine industry and commerce like no other (García Montoro, 2005).

In the inventory of his assets compiled after his death, they were valued at 60 million *reales*. His net capital was divided between ships, factories, warehouses, and rural and urban properties, worth almost ten million; and merchandise, credit, and cash, totalling more than 50 million. He had interests in industrial, mining, insurance, shipping, and banking companies. As García Montoro (1979) points out, his fortune was characterised by dynamism and risk, as evidenced by the fact that almost two-thirds of his assets were made up of working capital.

3 Heredia's Steelmaking Initiatives

Manuel Agustín Heredia's intense activity led him to be considered one of the great figures of his time, but also as a person who championed innovation and entrepreneurship, to the point of becoming one of Spain's greatest modernisers of the nineteenth century. In this regard, his most important initiative was the launch of a steelworks, *La Concepción*, which exploited the iron deposits near Marbella. Shortly after, this was expanded to include *La Constancia* ironworks in Málaga, where wrought iron was produced, pioneering in the country, using the indirect casting method. Until the mid-1850s, Málaga factories dominated Spanish cast iron production.

The mineral wealth of the region surrounding Marbella had long been known. Since the end of the eighteenth century, the mineral that generated the most interest in the area was graphite. As we saw, during the French occupation, general Ballesteros authorised Heredia to trade graphite through Gibraltar, an activity that continued until the Mining Law of 1825 reserved its control to the Royal Treasury.

The decline of graphite coincided with the growing interest in the exploitation of magnetic iron ore, or magnetite, from the El Peñoncillo mines, located about four kilometres northeast of Marbella, on the border with the municipality of Ojén. Nadal (1970) highlighted the pioneering role of Andalusia in establishing a modern capital goods sector in Spain, drawing attention to what he called the "Andalusian anticipation" in the modernisation of the Spanish steel industry. During the initial stage of iron mining in Marbella, the close relationship between extraction and the initial transformation of the metal was evident. This process was in the hands of Spanish entrepreneurs, and the production was entirely destined for the domestic market. The abundance of iron in the mines made it possible to extract it with limited investment (Parejo Barranco, 1997).

In 1826, Heredia formed a company called *La Concepción* with other shareholders. This company acquired an iron mine in the Peñoncillo district from the Irish merchant William O'Shea. The operation included a pile driver near the Verde river (Mendoza García, 2004). The company was incorporated into a public deed, in compliance with the recently published Commercial Code, on January 15, 1830. The founding partners were Heredia, Pedro Pablo del Valle, Jaime Setta, Juan Mirasol, Juan Giró, Jorge Loring, Domingo de Orueta, Manuel Enríquez, Diego María López, and Francisco Elorza. The first nine were listed as capital partners, and the last as an industrial partner (García Montoro, 1978).

Several factors explain why Manuel Agustín Heredia promoted the steel industry in the province of Málaga: the facilities granted by the mining legislation of 1825 for the exploitation of mining deposits; the tariff measures that protected steel goods manufactured in Spain; the existing demand in Andalusia for steel products, supplied until then by the ironworks of the north; the unique resource endowment of the Marbella area (iron ore, wood for charcoal, and hydraulic power); and the enormous entrepreneurial capacity of Heredia himself (Rodríguez Feijóo, 2007). Thus, although Spain was a country lagging behind the model of economic growth driven by Great Britain and based on industrialisation, the province of Málaga, and Marbella in particular, was a pioneer in the attempt to establish a modern industry, with the creation of the first blast furnaces initiated by civilians in the country.

The initial years of trials and tests were difficult and discouraging, but Heredia's perseverance and effort helped his industrial initiative move forward. Most of the partners abandoned the business and sold their shares when their capital was threatened, but Heredia sought out the best foundry expert in Spain. The technological knowledge needed to launch the Málaga steel industry was provided by the Basque military officer Francisco Antonio Elorza (1798–1873), who, during his exile due to his liberal ideas, had studied the modern steelmaking techniques being applied in Europe. Alcalá-Zamora y Queipo de Llano (1974) defined him as "the most important name in the origins of the steel industry in contemporary Spain". The contribution of the gunner Elorza, related to Orueta, another of the initial shareholders of *La Concepción*, was key to the success of Marbella steel industry from 1828 onwards (García Montoro, 1997).

The mineral's characteristics influenced the technological evolution of the local steel industry, as the Ojén magnetite, rich in metallic content and easy to mine, was difficult to melt with the low heat required by traditional low-flow furnaces. Various direct methods were tried, such as the Catalan or Walloon forging, but with poor results. Then, under the direction of Elorza, a new indirect method was adopted, the so-called English or puddling method, which used coal to refine the metal. This process led to the splitting of production: the initial ore smelting process continued at the Verde river factory, and pig iron or cast iron was obtained using charcoal. *La Constancia* ironworks was established in Málaga in 1833, intended to refine, mould, and forge iron from Marbella to obtain soft iron useful for multiple uses. For its construction, engineer Tomás Cortés was responsible for designing and supervising the works. The machinery was purchased in England, and Heredia hired British technicians to get the factory up and running and train local workers.

In *La Constancia*, the second smelting process was carried out to obtain wrought iron by refining it in reverberatory furnaces using the puddling method to remove impurities from the ore. This process used coal arriving at the port of Málaga from Asturias or Great Britain (Nadal, 1972). Later, another company that exploited the iron from Ojén, called *El Ángel*, replicated Heredia's model by installing puddling blast furnaces in Málaga, in 1841. In this case, the driving force behind the company was Gibraltarian Juan Giró, one of the original partners of *La Concepción* (García Montoro, 2011).

Heredia became the country's leading iron manufacturer and one of the most prominent Spanish businessmen, both in terms of the production volume of its factories and the number of workers. The Marbella and Málaga facilities permanently employed 1911 people (Heredia, 1841).

La Constancia offered an image of modernity to the Málaga landscape that inspired admiration among foreign visitors (García de Cortázar, 2006). The spectacular increase in iron production in the 1830s, driven by Málaga's ironworks, has been explained by a series of factors, such as the paralysis of the northern iron industry due to the Carlist Wars, the skilful technological and business management of Elorza and Heredia, and the diversification of production towards common iron. This latter option, which was supported by a progressive growth in domestic demand for iron, allowed the Málaga iron and steel industry to maintain its dominant position in the national market for the following two decades, despite Elorza's departure and the normalisation of production in the north beginning in 1839. In 1844, the Heredia and Giró companies produced 7829 tons of pig iron ingots, accounting for almost 73% of national production. In 1855, when the forges of Asturias and

Vizcaya were operating normally, the Málaga iron and steel companies produced 10,792 tons, which at the time represented 47% of all Spanish cast iron, according to Nadal (1972).

However, Elorza already demonstrated in 1840 his conviction that charcoal foundries could not compete with the new methods using coal, which ensured the long-term success of the northern steel industry (Nadal, 1998). The Málaga iron-works' weakness lay in the supply of mineral fuel. The need to obtain coal at a good price to guarantee the operation and competitiveness of his factories was one of Heredia's main concerns, especially in his later years. He was aware that the future of his industrial businesses depended on it (Anderson & Pilling, 1990).

Heredia tried coal from Asturias and Great Britain and arguing that the former was not in a position to meet his needs, he fought to lower the tariffs on English imports. The tariff reforms proposed in 1841 generated a broad debate between protectionists and free traders. Heredia was aware that the main problem facing his steel industry was fuel. The inadequacy and irregularity of Asturian coal production made it necessary to import coal at reduced tariffs to maintain the competitiveness of the Málaga steel industry (Heredia, 1841). The coal battle continued until 1844, when the Tariff Advisory Board, of which Heredia was a member, agreed by a single vote to maintain the current tariffs.

The setbacks suffered in the tariff battle with the Asturians forced the businessman to seek other solutions. Heredia travelled to England in 1840 to see first hand the trials being carried out to smelt iron with anthracite, with a view to introducing this process in his factories. He visited the *Butterley Company* foundry in Derby County, which had been using this system for just 2 years (Anderson & Pilling, 1990). He commissioned a search for deposits of this mineral in Spain and even ordered the necessary machinery, but the trials did not yield the expected results. The failure of the anthracite experiment and the tariff defeat indicated that, despite its apparent splendour, the Málaga steel industry had received, at its most brilliant moment, "a fatal wound" (Nadal, 1972).

4 The Long Decline of the Málaga Steel Industry

Heredia stipulated in his will that after his death, a company would be established, run by his eldest sons, Manuel (1817–1852) and Tomás (1819–1893), and by his brother Martín Heredia Escolar (1802–1867). All three had been sent by Manuel Agustín Heredia to England to learn languages and further their studies, and the first two had trained in Paris as engineers.

The eldest son, Manuel, committed suicide in 1852, and his uncle Martín founded his own business 4 years later. Thus, the management of the numerous companies promoted by Manuel Agustín Heredia was concentrated under the leadership of Tomás Heredia Livermore. In the following years, he gradually divested himself of some activities (such as the textile industry and the Adra lead factory) and focused his family business on maintaining the steel industry, trading, and participating in the creation of the *Bank of Málaga* in 1856. The bank, which was incorporated under the banking law of that year, was established with a share capital of 20 million *reales*, divided into 10,000 shares of 2000 *reales* each. Tomás Heredia and his immediate family owned a total of 750 shares (Jiménez Quintero, 1977). The *Bank of Málaga* was eventually incorporated into the Bank of Spain in 1874.

Initially, Málaga's heavy industry relied almost exclusively on domestic demand due to the shutdown of northern ironworks during the Carlist Wars. However, it was always hampered by its dependence on imported coal, which was sought to be obtained at competitive prices by reducing tariffs on British coal or by promoting the construction of a railway line that would allow coal to be brought from Córdoba. The failure of these initiatives inevitably doomed the Heredia family's steelmaking experience due to its high production costs (Nadal, 1972). The Heredia family's commitment to maintaining their most emblematic business extended its life until almost the last decade of the century, when its viability had long been in question.

The progressive loss of Andalusian dominance in the steel sector is related to the cost and availability of the key element in the technological level of the foundries of the period: coal (Nadal, 1972, 1975, 1984). Heredia's initial efforts were directed at overcoming this clear disadvantage, of which he was fully aware. His repeated trips to England and his countless negotiations with the government were part of a strategy aimed at reducing operating costs, in which fuel accounted for around 75% of the total (Nadal, 1970). As long as the Spanish steel industry continued to use charcoal for the production of cast iron, Andalusia's advantage was maintained. However, when, from the 1850s onwards, northern ironworks began to use coal for the initial smelting process, the definitive crisis of the Málaga steel industry became evident, unable to compete due to its high production costs derived from the price of fuel. *El Ángel* was the first industry to shut down its furnaces in 1862 (García Montoro, 2011).

Tomás Heredia became convinced of the need to rethink the coal supply problem. He decided to invest in domestic fuel starting in 1856, hoping that the railroad would allow him access to coal from the northern basin of the province of Córdoba (Nadal, 1984).

The Mining Statistics for 1866 reported that the *La Constancia* ironworks in Málaga had accumulated a stock of finished iron worth 30 million *reales*, meaning that the blast furnaces in Marbella and Málaga were operating at half capacity. In 1867, Tomás Heredia stated that only one blast furnace remained lit at *La Concepción*. In his petition for continued protection of the national steel industry, he stated: "Our interest today would be to close the factory that produces nothing, thus freeing ourselves from a bad business", but he clung to the continued support of the population and the hopes placed in Córdoba coal once the railway to Belmez was completed (Nadal, 1970). However, recourse to Córdoba coal, which became available from 1873 onwards, was not a viable solution, as its cost remained very high. Furthermore, domestic demand was no longer growing at the same rate as in previous decades, and the tariff policy was relaxed, allowing the entry of foreign iron.

Tomás Heredia's contacts with the French engineer Paul Clervaux to promote a recovery plan for his industries demonstrate his interest in remaining in the steel industry, even ignoring Elorza's advice to invest in Asturias and get rid of the Málaga foundries (García Montoro, 1998). As late as the early 1870s, the Málaga ironworks accounted for just over a tenth of the national production of ingots and soft iron. Tomás Heredia expanded his activity to the production of capital goods and a wide range of metal constructions intended primarily for the agricultural and construction sectors. However, his production costs were so high that he was no longer competitive by then. Nadal (1984) has highlighted the Heredia family's determination to maintain the steel industry on the Málaga coast, despite the evidence of its insoluble structural problems.

The decline of the Málaga iron and steel industry continued for several more years. *La Concepción* continued smelting iron ore from the Ojén mines using vegetable fuel. The resulting cast iron was processed in Málaga using the puddling system with English coal. The Marbella smelter was finally shut down in 1884, and the Málaga ironworks continued operating using ingots imported from Biscay as raw material until the early 1890s, coinciding with the death of Tomás Heredia in 1893.

5 The Final Stage of Blast Furnaces

Immediately after the closure of the old Heredia steelworks, its owners began efforts to restart it. After the death of Tomás Heredia Livermore, his son, Tomás Heredia Grund (1848–1912), began negotiations in 1897 with Belgian businessman Emile Bonehill to revive *La Constancia*. During those years, a favourable economic situation arose thanks to the approval of protectionist tariffs and the creation of steel cartels by Basque and Asturian companies to control prices and domestic demand (Escudero & Parejo, 2015). The restart of the Málaga ironworks was linked to its focus on steelmaking using technology based on the Bessemer converter and Martin-Siemens furnaces.

As a result of negotiations between Heredia and Bonehill in 1899, the company *Hauts Fourneaux, Forges et Aciéries de Málaga* was established, with its headquarters in Marchienne-au-Pont, Belgium. The new company acquired the ironworks by paying the Heredia family 15,000 shares and issued another 20,000, with a total capital of 3.5 million francs. The largest shareholders in the new company were the Heredias, with 42% of the capital, and Bonehill, with 11%. The remaining shares were distributed among Belgian and French bankers and businessmen. The board of directors included Tomás Heredia and his relatives Jorge Loring and Francisco Silvela. Silvela combined this position with the presidency of the Spanish government for several years (Escudero & Parejo, 2015).

The revitalised factory absorbed a large part of the regional demand for iron in the early years of the twentieth century. In 1903, the Málaga factory achieved a 17.6% market share in Spain, thanks to its prices being below those set by the two cartels operating in the country. But the situation soon deteriorated, and by 1905 the crisis had become irreversible. Overproduction had led to a drop in prices, and once again, Málaga's disadvantage stemmed from the price of coke, which translated into fuel costs far higher than those of the Basque and Asturian factories. Losses accumulated, with high debt, and work was finally halted in March 1907 (Escudero & Parejo, 2015).

The forge enjoyed a third opportunity, again subject to favourable but short-lived circumstances. French businessman Henri Jonqueres d'Oriola bought the factory in 1911 and the following year created the company *Altos Hornos de Andalucía*. With the outbreak of World War I, international demand for steel products, as well as prices, increased, leading to a revaluation of the Málaga facilities and their purchase by the French company *Aciéries et Forges de Firminy*. In September 1915, it began producing steel from ingots and scrap, and in January 1916, *Firminy* leased the factory to the *Sociedad Minera y Metalúrgica de Málaga*. With the end of the war in November 1918, the lease ended, and the blast furnace was shut down. It was dismantled in 1921 and finally decommissioned in 1924.

The factory failed in this final attempt due to its lack of competitive advantage due to the coal problem, compounded by its isolation. The fact that it was not located in an industrial district prevented it from benefiting from the advantages of agglomeration economies. In other words, the structural problems it had suffered from since its inception persisted. According to Escudero and Parejo (2015), "the factory failed due to its lack of competitive advantage" due to the coal problem. Something Manuel Agustín Heredia himself was well aware of before his death.

Competing Interests The author has no conflicts of interest to declare that are relevant to the content of this chapter.

References

Alcalá-Zamora y Queipo de Llano, J. (1974). Producción de hierro y altos hornos en la España anterior a 1850. *Moneda y Crédito, 128*, 117–218.

Álvarez de Linera, A. (1857). Memoria histórica, científica y estadística sobre las minas de grafito del partido de Marbella pertenecientes al Estado. *Revista Minera, VIII*, 648–656.

Anderson, B. L., & Pilling, P. W. (1990). Spanish entrepreneurs and British Technology in Early XIXth century Andalucia. *Journal of European Economic History, 19*, 35–72.

Bejarano, F. (1947). *Historia del Consulado y de la Junta de Comercio de Málaga*. CSIC.

Escudero, A., & Parejo, A. (2015). La siderurgia malagueña (1899-1924). *Revista de Historia Industrial, 58*, 319–347.

Gámez Amián, A. (1994). *Málaga y el comercio colonial con América (1765–1820)*. Miramar.

García de Cortázar, F. (2006). *Los perdedores de la Historia de España*. Planeta.

García Montoro, C. (1978). *Málaga en los comienzos de la industrialización: Manuel Agustín Heredia (1786–1846)*. Universidad de Córdoba.

García Montoro, C. (1979). La fortuna de Manuel Agustín Heredia. In *Actas del I Congreso de Historia de Andalucía, Andalucía Contemporánea, tomo I* (pp. 367–375). Caja de Ahorros de Córdoba.

García Montoro, C. (1997). Francisco A. Elorza en los comienzos de la industrialización andaluza. *Baetica, 19*(2), 243–253. https://doi.org/10.24310/BAETICA.1997.v2i19.579
García Montoro, C. (1998). *Sociedad y negocios en Málaga (Siglos XVIII-XIX)*. Universidad de Málaga.
García Montoro, C. (2005). La siderurgia malagueña en su momento de apogeo: Un texto de Ramón de la Sagra (1845). *Revista de Estudios Regionales, 73*, 223–234.
García Montoro, C. (2011). *El mundo de los negocios en Málaga. Siglo XIX*. Universidad de Málaga.
Heredia, M. A. (1841). *Exposición dirigida al Excmo. Sr. Secretario de Estado y del despacho de Hacienda sobre aranceles*.
Jiménez Quintero, J. A. (1977). El triángulo financiero Heredia-Larios-Loring. *Jábega, 19*, 35–46.
Madoz, P. (1848). *Diccionario geográfico-estadístico-histórico de España y sus posesiones de ultramar*. Tomo IX.
Mendoza García, E. M. (2004). Guillermo O'Shea y los inicios de la industrialización en Málaga en el siglo XIX a través de los documentos notariales. *Isla de Arriarán, 23–24*, 317–332.
Moreno, J. R. (2001). El impacto del liberalismo sobre la ganadería de montaña: La Sierra de Cameros (La Rioja) entre los siglos XVIII y XIX. *Ager, 1*, 113–158.
Nadal, J. (1970). Los comienzos de la industrialización española (1832–1868): la industria siderúrgica. In *Ensayos sobre la economía española a mediados del siglo XIX* (pp. 203–233). Ariel.
Nadal, J. (1972). Industrialización y desindustrialización del sureste español. *Moneda y Crédito, 120*, 3–80.
Nadal, J. (1975). *El fracaso de la revolución industrial en España, 1814–1913*. Ariel.
Nadal, J. (1984). Los dos abortos de la Revolución Industrial en Andalucía. In A. D. Ortiz (Ed.), *Historia de Andalucía. VI. La Andalucía liberal (1778–1868)* (pp. 399–433). Planeta.
Nadal, J. (1998). Cartas de Elorza, siderúrgico en Andalucía (1828–1840). In A. Gómez Mendoza & A. Parejo (Eds.), *De economía e historia. Estudios en homenaje a José Antonio Muñoz Rojas* (pp. 97–138). Junta de Andalucía & Unicaja.
Ordóñez Vergara, J. (1991). *Ciudad y gestión privada (M.A. Heredia. Málaga. 1ª mitad del siglo XIX)*. Universidad de Málaga.
Parejo, A. (2009). *Historia económica de la provincia de Málaga (1833–2008)*. CEDMA.
Parejo Barranco, A. (1990). *Málaga y los Larios. Capitalismo industrial y atraso económico (1875–1914)*. Arguval.
Parejo Barranco, A. (1997). *La producción industrial de Andalucía (1830–1935)*. Instituto de Desarrollo Regional.
Pérez de Perceval Verde, M. A. (2018). La fábrica de San Andrés de Adra (Almería). Un hito de la metalurgia del plomo en la primera mitad del s. XIX. *De Re Metallica, 31*, 73–82.
Rodríguez Feijóo, A. (2007). Las ferrerías de Río Verde y el efímero protagonismo industrial de Marbella. In F. López Serrano & J. L. Casado Bellagarza (Eds.), *Estudios en homenaje a Antonio Serrano Lima* (pp. 87–118). Asociación Cilniana.
Tedde de Lorca, P. (1999). *El Banco de San Fernando (1829–1856)*. Alianza Editorial & Banco de España.
Tortella Casares, G. (1975). *Los orígenes del capitalismo en España*. Tecnos.
Villar García, M. B. (1997). Los comerciantes extranjeros de Málaga en 1776. Culminación de una instalación secular. *Baetica, 19*(2), 191–207. https://doi.org/10.24310/BAETICA.1997.v2i19.575

Víctor M. Heredia-Flores is Associate lecturer of History and Economic Institutions at the University of Málaga. His research has covered fields such as the history of education in Andalusia, the reconstruction of regional historical statistical series, the history of industry and public services (especially water supply), and the early tourist infrastructure in the province of Málaga.

Leopoldo Calvo-Sotelo, Businessman and Politician: A Technocratic President?

Jorge Lafuente del Cano and Pedro Pablo Ortúñez Goicolea

Abstract This chapter examines the career of Leopoldo Calvo-Sotelo, a key figure in the Spanish transition who combined business experience with political responsibility at the highest level. Before becoming Prime Minister in 1981, Calvo-Sotelo had a distinguished career in the private sector, particularly in energy and industrial companies, which shaped his technocratic and pragmatic approach. The text analyses how his economic training and experience in executive positions influenced his leadership style and policies as Minister of Industry and later as Prime Minister. It also addresses his role in Spain's economic modernisation and European integration. The chapter highlights the uniqueness of his profile in Spanish politics at the time, characterised by a business-oriented approach to state management.

1 Introduction

Leopoldo Calvo-Sotelo is a multifaceted figure in the economic and political history of Spain in the last century. On the one hand, he was an engineer with remarkable technical training who developed a professional business career over twenty-five years. On the other, he played an important political role in the final years of the Franco regime and, above all, in the decisive period of the transition to democracy in Spain, becoming Prime Minister in February 1981. His figure was eclipsed after the overwhelming socialist victory in October 1982, but recently a series of studies have examined his career in depth (Lafuente del Cano, 2017; Lafuente del Cano & Ortúñez Goicolea, 2023; Pelaz López & Díez Miguel, 2018; Pelaz López & Pérez López, 2025; Pérez López, 2014).

An early version of this chapter can be found in the journal Historia y Política 43, 121–155.

J. Lafuente del Cano (✉) · P. P. Ortúñez Goicolea
Department of Fundamentals of Economic Analysis and History of Financial Institutions, University of Valladolid, Valladolid, Spain
e-mail: jorge.lafuente@uva.es; portunez@uva.es

M. Vázquez-Fariñas, F. Cabrera-Gallardo (eds.), *Business Trajectories in the History of Spain*, Frontiers in Economic History,
https://doi.org/10.1007/978-3-032-16214-4_7

This chapter analyses a controversial aspect of his profile that ties in with one of the most interesting topics of study in Spain's contemporary economic development: the role of technicians in politics, their limits and influence. The study of technocracy in Spain has taken on particular importance in relation to the Franco regime and Spain's economic opening from the 1950s onwards (Sánchez Recio, 2008; Zaratiegui Labiano, 2012; Zaratiegui Labiano, 2016). In this sense, Calvo-Sotelo's role could serve as a *laboratory* for analysing this specific period. He was a civil engineer who did not work in the civil service, but in the private sector, at the head of several companies belonging to the *Banco Urquijo* conglomerate. This business work allowed him to position himself in a position of some public prominence, which became visible at the time of Franco's death (1975), when he held a ministerial position for the first time and began his short but intense political career. It is therefore interesting to analyse two deeply intertwined aspects of his career: firstly, to assess the extent to which his technical training and business background influenced his entry into Spanish political life. Secondly, whether his political performance can be representative of a technocrat or whether, on the contrary, he held profound political ideas that were combined with his previous knowledge and experience. After analysing his technical training and business career, special mention will be made of two key moments in his political career: firstly, his position as Minister for Relations with the European Communities (1978–1980), from which he began negotiations for Spain's accession to the Common Market, an enormous challenge that took place in parallel with the democratisation of the Spanish political system; secondly, his time as Prime Minister (1981–1982), where he faced countless challenges and difficulties, as his tenure began with an attempted coup d'état in February 1981.

2 Engineer and Businessman

Leopoldo Calvo-Sotelo was 10 years old when his uncle José—a member of parliament and former minister during the dictatorship of Primo de Rivera—was assassinated on the eve of the civil war. His surname thus became linked to that of the "first martyr" of Francoism. However, his childhood and youth were not easy due to the premature death of his father. Thus, his family situation—a widowed mother with five children—determined that, when he began his university studies in 1946, he would choose those that offered good career prospects.[1] Engineering studies were highly prestigious in Spain at the time, and their predominance was soon to be accentuated by the economic growth that began in the 1960s. Various studies

[1] Calvo-Sotelo was familiar with the profession through his maternal uncle, Francisco Bustelo, an engineer in the same corps (Calvo-Sotelo, 2003, p. 51). In the May–June 1946 intake, Leopoldo Calvo-Sotelo entered the School of Civil Engineering, which at that time was under the Ministry of Public Works. Leopoldo Calvo-Sotelo Archive (ALCS), School of Civil Engineering, 6. Madrid, 1 July 1948.

(Camprubí, 2017; Martykánová, 2007, 2020) have highlighted the prominent role of these professionals in the political and economic development of contemporary Spain.

The greatest sign of the exclusivity and prestige of the School of Engineering was the *numerus clausus*, which meant that only a small number of applicants were able to enter, after a tough selection process following a preparatory course. In Calvo-Sotelo's class, which graduated in 1951, there were 36 engineers, all of them male. The content of the respective academic programmes was adapted in line with advances in technical and scientific knowledge. The most profound change in the curriculum did not occur in the immediate post-war period, but in 1957, when the School came under the authority of the Ministry of Education. It is worth noting the importance of certain exact sciences, such as mathematics, as well as the professional orientation that appeared across the programmes of various subjects throughout the degree course (Alarcón & Martínez-Val, 2010, p. 321).

It is also necessary to take a look at Leopoldo Calvo-Sotelo's academic record. He finished his degree at the top of his class with a grade of "Very Good".[2] This marked the end of his training, during which he had acquired remarkable technical knowledge and a sense of belonging to a group. The next logical step was to find a job. Engineers from the School of Civil Engineering automatically joined the Ministry of Public Works as civil servants. Calvo-Sotelo received his appointment as second Engineer of the Corps in November 1952[3] and his first position in the Administration a month later, specifically as a junior engineer in the *Guadiana Hydraulic Services*.[4] However, his professional future would not go in that direction. It is therefore interesting to find out what career paths his classmates took to see whether most of them followed the same path as him or chose a different one. The aim here is not to generalise about the situation of all engineers, but it is necessary to note the presence of companies that, from the final year of the degree course, hire some students and then offer them the opportunity to stay and work for them. This reinforces the idea of the prestige associated with the studies they were pursuing.

Among Calvo-Sotelo's classmates, the idea of mobility stands out: a good number of them will work in private companies and later in the public sector, and some will even move in various directions between both options throughout their professional lives[5]: of the 36 colleagues, 11 became civil servants, 10 joined private companies, 11 moved from private companies to the civil service, 1 moved from the civil service to a private company, and 3 moved from the civil service to private companies and then back to the civil service.

[2] He also obtained his doctorate on 21 March 1968, Alarcón and Martínez-Val (2010), p. 322.

[3] ALCS, School of Civil Engineering, 6. Madrid, 9 November 1952.

[4] ALCS, School of Civil Engineering, 6. Madrid, 12 December 1952.

[5] Prepared by the author based on information from "Historia de la Promoción de 1951" (History of the Class of 1951) by Fernando Mejón. ALCS, School of Civil Engineering, 5.

Of particular interest are the 10 engineers who worked exclusively in the private sector. Their destinations were also diverse, but their CVs highlight the following companies: *Dragados*; *Entrecanales*; *Fenosa*; *Unión Española de Explosivos*; *Vías y Construcciones*; *Endesa*; *Agromán*; *Termac*. Several of these companies were directly related to the world of engineering, but others had a different focus. The latter are those that fit the profile of demand for engineers due to their prestige, and among them is the professional career of Calvo-Sotelo, which is studied below.

Leopoldo Calvo-Sotelo spent most of his professional career, between 1951 and 1975, in the private sector, always linked to *Banco Urquijo*.

While still studying civil engineering in 1950, he joined the bank's Industrial Studies Department, created by Juan Lladó, the CEO. Lladó's incorporation into the entity had brought about a profound change in the concept and structure of the bank's management: he intended to transform it into a true industrial bank (Puig Raposo & Torres Villanueva, 2008, p. 107). The purpose of the Service was to promote the creation of companies, especially in the chemical industry. At the same time, as part of Lladó's drive for modernisation, Urquijo had also distinguished himself by hiring prestigious individuals from various social spheres to enrich the structure of the institution; the names of Xavier Zubiri, Luis Díez del Corral, Manuel Aznar, and Luis Solana are good examples of this.

It was Lladó himself who contacted him to offer him the job. As a fifth-year student, this clearly reflects the policy of hiring prestigious students in fields such as civil engineering. However, his status as an engineer was probably not the only factor that facilitated his recruitment. The surname "Calvo-Sotelo" may also have been an incentive. In addition, his uncle Francisco Bustelo had run one of Urquijo's companies: *Energías e Industrias Aragonesas*.

It seems appropriate to recall the importance of personal relationships within a small circle of professionals in the face of a shortage of available technicians during the early post-war years in Spain, which was still evident in 1951, the year in which Leopoldo Calvo-Sotelo completed his studies. At a time when industry was beginning to become the essential element of national economic policy (Barciela López, 2002, p. 362), "having good connections was key to prosperity" (Cabrera & Del Rey, 2011, p. 267). This strengthened the relationship between technical experts and a Francoist state imbued with an engineering mentality (Barciela López et al., 2001, p. 119): the senior bodies of the administration became a breeding ground for cadres for the regime (Cabrera & Del Rey, 2011, p. 317) and, in turn, the presence of technicians would give it a certain ideological justification (Camprubí, 2017; Velasco, 1984). In this context, Lladó proposed that a reluctant Calvo-Sotelo join the Study, who at that time believed that his professional future lay in engineering, specifically in hydraulic works. He remained in the Research Department until he was asked to lead one of the proposals that the Department itself had analysed and accepted. At just 30 years of age, he had become one of the youngest managers in Spanish private enterprise. And so, in 1954, Calvo-Sotelo took the helm at *Perlofil*. This was a company whose capital was divided between Urquijo, Hispano, and Mexican businessman Pablo Díez (Calvo-Sotelo, 2003, p. 199), and which was responsible for marketing nylon, a product that had undergone remarkable development during the

Second World War. This professional activity required him to undertake numerous trips throughout Spain and Europe, during which he gained knowledge not only of the European business network, but also of the national and community institutions that explained the economic prosperity and political stability of the Common Market countries. However, it was not all plain sailing, as after its launch *Perlofil* had not developed as expected and was in a delicate financial situation: Urquijo and Hispano planned to sell their shares at 30% of their nominal value (Nogueira, 2015, p. 74). Calvo-Sotelo started a new project, practically from scratch, and formed a team. After achieving a degree of financial stability with an additional injection of money from Díez, Calvo-Sotelo reached an agreement to protect the future of the company: specifically with the Dutch industrial group *AKU*, owner of *La Seda de Barcelona*, a company that merged with *Perlofil* in 1963, when it bought 45% of the capital from the two banks at 335% (Calvo-Sotelo, 1990, p. 158; Nogueira, 2015, p. 74).

Sometime later, Calvo-Sotelo (2003, p. 200) received an offer from Díez himself to move to Mexico to run one of his businesses, but he ended up rejecting it. However, he had achieved a considerable internal promotion, as he went on to head *Unión Española de Explosivos* after Carlos Botín resigned from his position as CEO. He combined this position with that of director of *Banco Urquijo* (Puig Raposo & Torres Villanueva, 2008, p. 312). The situation was similar to that of his former company: poor financial health—it sold 2.5 billion pesetas a year without making any real profit (Calvo-Sotelo, 1990, p. 259), which he tried to reverse. To do so, he used a precise strategy: expansion and diversification were necessary for the company to become profitable again, and to achieve this, a policy of acquisitions had to be implemented (Gómez-Santos, 1982, p. 151). This led to the merger with *Compañía Española de Minas Río Tinto* in 1970, which gave rise to *Unión Explosivos Río Tinto*. From then on, the policy of acquiring other companies and the process of diversification continued, especially in the plastics and pharmaceutical sectors. In 1975, the company had sales of 50 billion pesetas, generated 4 billion and earned 2.3 billion (Calvo-Sotelo, 1990, p. 159).

With his technical training as a civil engineer, Calvo-Sotelo had made the leap to private enterprise, proposing a management strategy based on three pillars: teamwork, mergers, and confidence in technology. This period of business consolidation coincided with the strengthening of his interest in politics, which had probably already become a vocation. As mentioned earlier, personal relationships were of great importance in the economic context of the 1950s, and Calvo-Sotelo also built up a network of personal contacts that later facilitated his entry into politics. In this way, he began to position himself politically in the final years of the dictatorship: he held his first public office as president of *RENFE* between 1967 and 1968 (Muñoz Rubio, 1995, p. 103). In addition, in 1971 he obtained a seat in the Cortes representing the Chemical Industries Union.

3 Prime Minister

Given all this, it was not surprising that, at the end of the regime, he was well placed to become a member of the first government of the monarchy. He successively held the portfolios of Trade (1975–1976), Public Works (1976–1977), and parliamentary spokesperson (1977–1978) for the Union of the Democratic Centre, the party with which Adolfo Suárez won the 1977 elections. In February 1978, Calvo-Sotelo was appointed Minister for Relations with the European Communities, a new body created by the Prime Minister to initiate Spain's long-awaited accession to the Common Market. The role of negotiator was a key position in Calvo-Sotelo's career, and in it he put to use both his technical training and the experience he had gained during his time in business. Two aspects stand out that laid the foundations for the new Ministry and which, to a large extent, remained in place over time. Firstly, the creation of the negotiating team: it was not the first time that Calvo-Sotelo had undertaken a project from scratch; he had done so, as mentioned above, at the *Perlofil* company. In choosing his team, he emphasised the technical profile of its members. He was assigned twenty-five senior civil servants, experts in the various subjects considered vital for negotiations with the Community, attached to different government ministries, as well as diplomats. Secondly, the procedure to be followed in the Community negotiations: Calvo-Sotelo created working teams in which both his own Ministry and other government departments were represented, with the aim of involving the entire Spanish administration, unifying criteria and achieving specialisation in the technical aspects of each of the areas in which the negotiations would take place.[6] However, the negotiators were aware that the negotiations would be guided by technical considerations, but that the final decision could be political. The interests of the other countries would prevail over the historical expectations of a country such as Spain, which needed recognition and equal treatment with the Community countries. There was a degree of disappointment within the Spanish government at this reality (Bassols, 1995, p. 7), but the complicated circumstances facing the Community at that time and the position of some countries (Moreno Juste & Sanz Díaz, 2023) prevented Calvo-Sotelo from completing the negotiations. Nevertheless, his almost 3 years in office were viewed positively, as in September 1980 he was promoted to the position of economic vice-president of the government and, just a few months later, he became prime minister following the resignation of Adolfo Suárez.

To analyse Calvo-Sotelo's performance as head of government, we must first examine his inaugural speech, which began on 18 February 1981. This speech clearly reveals some of the characteristics of the businessman who had become president: realism in the face of an unexpected situation that had an expiry date—the end of the legislative term—an emphasis on a series of issues that could be defined as technical—relating to the difficult economic situation the country was experiencing—but also a series of other aspects of clear political significance, in

[6] ALCS, Economics, 4a, 52.

which he managed to establish his own profile, different from that of Adolfo Suárez; particularly with regard to regional policy—since he was confident of definitively finalising the new configuration of the decentralised state—and foreign policy—in which he emphasised the political and strategic importance of joining the European Community and the Atlantic Alliance. It did not, therefore, seem to be the speech of a technician willing to offer mere expert solutions to the country's problems, but rather that of a politician trying to address issues of substance. Whether some of these initiatives would be successful during his term of office is another matter.

It should be noted that one event radically changed the scenario facing the Calvo-Sotelo government. On the second day of the investiture, 23 February, there was an attempted coup d'état by a group of civil guards and military personnel. This event meant that the new government's priorities had to be changed: from then on, the priority was to consolidate the democratic system, which had only been in place for a few years since Franco's death. All operations were subordinated to this new reality, but they were not abandoned: the choice was not made to form a caretaker government, nor to form a coalition with the main opposition party, nor to call early elections—all options that were on the president's table—but rather to try to push through a series of necessary measures that would also contribute to the stabilisation of the system.

The first of the important issues on the presidential agenda before the coup was the economy. This was an area that could apparently be considered the new president's strong point, given his professional experience and his time as deputy prime minister before becoming head of government. The Spanish economic situation, exacerbated by the impact of the oil crisis, was worrying, with striking growth in unemployment and inflation (Vázquez-Fariñas, 2023). The Calvo-Sotelo government designed the country's first industrial restructuring programme; however, the country's economic situation and the parliamentary weakness of his executive meant that it could not be carried out in its entirety, and instead a pragmatic solution was chosen to offer financial aid to companies in the most affected economic sectors.[7] By October 1982, a total of 234 billion pesetas had been allocated to these items. In fact, the economic stagnation could only be addressed with specific measures that failed to change the course of the situation. It was the next government, now led by the Socialist Party, that managed to develop a comprehensive restructuring plan.

Another important issue was regional policy, which combined technical needs and political momentum (Pelaz López & Pérez López, 2025). After Franco's death, Spain began a process of territorial decentralisation based on this general idea, but without a master plan. As a result, a number of communities (Catalonia, the Basque Country, Galicia) that had had their own institutions during the Second Republic were clearly defined and at a faster pace than the others. The rest were designed in a sometimes improvised manner, with political and economic interests that did not always coincide. Upon becoming Prime Minister, Calvo-Sotelo attempted to

[7] Juan Antonio García Díez Archive (AJAGD), Industrial Restructuring, 29, 4 October 1982.

finalise the map of autonomous communities. On the one hand, he defined the definitive number of autonomous communities and their size; on the other, he adjusted the powers of the state and those of the autonomous bodies. It was not an easy task and, certainly, behind it laid a political idea: to clearly define the limits of the decentralisation process and the exclusive powers of the state. Evidence of this political impetus was particularly evident in the search for agreements with the other political forces, although in the end only the main opposition party, the PSOE, signed the regional pact. This pact was partially successful (in that it managed to finalise the configuration of the 17 autonomous regions that currently exist in the Spanish political system), but it suffered a major setback when the Constitutional Court did not validate some sections of the law presented by the government. As a result, various problems regarding the powers and limits of the autonomous regions' self-government have continued to arise in the Spanish political arena in recent years.

One final aspect also deserves attention, as it shows how Calvo-Sotelo managed to combine technical and political aspects without opposition. During 1981 and 1982, Spain's foreign policy had a clear objective: to ensure that the country assumed the international position and commitments that had not been possible during the Franco regime for political reasons, in particular, entry into the Common Market and the NATO (Pérez López & Lafuente del Cano, 2014). Calvo-Sotelo's personal involvement was mentioned above in the first section, as he was Spain's chief negotiator with the European Communities. From his position, he defended the need for the country to join the Community bodies because it was economically necessary, but also for strategic reasons: Spain had to occupy its rightful place in the European environment. Politics and economics were complementary dualities on the path to accession to the Common Market. This approach was even more evident in the process of Spain's entry into NATO. The ruling party, the Union of the Democratic Centre, had shown some ambiguity on this issue, especially due to the reluctance of its former president, Adolfo Suárez. However, the new president defended the need for Spain to join the Atlantic Alliance definitively in his inauguration speech, as this was its rightful place in the bipolar world of the Cold War. The decision to join NATO was highly political in nature, reflecting the president's Atlanticist stance. Moreover, it caused considerable friction with part of his party, with the opposition, which was vehemently opposed to the measure (despite being able to reach agreements on other matters, such as regional policy), and with part of the public, as over the following months a section of Spanish society mobilised against joining the Alliance. Despite all the obstacles, the government achieved its goal and Spain officially joined in May 1982.

Several other projects of the Calvo-Sotelo government confirm the political momentum behind major decisions: the divorce law (which notably divided the centrist party and was in the process of being passed when Adolfo Suárez resigned); the new University Law; and the Administrative Reform Law. The latter two could not be completed due to the progressive deterioration of parliamentary support for the UCD government, including an exodus of MPs (both to the left and to the right), which ultimately led to the general election being brought forward to October 1982. In these elections, the PSOE won a resounding victory and Calvo-Sotelo's party ended up dissolving. This was a melancholic epilogue to a decisive period in Spanish history, the transition to democracy, which counted among its protagonists Leopoldo Calvo-Sotelo, the last president of the business-friendly government.

4 Conclusions

The preceding pages have examined the career of Leopoldo Calvo-Sotelo, which was unique but also representative of a particular moment in Spain's economic and political history. He was an engineer who spent his entire professional career at the helm of various companies and later pursued an intense political career that led him to the presidency of the government.

This career took place, on the one hand, during the years of economic openness in Spain after the civil war and the autarkic period, which enabled the greatest relative growth in the country's economic history in the 1960s and coincided with an increased need to recruit specialised technical personnel in both the public and private sectors. On the other hand, the end of growth and the onset of the oil crisis coincided with political change in Spain after Franco's death, leading to the creation of a democratic system comparable to that of its European neighbours.

Amidst both contexts, the figure of Calvo-Sotelo emerged. With outstanding technical qualifications as a civil engineer, he opted for private enterprise, joining the *Urquijo Group*, where he led some of its business projects. In these projects, he made good use of the resources acquired during his years of training, also taking advantage of the social prestige of his status as an engineer. His good results at the helm of several companies earned him the position of advisor to the Bank and placed him in a privileged position to participate in the process of political change that was beginning in Spain. He was able to apply his acquired technical knowledge and business experience in the various ministerial responsibilities he held, successively as Minister of Trade, Public Works and Relations with the European Communities. He was particularly visible in the latter field, where he had to create a negotiating team from scratch and where he used some of the European contacts he had acquired during his business trips in the 1950s and 1960s. At the same time, however, this position also shows how Calvo-Sotelo was not simply a technician in politics, as in his view Spain's entry into the European Community was not simply economic (although it was that too), but a state strategy with a political basis: Spain was not joining the Common Market solely to solve the country's economic problems, but for political and strategic reasons and because the democratisation of the system would be incomplete without European membership.

During Calvo-Sotelo's presidency, this economic and political duality can be seen once again: on the one hand, some of the key issues of his government were economic problems requiring technical solutions, such as the industrial restructuring plan. However, a significant number of other initiatives were markedly political in nature: Spain's entry into the Atlantic Alliance, the completion of the country's autonomous configuration, educational reform, the divorce law... Some of these initiatives were successfully completed, while others foundered due to the government's loss of parliamentary support, which ultimately led to the electoral debacle of the centrist party.

We can therefore conclude that in the career of Calvo-Sotelo, engineer, businessman, and politician, technical and political issues were intertwined without opposition: he was a man with a technical profile—at a time when the Spanish economy and institutions demanded it—but also a politician with profound ideas that he tried to apply, with varying degrees of success, during his public life in a decisive period of the country's recent history.

Competing Interests The authors have no conflicts of interest to declare that are relevant to the content of this chapter.

Sources Leopoldo Calvo-Sotelo Archive (ALCS).
Juan Antonio García Díez Archive (AJAGD).

References

Alarcón, E., & Martínez-Val, J. M. (2010). La biblioteca de matemáticas y física. In P. Calvo-Sotelo Ibáñez-Martín (Ed.), *Leopoldo Calvo-Sotelo: un retrato intelectual* (pp. 317–359). Ortega Marañón-Marcial Pons Foundation.

Barciela López, C. (2002). Guerra civil y primer franquismo (1936-1959). In F. Comín Comín, M. Hernández Benítez, & E. Llopis Agelán (Eds.), *Historia Económica de España, siglos X-XX*. Crítica.

Barciela López, C., López Ortiz, I., Melgarejo Moreno, J., & Miranda Encarnación, J. A. (2001). *La España de Franco (1939–1975). Economía*. Síntesis.

Bassols, R. (1995). *España en Europa. Historia de la adhesión a la CE, 1957–85*. Política Exterior.

Cabrera, M., & Del Rey, F. (2011). *El poder de los empresarios: Política y economía en la España contemporánea (1875–2010)*. RBA.

Calvo-Sotelo, L. (1990). *Memoria viva de la Transición* (p. 16). Plaza & Janés/Cambio.

Calvo-Sotelo, L. (2003). *Pláticas de Familia. 1878–2003*. La Esfera de los libros.

Camprubí, L. (2017). *Los ingenieros de Franco. Ciencia, catolicismo y Guerra Fría en el Estado franquista*. Crítica.

Gómez-Santos, M. (1982). *Conversaciones con Leopoldo Calvo-Sotelo*. Planeta.

Lafuente del Cano, J. (2017). *Leopoldo Calvo-Sotelo y Europa. Historia de una convicción política y económica*. Sílex.

Lafuente del Cano, J., & Ortúñez Goicolea, P. P. (2023). El Plan Francia ante el intento de frenar el ingreso de España en la CEE. *Ayer. Revista de Historia Contemporánea, 129*(1), 299–324. https://doi.org/10.55509/ayer/1179

Martykánová, D. (2007). Por los caminos del progreso. El universo ideológico de los ingenieros de caminos españoles a través de la Revista de Obras Públicas (1853-1899). *Ayer. Revista de Historia Contemporánea, 68*(4), 193–219.

Martykánová, D. (2020). Los ingenieros y el poder en la España contemporánea (presentación). *Historia y Política, 43*, 17–26. https://doi.org/10.18042/hp.43.01

Moreno Juste, A., & Sanz Díaz, C. (2023). Las Comunidades Europeas y la ampliación al Sur. In A. Moreno, C. Sanz, & R. M. de la Guardia (Eds.), *Memoria de Europa. La adhesión de España a las Comunidades Europeas* (pp. 65–84). Centro de Estudios Políticos y Constitucionales, Ministerio de la Presidencia.

Muñoz Rubio, M. (1995). *RENFE (1941–1991), medio siglo de ferrocarril publico*. Ediciones Luna.

Nogueira, A. (2015). *El nuevo estado industrial en España: la profesionalización de los directores de empresa durante el desarrollismo* [doctoral thesis]. Complutense University of Madrid. https://eprints.ucm.es/40726/
Pelaz López, J.-V., & Díez Miguel, D. (2018). Las Comisiones Provinciales de Incautación de Bienes en Galicia (1936-1939). *Ayer. Revista de Historia Contemporánea, 109*(1), 325–348. https://doi.org/10.55509/ayer/109-2018-12
Pelaz López, J.-V., & Pérez López, P. (2025). *Consolidar la democracia. El Gobierno de Leopoldo Calvo-Sotelo (1981–1982).* Marcial Pons.
Pérez López, P. (2014). El lector que presidió el gobierno. *Nueva Revista de Política, Cultura y Arte, 147*, 43–53.
Pérez López, P., & Lafuente del Cano, J. (2014). Leopoldo Calvo-Sotelo y la Transición exterior: la prioridad europea. *Arbor, 190*(769), a169. https://doi.org/10.3989/arbor.2014.769n5008
Puig Raposo, N., & Torres Villanueva, E. (2008). *Banco Urquijo. Un banco con historia*. Turner.
Sánchez Recio, G. (2008). Católicos y tecnócratas al servicio del régimen. La ampliación del personal político. In A. Mateos López (Ed.), *La España de los cincuenta* (pp. 225–236). Eneida.
Vázquez-Fariñas, M. (2023). La economía española en los inicios de la democracia (1976-1996). In L. Garrido-González & M. Castro-Valdivia (Eds.), *España (1923–2023): un siglo de economía* (pp. 159–200). Marcial Pons. https://doi.org/10.2307/jj.4908201.5
Velasco, C. (1984). El "ingenierismo" como directriz de la política económica durante la autarquía (1936-1951). *Información Comercial Española, ICE: Revista de Economía, 606*, 97–106.
Zaratiegui Labiano, J. M. (2012). La tecnocracia en España. In A. F. Ojeda & A. Cañellas (Eds.), *El régimen de Franco: unas perspectivas de análisis* (pp. 187–218). University of Navarra.
Zaratiegui Labiano, J. M. (2016). Los orígenes ideológicos de la tecnocracia en España (1940-1962). In A. Cañellas Mas (Ed.), *La tecnocracia hispánica: ideas y proyecto político en Europa y América* (pp. 49–80). Trea.

Jorge Lafuente del Cano is a Lecturer in Economic History and Institutions at the University of Valladolid. He holds a degree in History, a degree in Journalism and a PhD in History. He has conducted research at the University of Oxford and the University of Rome-La Sapienza. He is the coordinator of the Studies on Economic History Research Group and a member of the Studies on Recent History Research Group. He has published two books and numerous articles on entrepreneurship, the economic history of Spain's transition to democracy, negotiations for Spain's entry into the EEC and the figure of former Spanish Prime Minister Leopoldo Calvo-Sotelo.

Pedro Pablo Ortúñez Goicolea (PhD, University of Valladolid, 1999) is Professor of History and Economic Institutions at the University of Valladolid. His research interests include the Spanish railway system and the public sector before nationalisation of the railway, regulation and business history. He has published his research in books (with first quartile publishers such as Oxford University Press, Ariel, Pirámide, Comares) and specialised journals (indexed in JCR or Scopus) and has participated in conferences in these fields. He has undertaken research during several stays at the London School of Economics and at the École des Hautes Etudes en Sciences Sociales (Paris).

Hotel Companies and Entrepreneurs in Twentieth-Century Spain

Marta Laguna-García and Carlos Larrinaga Rodríguez

Abstract This chapter analyses the transformation of Spain's hotel sector throughout the twentieth century, from modest, traditional lodgings to the consolidation of a modern, professionalised tourism industry. It examines how certain visionary entrepreneurs and pioneering companies adapted to the growth of tourism, particularly following the boom in international tourism in the 1950s and 1960s. The text explores notable cases of business evolution, highlighting figures that established hotel chains, modernised infrastructure, and professionalised management. It also considers the influence of the state, coastal development, and foreign investment on the development of the new tourism model. Ultimately, the chapter reveals how Spanish hoteliers evolved from innkeepers to globalised entrepreneurs and key players in the national and international hospitality sector.

Project PID2021-122476NB-I00, funded by MICIU/AEI /10.13039/501100011033 and by FEDER/EU.

M. Laguna-García
Department of Business and Marketing, University of Valladolid, Valladolid, Spain
e-mail: marta.laguna@uva.es

C. Larrinaga Rodríguez (✉)
Department of Economic Theory and Economic History, University of Granada, Granada, Spain

Instituto Andaluz de Investigación e Innovación en Turismo (IATUR), Granada, Spain
e-mail: clarrinaga@ugr.es

M. Vázquez-Fariñas, F. Cabrera-Gallardo (eds.), *Business Trajectories in the History of Spain*, Frontiers in Economic History,
https://doi.org/10.1007/978-3-032-16214-4_8

1 Hospitality and Tourism

Regardless of climatic conditions, scenic beauty, monuments, the media, or even the advertising of a particular place, the lack of sufficient accommodation is a clear obstacle to the consolidation of a tourist destination. When studying the travel industry, Lickorish and Kershaw (1958, p. 3) identified transport, hotels, and catering as the most important aspects. Indeed, tourists seek the best way to travel to a tourist destination and hotel accommodation that suits their budget. Today, a large part of the hotel industry in Spain is suitable for tourists, but this was not always the case (Larrinaga Rodríguez, 2021).

At the beginning of the twentieth century, not all existing hotels were specifically geared towards tourists, so for those years, it is necessary to differentiate between accommodation in general and establishments for tourists. Therefore, two types of hotels must be distinguished. On the one hand, there were those with traditional hospitality functions, which were aimed at a clientele linked to travel for various reasons (trade, business, health, administrative procedures, etc.), and on the other hand, there were those geared towards tourism. The latter were accommodations heavily influenced by the comfort elements found in large foreign hotels (Harismendy, 2016).

It was these establishments that gradually incorporated the great advances of the time (hot water, heating, individual bathrooms, electric lighting, lifts, etc.) to make their guests' stay increasingly comfortable. However, this distinction was not always so clear, as in cities such as Barcelona, Madrid, and San Sebastián, for example, some of the existing hotels came to have a dual function, insofar as they began to receive tourists attracted by the importance of their monuments, their natural attractions or certain international events, such as the exhibitions in Seville and Barcelona in 1929–1930. Hence the enormous importance of the role played by hotel companies and entrepreneurs within the tourism market.

2 The Accommodation Industry Around 1900: The Case of Madrid

At the end of the nineteenth century, most of the accommodation available in Spain could not be classified as tourist accommodation. However, in many cases, the first tourists had no choice but to stay in this type of establishment. In such circumstances, many travellers of the time, mainly foreigners, and the guidebooks published in those years complained about the poor quality of the accommodation. These establishments were not designed for tourism, as a solid tourist hotel offering had not yet been established.

In the case of Madrid, Gutiérrez Ronco (1984, pp. 35–46) has established the following typology of accommodation for most of the nineteenth century and early twentieth century, namely: inns (*mesones*), lodging house (*posadas*) and *paradores*, guest houses, rental houses, *fondas* (inns) and hostels (*hosterías*), and hotels. Briefly, inns (*mesones*) were the most sordid, noisy, and ordinary lodgings, where commoners or the poor stayed. In inns, strangers were only given a room, where they stayed alone or in company. Inns also usually had a courtyard where the stables were located. Inns also had a kitchen where customers could prepare their meals. Very popular in the seventeenth and eighteenth centuries, inns were almost non-existent by the end of the nineteenth century.

In contrast, lodging houses (*posadas*) were for wealthier groups. However, not all inns were the same, and it is possible to distinguish between two types: public lodging houses, which were advertised, and secret lodging houses. The former were the best and accommodated people of a certain social standing. Secret lodging houses, on the other hand, were not advertised and resembled private homes, offering travellers more familiar comforts and services. *Paradores*, on the other hand, were establishments where travellers could find accommodation and, generally, food and drink. By the mid-nineteenth century, inns and *paradores* were already being identified.

As for guest houses, they were the most economical means available to foreigners to live in the Spanish capital. They were private homes where the owners rented one or more rooms to guests, who were provided with food in addition to furniture and furnishings. The owners were not professional innkeepers but rather sought extra income from this business. In many cases, these guest houses were run by widows who earned their living in this way. They used to select their guests, so it was necessary for some people to introduce them. This form of accommodation lost importance in the last third of the nineteenth century as a result of competition from other types of accommodation.

Another option for a stranger wishing to spend a long period in Madrid was to stay in a rented house. It was possible to rent the entire house or just some of the rooms. It was also common for houses to be rented unfurnished, in which case it was possible to buy or rent used furniture from specialist shops.

Finally, the *fondas* (inns) emerged in Madrid in the nineteenth century, following on from establishments that only served food and drink. *Fondas* came in different categories, and some of them provided accommodation for guests. In Barcelona, the first *fondas* date back to the late eighteenth century and can be linked to the economic expectations of the time, particularly colonial trade and the expansion of industrial activity, especially in the textile sector. In general, they offered more convenient and comfortable services than other types of accommodation (Rosselló & Valdívia, 2016). In fact, the *fonda* became the most upmarket establishment in Spain in the mid-nineteenth century. So too were the stagecoach inns (*paradores*), located at strategic points along the transport routes. Thus, what differentiated the *fondas* and the new stagecoach inns from other types of accommodation was that they offered dining services, in addition to the quality of their facilities. Both types of accommodation arose as a result of increased traveller traffic and the necessary improvements that were imposed in this sector.

3 The Birth of Modern Hotels

At the end of the nineteenth century and the beginning of the twentieth, a new type of accommodation began to gain momentum and would eventually dominate the tourism industry: the hotel. These were establishments offering lodging, meals, and other services to guests. They were therefore more comprehensive establishments, with more services and higher quality than the traditional accommodation available at the time. As they offered more and better services, these establishments required greater capital investment, giving rise to the first entrepreneurs and the first companies in the Spanish hotel industry. Thus, during the first decades of the twentieth century, Spain experienced a considerable increase in this type of accommodation. Following the model of the grand hotels of Paris and London, the first hotels designed for tourists appeared in Spain in the last decades of the nineteenth century. In view of the criticisms mentioned above, it is not surprising that one of the main objectives of Spanish tourism at the beginning of the twentieth century was precisely to improve the range of hotels designed for tourists (Arcos, 1909).

To achieve this objective, it was necessary to introduce significant changes to the deficient hotel industry that existed in Spain at the beginning of that century, increasing investment in hotel establishments. Thanks to the efforts of entrepreneurs and companies in the sector in the early decades of the twentieth century, a modern hotel network designed for tourists was successfully developed, so that when the Civil War broke out in 1936, significant achievements had already been made in this area. For example, it was possible to create the first luxury hotel system (Larrinaga Rodríguez, 2019). Not only that, but during these years we also saw the first signs of concern for the hotel industry from both trade associations and the state, which contributed not only to its improvement but also to its expansion. Thus, the perception of the hotel industry from outside began to improve progressively in the years leading up to the First World War, giving way to an increasingly high-quality hotel industry in a process that would culminate in the 1920s (Vallejo et al., 2016, pp. 156–157).

An important step for the Spanish hotel industry was taken with the establishment of hotel corporations, a phenomenon that emerged at the beginning of the twentieth century. This can be seen as a sign of the modernisation of the sector and, above all, of an industrial conception of tourist accommodation. This reality can be clearly seen in two tourist destinations in northern Spain, San Sebastián and Santander. In 1901, *El Sardinero, Sociedad Anónima* was established in the latter, and in 1902, *Fomento de San Sebastián*. The former aimed to exploit the concession of Sardinero beach, the bathing establishment that had been built there, the steam tram to Sardinero, the *Hotel de Castilla*, the *Casa de Sarabia* café and casino, the *Hotel de París*, the *Hotel de Hoyuela*, and the *Gran Hotel*. The second company was responsible for the construction of a theatre and a hotel, the future *Victoria Eugenia* and *María Cristina*, both of which opened in July 1912.

Alongside these establishments, we find new initiatives in other Spanish cities. For example, in Madrid, with the opening of the *Ritz* and *Palace* Hotels, two luxury establishments particularly suited to the international tourism that was beginning to visit the Spanish capital at that time. We can also mention important initiatives in Santander (*Hotel Real, S.A.*), Malaga (*Hotel Regina, S.A.*), Barcelona (*Hotel Meublé*), and Oviedo (*Hotel Covadonga, S.A.*). As far as hotel offerings are concerned, Barcelona, in addition to an initial investment cycle detected between the late nineteenth and early twentieth centuries, experienced a second investment cycle that would run from 1908–1910 to 1914–1915.

During those years, the number of hotels increased significantly, although the most notable initiative was the creation in 1917 of the *Hotel Ritz de Barcelona, S.A.*, established with local capital and which, due to the turbulent political and economic situation at the time, did not open until January 1920 (Larrinaga & Vallejo, 2021). However, some inland towns also saw a clear improvement in their hotel facilities, with a view to attracting tourists. This was the case in Granada, for example, with its extraordinary monumental heritage. In 1911, there were at least four high-end hotels. Among them, the *Alhambra Palace Hotel* stood out, inaugurated by King Alfonso XIII in 1910.

4 From the Hotel Expansion of the 1920s to the Boom of the 1950s

Once the First World War was over, a new cycle of investment in luxury hotels began in Spain, undoubtedly most closely associated with the great tourists of the time. There were various initiatives, although Barcelona stands out, not only because of the aforementioned *Hotel Ritz*, but also because of the establishment of the *Majestic Hotel de Inglaterra* public limited company with local capital, which was created with the aim of operating one of the most luxurious hotels in the city. In general, it can be said that the 1920s were good years for the Spanish hotel industry. From 1922 onwards, we see a new phase of investment, although it was not until the end of that decade, thanks to the Ibero-American Exhibition in Seville and the International Exhibition in Barcelona, that this tourist hotel industry grew and became consolidated. These exhibitions were a real boost for the hotel industry during those years, to the extent that their impact transcended both cities, affecting other locations in the country.

During this investment boom, it is worth mentioning the addition of new luxury hotels. In 1926, the King and Queen inaugurated the *Hotel Príncipe de Asturias* in Málaga. That same year, the *Hotel Carlton* in Bilbao opened its doors, followed shortly afterwards, in 1928, by the *Hotel Alfonso XIII* in Seville. Obviously, these hotels catered to a very specific sector of demand, that of the most affluent, still in line with what was known as elite tourism. However, in the 1920s and even more so in the 1930s, it is possible to speak of a certain democratisation of tourism, when increasingly broad sectors of society began to take up the practice of tourism. Through a process of social mimicry, the middle classes began to imitate the tourist behaviour and practices of the privileged classes (Boyer, 2002, p. 15). In fact, the Official Hotel Guide of 1929 clearly reflects this phenomenon, with a very considerable increase in the number of hotel establishments throughout Spain.

The outbreak of the Civil War in 1936 had a profound effect on the hotel sector, as many establishments suffered extensive damage or were confiscated and converted into hospitals, headquarters for trade unions, or revolutionary parties to house government or political representation bodies, foreign delegations, etc. (Fernández Casado, 2018). Hotels in Barcelona, Bilbao, and Madrid are good examples. The *Carlton Hotel* in Bilbao was the headquarters of the first Basque Government after the 1937 Statute was approved. With all these vicissitudes, when the war ended and Franco was in power, it was necessary to recover a large part of all these buildings for hotel services and to reorganise the Spanish tourism system, now conditioned by the heavy influence of the Administration. In the hotel industry, there was control not only over the business itself, but also over the organisation of entrepreneurs in the sector. An Order from the Ministry of the Interior dated 8 April 1939 established regulations for hotel accommodation, so that any company or individual wishing to provide accommodation had to first apply to the Head of the National Tourism Service, the new public body responsible for tourism. Among other aspects, this Order also regulated prices, thus restricting business freedom. The idea was that Spain could compete on price, as indeed it ended up doing, setting rates that were considerably cheaper than in other neighbouring countries, such as France or Italy (Larrinaga Rodríguez, 2021).

Despite everything, the 1940s were not a good decade for the sector. For example, in Barcelona, there were 3542 beds in 1936, 3002 in 1939 and 3287 in 1949 (Palou, 2012, p. 264). What is more, in 1950 there were only 28 hotels, whereas the 1929 guide listed 45 establishments. The double impact of the Civil War and the Second World War seriously damaged both the Spanish and European tourism industries, and it was not until the 1950s that tourist flows regained their vigour. In Spain, in the early 1950s, tourism became the main item compensating the balance of payments. In addition, it is worth mentioning the incorporation of Spaniards into tourism, which was rooted in the growth in national income, especially between 1950 and 1959, with an annual rate of 4.4% (Vallejo, 2013). It was then that business opportunities for entrepreneurs in the hotel sector increased and they were able to feel encouraged (Pack, 2006). Practically 40% of all hotel establishments in 1960 were less than 10 years old, making it the youngest hotel industry in Europe (Aguirre, 1963, p. 108). It was in the late 1940s that private investment began to gain momentum, and the hotel industry began to recover, affecting not only traditional urban destinations, but also others that were joining the mass tourism and sun and beach tourism sectors, with mid-range and lower-end establishments.

5 *Paradores*, Spain's Public Hotel Chain

However, beyond private initiative, it is also worth mentioning the existence of public hotels, grouped together under the *Paradores* brand (Moreno & Pellejero, 2015; Rodríguez, 2018). We are talking about the state as an entrepreneur. On 9 October 1928, King Alfonso XIII inaugurated the *Parador de Turismo de Gredos*, the first hotel establishment owned by the state. With thirty beds, this accommodation was intended for lovers of hiking and hunting. The construction of this accommodation laid the foundations for the State to set up new establishments where there were none. In fact, with the Seville and Barcelona exhibitions on the horizon, in the summer of 1929, at the request of the Patronato Nacional de Turismo, the official tourism body in Spain created in 1928, a decree was passed to create a network of twelve roadside hostels with the first motorists in mind, who would travel around Spain once its roads had undergone a notable improvement thanks to investments in the Special Road Surface Circuit during the dictatorship of Primo de Rivera. Finally, eight were opened between 1932 and 1935. Within this network, the *Hotel Atlántico* in Cádiz was inaugurated in 1929, with a clear focus on tourism. When the Civil War broke out, *Paradores* had 17 establishments, including tourist inns, the aforementioned hotel, roadside hostels, two inns, and a mountain refuge.

Once the war was over, it was necessary to repair the buildings that had been damaged during the war years and to complete some that had been left unfinished when the war broke out. Thus, by 1942, a large part of the network was already open, and a new phase of creating new establishments began. Between 1939 and 1959, another 20 buildings were added, its prestige grew, although the percentage of hotel rooms represented by the chain rarely exceeded 1% of the total available in Spain.

6 From the Hotel Boom of the 1960s to the Present Day: The Origin and Evolution of the Large Hotel Chains

In the 1950s, the emergence of tour operators was key to the expansion of mass sun and beach tourism, as they drove tourism development and the creation of hotels, helping to cover the structural accommodation deficit that existed in Spain. Growing demand, good economic results, and high returns on invested capital led to the tourism boom of the 1960s. This led to the emergence of major holiday destinations (Mallorca, the Canary Islands, the Costa del Sol), driven by good business prospects and the initiative of local entrepreneurs who laid the foundations for what would become major Spanish hotel chains decades later.

6.1 *Sol Meliá: From a Small Mallorcan Hotel to a Global Empire*

In 1956, at the age of just 21, Gabriel Escarrer opened his first establishment in Palma de Mallorca: the *Hotel Altair*. The success of the business led to its expansion with the purchase of thirteen more establishments, which would form part of *Hoteles Mallorquines* (1966).

In the 1970s, agreements with tour operators—who made advance payments for the purchase of accommodation services—facilitated the rapid growth of the company and the incorporation of new hotels on a rental basis. During this decade, the *Sol Hoteles* brand was created, leading to a change of name for *Hoteles Mallorquines*. In 1976, the Mallorca market began to become saturated, leading to expansion into other holiday destinations such as the Costa del Sol and the Canary Islands.

In the 1980s, the company took a strategic leap forward by purchasing two of the largest Spanish hotel chains of the time. In 1984, it bought 32 hotels from HOTASA, expropriated from RUMASA, becoming the largest chain in the country with 92 hotels and more than 50,000 beds (Laguna & Larrinaga, 2024). Three years later, it acquired the *Meliá* chain, with 22 high-end hotels, which became its flagship brand. Its international journey began in 1985 with the opening of the *Hotel Bali Sol*. This marked the company's foray into a new continent and a new destination for honeymoons, exotic, with high-quality facilities and at a good price (González, 1996).

In the 1990s, the company continued its expansion throughout the Caribbean and Latin America. It was the first company to open hotels in Cuba, despite the complicated context of the destination due to the US blockade, becoming a benchmark for tourism development on the island. This expansion also extended to Southeast Asia and major European cities through management contracts and franchises, opening 25 hotels per year. In 1993, it signed an agreement with the German company AGIB and created the *Sol Inn Hotels* brand. A year later, it launched its loyalty programme with the Mas card (now Meliárewards) and created its own reservation centre (Solres), connected to major reservation systems such as Amadeus, Apolo, etc. (González, 1996). In 1995, the *Paradisus* brand was created for its resorts in the Caribbean (Meliá, 2025).

In the second half of the 1990s, it continued to grow in Europe and South America, one of its key markets. The incorporation of the founder's son, Sebastián Escarrer Jaume, boosted and transformed the management of the company. In 1996, *Sol Meliá* became the first European chain to go public. This provided a significant injection of liquidity that allowed it to reduce the debt incurred during its expansion. Previously, the hotel business (*Sol Meliá, S.A.*) had been separated from the real estate business (*Inmotel*, the company that owned the properties) (Guitart Pascual, 1999). With this asset-light management model, the company gained profitability and financial flexibility, favouring its international growth through franchise and/or management agreements. In 1997, *Sol Meliá* and *Inmotel* created MIA (*Meliá Inversiones Americanas*) to drive growth in Latin America, which became the priority area for expansion. *Sol Meliá* was then already present in 25 countries and had 205 hotels on four continents.

In 2000, the company acquired the *Tryp* chain, which it would sell 10 years later to *Wyndham Worldwide*, entering the top ten in the global hotel industry. It then created the *Me by Meliá* brand (2006) and relaunched the *Meliá* (2008), *Sol* (2014), and *Club de Vacaciones* brands, which would become *Circle by Meliá*.

Throughout the first decade of the 2000s, it continued its expansion, tripling its presence in Asia and entering the United States. In 2007, it launched the SAVE project to reduce the environmental impact of its business, one of the objectives for which the company sets itself more ambitious targets year after year. In 2011, *Sol Meliá* became *Meliá Hotels International*, reflecting its global nature, and 3 years later it began to drive the company's digital transformation with the Meliá Digital project.

A few years later, the Covid-19 crisis had a serious impact on its financial results, but it emerged stronger, consolidating its adaptability and resilience. In 2021, it posted revenues of €1.065 billion, up 65.6% on the previous year (Meliá, 2021). In recent years, *Meliá* has strategically focused on the holiday and bleisure (business and leisure) segments, as reflected in its slogan "Leisure in heart, business in mind". It has continued its expansion in Asia Pacific (Vietnam, Thailand, Dubai, China) and the Mediterranean (Albania, Malta) and has grown in established destinations such as the Canary Islands, where it has opened the first *Paradisus* all-inclusive resorts in Europe, Mexico, and Portugal. Its commitment to the luxury segment now accounts for 13% of its offering and one in three new openings. All of this has led to an ambitious expansion and repositioning plan focused on the premium and luxury segments, increasing its portfolio with *Meliá Collection*, a collection of unique luxury hotels where differentiation and quality are expressed to the fullest (Meliá, 2021, 2023). It currently has eight brands: *Gran Meliá*, *Meliá Collection*, *Me by Meliá*, *Paradisus*, *Meliá Hotels and Resorts*, *Innside by Meliá*, *Zel*—a brand created in collaboration with tennis player Rafael Nadal (2022)—and *Sol*, in addition to its affiliated establishments (*Affiliated by Meliá*) (Meliá, 2025).

Today, the company owns more than 400 hotels and almost 94,000 rooms (52% resort and 48% urban) in 43 countries and four continents. It is the leading hotel group in Spain, the third largest in Europe and among the top twenty worldwide. Its future strategy is based on innovation—with projects such as Robotics 360 for process automation—digitalisation, sustainability, and a brand architecture that projects the company's growth strategy focused primarily on the premium and luxury segment (Meliá, 2025). In 2024, it had revenues of €2.013 billion and a net profit of €162 million, representing annual growth of 24.5%.

6.2 Barceló: A Global Chain with a Family Feel

Barceló began its hotel venture in 1962 with the opening of the *Hotel Latino* in Palma de Mallorca, followed 3 years later by the *Hotel Barceló Pueblo Palma*. With it came a new hotel concept (the Pueblo hotel), considered the precursor of the resort-type hotel, with a more horizontal, economical design and services and facilities aimed at family customers.

The tourism boom led to expansion in the Balearic Islands with the construction of new hotels in Ibiza (1967) and the purchase of the *Barceló Hamilton Hotel* (1969) in Menorca. In 1970, it opened its first hotel on the mainland in Benidorm, later expanding to the main national destinations (the Canary Islands, Levante and Costa del Sol).

In the 1980s, it became the first Spanish chain to operate in the Caribbean when it opened its first resort in Punta Cana (Dominican Republic) in 1985. In the following years, in addition to strengthening its presence in this market, it began operating in other destinations in Central and South America, such as Costa Rica, Mexico (with hotels in Cancún and Acapulco), Guatemala, Nicaragua, Venezuela and Colombia (Guitart Pascual, 1999). At the same time, there was a strategic reorientation towards exclusivity, focusing on the opening of four- and five-star hotels.

In the early 1990s, *Barceló* entered the US market, one of the group's most important milestones, as it was the first Spanish chain to establish itself in Washington (1992) and Orlando (1994), where it opened a hotel very close to Disney World (Barceló, 2007). In 1993, it opened its first hotel in a European capital in Prague (1993).

In Spain, the company focused on the urban segment, adding hotels in Spanish cities (Barcelona, Bilbao, Vitoria, Badajoz, etc.) to the group, but without abandoning the holiday market, where it increased its presence in the Canary and Balearic Islands (Guitart Pascual, 1999). In 1998, in order to grow more quickly, but without abandoning property investment, it created the *Grubarges* joint venture with BBVA (*Gesinar*) and the company *Fomento de Construcciones y Contratas* (*Grucycsa*) (Adame Sánchez & Cruz Ros, 2012). With this venture, it sought to promote the construction of large tourist complexes, also acquiring sixteen hotels in the United States, which made it the Spanish chain with the largest presence in that competitive market.

The new millennium officially marked the beginning of the third generation of the family's leadership, Simón and Simón Pedro Barceló, thanks to a prior agreement between the founder's children to distribute his business assets equally among their families.

In 2001, the group reached the iconic figure of 100 hotels (Barceló, 2025). A year later, it purchased *Crestline Capital*, which operated 45 hotels and six convention centres in the United States, creating the subsidiary *Barceló Crestiline Hotels and Resorts*, which thus became the group's first market (Adame Sánchez & Cruz Ros, 2012). In 2003, it launched its website and created its own booking centre

(Barceló-Res) (Barceló, 2007). This allowed it to reduce commission costs, have a more direct relationship with its customers and greater control over bookings.

In 2005, it launched a Strategic Plan (2005–2010) with the aim of growing to two hundred four- and five-star establishments, which meant opening twenty per year through various formulas (ownership, management, etc.). In this way, *Barceló* positioned itself in the top 30 worldwide with 52 hotels in Europe, 46 in the United States, 32 in Latin America, 2 in Africa and 2 in Asia (Barceló, 2007). Two years later, it rose to twenty-fourth place and in 2010 it was in the top twenty.

After this strong growth and as a result of the severe economic recession (2008–2014) caused by the subprime crisis—which in Spain was exacerbated by the property bubble—the group changed its strategy, prioritising the renovation of its establishments over expansion, reorganising its portfolio and disposing of its least profitable hotels. In the following years, *Barceló* continued to grow with the purchase of *Occidental Hotels* and other acquisitions and agreements, such as the one signed with the Chinese giant *Plateno* (2016) to exploit the *Barceló* brand through franchises in that market.

In recent years, the group has developed new business models by adopting oil-spill strategies, which have allowed it to enter new destinations (Maldives, Sri Lanka) slowly but deeply through the creation of joint ventures with local partners. In addition, it has continued its process of expansion, improvement, and repositioning, increasing its presence in new segments (spa, golf) and developing a multi-brand strategy with brands positioned in strategic targets: *Royal Hideaway Luxury Hotels and Resorts* (luxury), *Barceló Hotels and Resorts* (upper upscale), *Occidental Hotels and Resorts* (upscale), and *Allegro Hotels* (upper midscale).

In 2019, it opened its first European hotel under a foreign brand, the *Canopy by Hilton*, in Madrid. In recent years, it has made a firm commitment to haute cuisine, especially in its most iconic and exclusive hotels, such as the *Royal Hideaway Canfranc Estación*—a five-star luxury hotel located in an emblematic building declared a site of cultural interest—making it the Spanish hotel chain with the most Michelin stars (seven) (Barceló, 2023).

Today, the company continues to retain its family character. It has 300 urban and holiday hotels with more than 66,000 high-quality rooms (four and five stars) in 30 countries, employing more than 38,000 people (Barceló, 2025). It is the second largest hotel chain in Spain and is among the 30 largest in the world in terms of number of rooms. In recent years, it has made a firm commitment to regenerative, sustainable, and responsible tourism. In 2024, its turnover reached 7.5 billion with a net profit of over 300 million euros (Barceló, 2023). In 2025, it acquired 80% of *Rusticae*, a leading company in the rural segment, which has allowed it to enter and position itself in a new market niche where other chains do not yet have a presence.

6.3 NH Hotels*: From Revolutionising Urban Hospitality in Spain to Becoming a Major International Group*

NH Hotels began operating in Pamplona in 1978, when Antonio Catalán opened his first establishment, the *Hotel Ciudad de Navarra*. Four years later, it began expanding into Spain's major cities (Madrid, Barcelona, Zaragoza, etc.). In just over a decade, NH became one of Spain's leading hotel chains, with modern hotels featuring functional, avant-garde décor that made it a benchmark for urban hotels in the country.

In 1988, NH carried out a capital increase, which was fully subscribed by COFIR (*Corporación Financiera, S.A.*), which thus became a shareholder by acquiring 49.5% of its shares. The corporation increased its stake until, in 1997, it acquired 100% of the capital (NH, 2025). This led to the departure of NH's creator and founder, who sold his stake due to differences in the strategic vision and management of the company with his then partner. Shortly afterwards, Antonio Catalán started his new project, *AC Hotels*.

With the merger of *NH Hoteles* and COFIR, the company began trading on the stock exchange (1997). During these years, the company's commitment to quality lived up to its slogan "A matter of detail", and *NH University* was created with the aim of promoting the continuous training of its employees (NH, 2025). In 1998, it launched its corporate website and began its international expansion in Latin America and Europe by acquiring part of the Italian chain *Jolly Hotels*. By the end of 1998, NH already had 71 hotels with more than 8000 rooms and four hotels (645 rooms) in the Mercosur countries. A year later, in 1999, it acquired 91.5% of *Sotogrande S.A.*, a company dedicated to residential property development, and created the Equity International Properties fund to boost its investments in Latin America.

At the start of the new millennium, NH intensified its internationalisation strategy by purchasing the Dutch chain *Krasnapolsky* (2000), which allowed it to double in size and reach the top three in the European business hotel sector, the Mexican chain *Chartwell* (2001) and the German chain *Astron Hotels* (2002) (De Diego Ruiz et al., 2016). In addition, during these years it signed collaboration agreements with non-hotel partners that improved and reinforced its image, such as Adolfo Domínguez, who designed its employees' uniforms; Jesús del Pozo, who developed fragrances for the chain's bathroom kits and amenities; and Ferrán Adriá, with whom it implemented a new and innovative gastronomic concept: fast-good.

In 2004, it entered new markets (the United Kingdom, France, Romania), becoming Italy's leading business chain after the purchase of *Framon and Jolly*. Five years later, it entered into an integration agreement with *Hesperia*, taking over the management of its 51 hotels and nearly 7800 rooms (De Diego Ruiz et al., 2016). In 2011, NH ranked among the top 25 worldwide with 400 hotels and 60,000 rooms. However, its financial results were poor, and the debt incurred by acquisitions and mergers, compounded by the economic crisis in some of its most important markets, eventually took its toll.

To resolve this complicated situation, the company undertook significant changes to its organisational structure, separating the roles of chairman and CEO, refinanced its debt (€800 million with 33 financial institutions) and restructured its assets. This involved the sale of some iconic hotels to generate liquidity, such as the *NH Grand Hotel Krasnapolsky* in Amsterdam (De Diego Ruiz et al., 2016). In addition, it launched a Strategic Plan (2014–2019) (NH, 2013) to optimise its portfolio, divesting non-strategic hotels, renegotiating leases and selling non-value-generating businesses, such as the real estate company *Sotogrande*. The customer experience and brand were also redefined, the pricing strategy and distribution channels were changed—giving greater prominence to the company's own channels—and its segmentation and asset repositioning strategy was rethought, involving a significant investment in the refurbishment and renovation of its hotels, which made it possible to increase the average room rate and revenue.

During these years, the company made a strong commitment to innovation, with initiatives such as the Living Lab, where technology was applied to create value and improve the customer experience, and to gastronomy by partnering with renowned chefs such as Dabiz Muñoz, who opened his famous restaurant *Diverxo* (2014) in the *NH Eurobuilding*. In addition, the expansion and growth strategy was redefined. In 2015, it acquired the Colombian chain *Hoteles Royal*, strengthening its presence in Latin America (Chile and Ecuador). In the following years, NH improved its financial results and regained its leading position in urban hospitality. In 2018, *Thailand's Minor International* launched a takeover bid, acquiring 94% of NH's capital, a change that redefined NH's control and management. In 2025, *Minor* approved a takeover bid to acquire 100% of *NH Hoteles*' share capital.

Its revenue reached €2.163 billion, 23% more than the previous year (NH, 2023). It currently has 357 hotels in 36 countries around the world (NH, 2025). Since 2024, it has adopted the name of its owner (*Minor Hotels Europe and America's*), although it retains its trademark and those of its establishments: *NH Collection Hotels* (premium urban), *NH Hotels* and *Nhow*.

Competing Interests The authors have no conflicts of interest to declare that are relevant to the content of this chapter.

References

Adame Sánchez, C., & Cruz Ros, S. (2012). El grupo Barceló. In D. R. Soriano, F. S. Parellada, F. M. Verdú, J. L. Taverner, & M. Peris-Ortiz (Eds.), *Casos de Dirección Estratégica* (pp. 107–115). Pearson.

Aguirre, R. (1963). *El turismo en Guipúzcoa*. Diputación de Guipúzcoa.

Arcos, C. (1909). *De las grandes ventajas que produciría el desarrollo del turismo en España*. Nemesio Aramburu.

Barceló, S. P. (2007). Trajectòria empresarial d'èxit: l'empresa Barceló, 75 anys del *bon fer* [Conferencia]. *II Semana del emprendedor de la empresa, Universidad de las Islas Baleares*. Retrieved September 25, 2025, from https://fci.uib.es/digitalAssets/177/177047_barcelo.ppt

Barceló. (2023). *Memoria anual 2023*. Grupo Barceló.
Barceló. (2025). *Grupo Barceló*. Retrieved September 12, 2025, from https://www.barcelogrupo.com
Boyer, M. (2002). El turismo en Europa, de la Edad Moderna al siglo XX. *Historia Contemporánea, 25*, 13–31. https://doi.org/10.1387/hc.5916
De Diego Ruiz, E., Susaeta Erburu, L., Pin Arboledas, J. R., & Suárez Ruz, E. (2016). Nuevo Rumbo Estratégico y Reestructuración: El Caso NH Hotel Group. *UCJC Business and Society Review (formerly known as Universia Business Review), 52*, 114–167. https://doi.org/10.3232/UBR.2016.V13.N4.03
Fernández Casado, A. (2018). *Hospitales de sangre o cuarteles. Guía de hoteles durante la Guerra Civil 1936–1939*. Editorial la Cátedra.
González, G. (1996). El mejor birdie de un consumado golfista. In F. G. Urbaneja & F. Vicente (Eds.), *Historias de éxito: empresas y empresarios que saben hacer las cosas* (pp. 248–259). El País Aguilar Ediciones.
Guitart Pascual, C. (1999). Cadenas hoteleras nacionales e internacionales. In F. B. Mariné (Ed.), *50 años del Turismo español: un análisis histórico y estructural* (pp. 899–926). Centro de Estudios Ramón Areces.
Gutiérrez Ronco, S. (1984). *La función hotelera de Madrid*. CSIC.
Harismendy, P. (2016). Introduction. In J.-Y. Andrieux & P. Harismendy (Eds.), *Pension complète! Tourisme et hôtellerie (XVIIIe-Xx^e siècle)* (pp. 9–29). Presses Universitaires de Rennes.
Laguna, M., & Larrinaga, C. (2024). Hotelería urbana. In E. de Quesada (Ed.), *Centenario del Turismo Español* (pp. 59–70). Nexo Editores.
Larrinaga Rodríguez, C. (2019). La hotelería turística de lujo en España en el primer tercio del siglo XX. *Ayer. Revista de Historia Contemporánea, 114*(2), 65–94. https://doi.org/10.55509/ayer/114-2019-03
Larrinaga Rodríguez, C. (2021). *De la fonda al hotel*. Comares.
Larrinaga, C., & Vallejo, R. (2021). The origins and creation of the tourist hotel industry in Spain from the end of the 19th century to 1936. Barcelona as a case study. *Tourism Management, 82*, 1–12. https://doi.org/10.1016/j.tourman.2020.104203
Lickorish, L. J., & Kershaw, A. G. (1958). *The travel trade*. Practical Press Ltd..
Meliá. (2021). *Informe de gestión 2021*. Meliá Hotels International. Retrieved October 7, 2025, from https://www.meliahotelsinternational.com/es/ourCompany/Documents/HistoricoInforme/Informe_de_Gestion_2021_Melia_Hotels_International.pdf
Meliá. (2023). *Informe de gestión 2023*. Meliá Hotels Internacionational.
Meliá (2025). *Perfil de la compañía*. Retrieved October 12, 2025, from https://www.meliahotelsinternational.com/es/perfil-compania/sobre-nosotros/premios-y-reconocimientos
Moreno, A., & Pellejero, C. (2015). La red de establecimientos turísticos del Estado (1928–1977), ¿necesidad hotelera o política turística? *Revista de Historia Industrial, 59*, 147–178.
NH. (2013). *Informe anual 2013. Memoria de responsabilidad social corporativa*. Retrieved September 12, 2025, from https://www.nhotels.com/corporate/assets/uploads/2016/06/memoria_rc_2013_esp.pdf
NH. (2023). *Estado de información financiero no consolidado. Memoria de sostenibilidad*. Retrieved September 12, 2025, from https://www.nh-hotels.com/corporate/assets/uploads/2024/02/12125557/NH-Hotel-Group-EINF-2023-Memoria-de-Sostenibilidad.pdf
NH. (2025). *Historia de NH Hotels Group*. Retrieved September 12, 2025, from https://www.nh-hotels.com/es/corporate/sobre-nh/historia
Pack, S. D. (2006). *Tourism and dictatorship. Europe's peaceful invasion of Franco's Spain*. Palgrave Macmillan. https://doi.org/10.1057/9780230601161
Palou, S. (2012). *Barcelona, destinació turística*. Vitel.la.
Rodríguez, M. J. (2018). *La red de paradores*. Taurus.
Rosselló, M., & Valdívia, P. (2016). Els primers establiments hotelers. In S. Palou (Ed.), *Història del turisme a la ciutat de Barcelona* (pp. 48–67). Efadós y Ajuntament de Barcelona.

Vallejo, R. (2013). Turismo y desarrollo económico en España durante el franquismo, 1939–1975. *Revista de la Historia de la Economía y de la Empresa, 7*, 423–452.
Vallejo, R., Lindoso, E., & Vilar, M. (2016). Los antecedentes del turismo de masas en España, 1900–1936. *Revista de la Historia de la Economía y de la Empresa, 10*, 137–188.

Marta Laguna García PhD in Business Administration, is an associate professor at the University of Valladolid (Spain). She has been dean of the Faculty of Social Sciences, Law and Communication and vice-dean of Economics and Infrastructure. She has also worked as a researcher at the General Subdirectorate for Tourism Planning and Forecasting and at the Institute for Tourism Studies (Ministry of Trade and Tourism). Her research areas are closely connected to tourism and marketing. She has undertaken research stays at London Metropolitan University, Bournemouth University, Shizouka University and International Hellenic Univeristy among others. She has published in several international refereed journals as *Tourism Management, Journal of Hospitality Marketing and Management, Journal of Travel Research, International Journal of Tourism Research*, and *Current Issues in Tourism.*

Carlos Larrinaga Rodríguez PhD in History, is full professor at the University of Granada (Spain). His research is in the history of tourism, railways in the nineteenth century, and the service sector. He has undertaken research in several stays at Bordeaux-Montaigne University and at Aberystwyth University. He is the Main Researcher of the four research projects about history of tourism, funded by the Ministry of Science and Innovation of the Government of Spain. He has published in several international refereed journals as *Historia y Política, Ayer. Revista de Historia Contemporánea, Tourism Management, Business History, Management & Organizational History*, or *European History Quarterly*. He has also published numerous books. The last one is *Tourism and economic development*, edited by P. Battilani, C. Larrinaga, and D. Srangio (Routledge, 2026).

The Figure of the Executive in the Management of the Modern Company: Pedro Durán Farell and *Catalana de Gas* (1950–1970)

Juan Manuel Matés-Barco, María Vázquez-Fariñas, and Mariano Castro-Valdivia

Abstract This chapter examines the professional trajectory of Pedro Durán Farell, a pivotal figure in the modernisation of *Catalana de Gas* and the development of the natural gas sector in Spain between 1950 and 1970. Amidst the broader historiographical shift in Spain from collective institutions to individual entrepreneurs, Durán's career exemplifies the integration of innovation, risk-taking, and managerial acumen within a transforming economic landscape. Beginning his career in the construction of hydroelectric plants in Catalonia, Durán quickly emerged as a skilled negotiator and strategic leader, fostering collaborations with both national institutions and international actors, notably in Algeria and across Europe. His engagement with emerging technologies, particularly in gas liquefaction and distribution, positioned *Catalana de Gas* at the forefront of energy modernisation. The study highlights Durán's role in the creation of *Gas Natural, S.A.*, illustrating the intersection of corporate governance, technological innovation, and international business relations. Furthermore, his extensive personal networks, including close ties with political and banking figures, facilitated industrial development and policy influence. By analysing Durán's entrepreneurial biography, this work underscores the significance of individual agency in economic and technological change, emphasising the interplay between leadership, organisational structure, and strategic decision-making within Spain's mid-twentieth-century energy sector.

J. M. Matés-Barco · M. Castro-Valdivia
Department of Economics, University of Jaén, Jaén, Spain
e-mail: jmmates@ujaen.es; mcastro@ujaen.es

M. Vázquez-Fariñas (✉)
Department of Economic Theory and Economic History, Faculty of Economics and Business Studies, University of Málaga, Málaga, Spain
e-mail: maria.vazquez@uma.es

M. Vázquez-Fariñas, F. Cabrera-Gallardo (eds.), *Business Trajectories in the History of Spain*, Frontiers in Economic History,
https://doi.org/10.1007/978-3-032-16214-4_9

1 Introduction

In recent decades, Spanish historiography, following similar developments in other traditions such as the French and the British, has devoted particular attention to the biography of entrepreneurs (Burdiel Bueno & Pérez Ledesma, 2000; Núñez García, 2013). To a considerable extent, the influence of the Marxist perspective in the last century had generated a generalised interest in collectives and institutions. Gradually, however, individuals have gained increasing weight as a subject of study. Traditional historiography concentrated its attention on emperors, kings and heads of government as the sole protagonists of history. By contrast, more recent research has shifted its focus towards figures who were representative of a specific epoch and a particular moment within the sphere of economic and social life. Undoubtedly, the influence of liberalism and, by extension, of individualism, encouraged many historians to restore the individual as an object of inquiry. On occasion, such individuals had not previously enjoyed prominence or were virtually forgotten and absent from historical manuals. For this new historiography, such omissions were no longer significant, for what mattered was the role played by the individual in the ongoing course of history.

Interest in biography has not been confined to the political realm but has extended to other previously unexplored fields. It is within this framework that the biographies of entrepreneurs and figures from the business world are to be situated. Whereas until only a few decades ago the entrepreneur was primarily depicted as an exploiter of labour, more recent scholarship has incorporated a more dynamic perspective, one in which innovation, risk, and, in some cases, a sense of adventure occupy a prominent place.

The changes prompted by the Welfare State, together with the failure of the Soviet economy, led some historians to engage with Anglo-Saxon historiography, which had long recognised the central role of the entrepreneur. As early as 1911, Schumpeter, in his theory of economic development, set out the entrepreneur's role in the economic advance of the United States and Great Britain (Tortella, 2000, pp. 13–14). In Spain, however, this image deteriorated even further. Firstly, because of the support given by large entrepreneurs to the Franco regime; and secondly, because of the massive bankruptcy of many firms during the transition to democracy, which substantially increased unemployment and produced a discouraging scenario for the Spanish economy. Numerous cases in Asturias, Cantabria, the Basque Country and Catalonia—also as a consequence of the crisis and industrial restructuring—are sufficiently illustrative. The work of Urrutia (2018) underlines this aspect.

More recent research has fostered a shift in the perception of the entrepreneur. The terminology employed is more innovative, distancing itself from the repertoire of the First Industrial Revolution, and it is now more common to analyse the entrepreneur (Matés-Barco, 2019). This expression, of Schumpeterian resonance, emphasises innovation, initiative, ingenuity, and spill-over effects, and places less weight on the ownership of the means of production. In any case, Spanish historiography has increasingly turned its attention towards this figure. The studies by Torres, among which his work on *Cien empresarios españoles del siglo XX* (Torres Villanueva, 2000) stands out, as well as those focused on various geographical regions—Catalonia, Valencia, Madrid, Andalusia—and even the *Diccionario Biográfico Español de la Real Academia de la Historia* (available online), are eloquent testimony of this reorientation. In addition, a significant number of recent studies further highlight the growing scholarly interest in firms and entrepreneurs (Fernández-Paradas & Larrinaga Rodríguez, 2021; Matés-Barco & Caruana de las Cagigas, 2021; Vázquez-Fariñas et al., 2021).

Furthermore, technological innovation is a predominant factor in entrepreneurship, understood in a broad sense, as accepted within the scientific community. This feature is essential in explaining the prominence of certain executives and entrepreneurs in the transformation that took place during the so-called "golden age of the Spanish economy" (Carreras & Tafunell, 2018). Business organisation is founded upon physical and human resources, which increase productivity, competitiveness, and profitability. As Hernández-Andreu (2019) observes, alongside the theories of the innovative entrepreneur postulated by Cantillon, Garnier, and Schumpeter, the theory of entrepreneurship has emerged, attributing to the company the causality of growth. This approach encompasses total factor productivity, which includes labour and capital, and highlights the importance of entrepreneurs' education in understanding economic growth (Matés-Barco & Caruana de las Cagigas, 2021; Tortella & Quiroga, 2013).

It is within this context that the present study of Pedro Durán Farell emerges. As a leading figure of the company *Catalana de Gas*, he constitutes a representative example of the changes experienced by Spanish firms in the final decades of the Franco dictatorship. He also presided over prominent companies such as *Hidroeléctrica de Cataluña* and *La Maquinista*, served as a board member of RENFE, and was managing director of the *Comisión Promotora de Autopistas,* among many other posts. A skilled negotiator, he reached agreements with governments of various countries and with several multinationals, invariably securing advantageous arrangements. His creative and optimistic disposition enabled him to perceive opportunities where others saw only problems. He approached the public–private dialectic from the perspective of efficiency and effectiveness, avoiding ideological disputes. His appointment as managing director of *Catalana de Gas* in 1961 generated a significant transformation in the company's activity and established him as a reference figure in the gas sector (Ballestero, 2017, p. 29).

The scarcity of entrepreneurial spirit in Spain has often been attributed to cultural legacies, an aversion to risk, and fear of failure. However, Pedro Durán believed that without entrepreneurs and the willingness to take risks, society would stagnate. For this reason, he advocated the promotion of creative leaders, willing to take risks and motivated by the aspiration to advance and improve the economy—individuals imbued with self-confidence and determined to counteract any sense of frustration.

This work provides an examination of the figure of Pedro Durán Farell and the role he played in the modernisation of *Catalana de Gas*, as well as in the development and dissemination of natural gas in Spain. The intense activity that he carried out at the head of the company demonstrated both his negotiating skills and his management capacity. To a considerable degree, his professional trajectory constitutes an example of the broader transformation that was taking place in the Spanish economy and business sector during the 1960s. Specifically, the study encompasses the period between 1950 and 1970, the years in which he concentrated his executive activity on technological transformation and the implementation of natural gas in Spain. In order to approach his figure, it is necessary to turn to the detailed studies of Pere Fàbregas and, in particular, to the biography he wrote of the Catalan engineer. Moreover, Alfonso Ballestero, in his incisive analysis of natural gas in Spain, also provides significant information on the subject of this chapter (Ballestero, 2017; Fàbregas, 2014). Likewise, a commemorative volume promoted by *Gas Natural* following his death offers insights into his thought and includes a selection of his speeches (Maluquer i Sostres, 2001). Finally, the company's Board of Directors' Minutes Book (*Libro de Actas del Consejo de Administración*) from those years have served as a substantial complementary source, contributing concrete data on the company, the sector, and the wider economy of the period.

Following this introduction, the second section briefly summarises his family origins and his first steps in professional life. The third describes his contacts and personal relationships, both nationally and internationally. The subsequent section reviews his incorporation into the management of *Catalana de Gas* and his ambitious business projects. Lastly, the fifth section offers some brief conclusions, followed by the sources and bibliographical references employed in the preparation of this study.

2 Family Origins and First Steps in Professional Life

Pedro Durán Farell was born into a family of agricultural landowners established in the Vallés Oriental, in the province of Barcelona. Among his ancestors were individuals connected to local political life and to institutions such as the Agricultural Chambers. His father served as mayor during various years of the reign of Alfonso XIII and was a member of the "Lliga Regionalista" during the Republican period. During the Civil War, the family estate was occupied by peasants and tenant farmers, and his grandfather was assassinated in Montcada on 19 December 1936. The decrees issued by the Generalitat of Catalonia mandated the collectivisation of companies with more than one hundred employees and the requisition of the property of those who had supported the military uprising (Fàbregas, 2014, pp. 14–15).

Amidst this violence and upheaval, the family sought refuge in Barcelona, staying in the homes of friends and acquaintances in order to avoid the fate suffered by the grandfather. During these years, the young Pedro Durán carried out tasks as a medical assistant and served in the infirmary of the company *Maquinista Terrestre y Marítima*. At the end of the conflict, he settled in Madrid to study at the School of Civil Engineering, where he obtained the degree of *Ingeniero de Caminos, Canales y Puertos in 1947, at the age of 26.*

The absence of rainfall and the possibility of provoking it artificially was a matter that greatly interested him from his student years onwards. While still a student at the School of Civil Engineering, he published several articles on this subject in the *Revista de Obras Públicas*. Although there were various theories on the subject, none had been tested empirically. After several attempts, his efforts to induce artificial rainfall ended in complete failure. Nevertheless, they revealed his entrepreneurial spirit, his capacity to seek alternatives, and his ability to bring together divergent interests (Fàbregas, 2014, pp. 29–30).

Another significant aspect of these early years was his involvement in the construction of dams in the Catalan Pyrenees. In the 1940s, electricity companies faced severe limitations. Despite these constraints, the sector was marked by vigorous entrepreneurial activity and promising prospects for growth. The creation of UNESA stimulated its development and facilitated the establishment of private companies as well as the entry of the public sector. Within this context, Pedro Durán undertook his first professional activities (Fàbregas, 2014, pp. 25–26).

By the late 1940s, a plan for the construction of hydroelectric plants was underway. Restrictions and frequent power cuts left no alternative. In Barcelona, two important groups were active: *Barcelona Traction* and *Catalana de Gas y Electricidad*, through the *Compañía de Fluido Eléctrico* (CFE). In 1946, the Catalan company, together with the banks *Urquijo* and *Hispano Americano*, promoted the creation of a company to build hydroelectric dams and plants. The new company, *Hidroeléctrica de Cataluña, S.A.* (HECSA), provided a field for the exchange of board members: Juan Bertrand Mata, president of *Catalana*, joined the *Banco Urquijo*, while the latter became a shareholder in the gas company (Díaz Hernández, 1998). It is worth recalling that *Catalana de Gas* had been founded in 1843 with the aim of supplying the city of Barcelona. To compete with the German firm AEG and its subsidiary *Barcelonesa de Electricidad*, it created the *Central Catalana de Electricidad*. A similar policy was later pursued against *Barcelona Traction*—its main competitor—which progressively absorbed all the electricity companies in Catalonia. In response to this offensive by *La Canadiense*, in 1928 *Catalana* leased its electrical assets to the *Compañía de Fluido Eléctrico* (CFE).

Hidroeléctrica de Cataluña, S.A. (HECSA) was founded with the participation of *Catalana de Gas* (53%) and a banking group (47%). As Fàbregas notes, its objective was to build hydroelectric plants and supply electricity to the *Compañía de Fluido Eléctrico*. Both companies made their respective concessions available to the new enterprise. Pedro Durán joined HECSA in 1947, the very year the company commenced operations. Shortly thereafter, he was already head of the team of engineers. The projects envisaged the construction of a hydraulic system in the basins of the Pallars Sobirà and the Noguera Pallaresa. Between 1953 and 1957, six hydroelectric plants were built with a combined capacity of 77,900 horsepower, while at the same time dams were constructed to regulate the Ter river. In September 1955, the Head of State, Francisco Franco, visited the Catalan Pyrenees to inaugurate the HECSA and ENHER hydroelectric plants (Fàbregas, 2014, p. 36).

Despite these advances and the momentum in construction, relations between *Catalana de Gas y Electricidad* and its banking partners in HECSA became increasingly tense as the years passed. Disagreements over the scale of investments were constant, and the banks exerted no effective control over the *Compañía de Fluido Eléctrico*, which was responsible for selling the electricity generated by the hydroelectric plants. The attempts by *Banco Urquijo* and *Banco Hispano Americano* to increase HECSA's control over this group of companies were unsuccessful. Ricardo Margarit, managing director of *Catalana de Gas*, strongly resisted such interference by the banks; in turn, they countered by threatening to transfer HECSA to the *Instituto Nacional de Industria* (INI), although they eventually promoted the acquisition by HECSA of the shares of the *Compañía de Fluido Eléctrico* previously held by *Catalana*.

In this new context, in 1956 the banks financially supported HECSA's expansion plan, seeking to exert greater control over the *Compañía de Fluido Eléctrico* (CFE). The new strategy required a restructuring of the company's board of directors. Pedro Durán, who at that time was general manager, was appointed managing director of HECSA. Simultaneously, a coordinating committee was established among the three companies: *Catalana de Gas y Electricidad* (CGE), *Compañía de Fluido Eléctrico* (CFE), and *Hidroeléctrica de Cataluña, S.A.* (HECSA). The committee was chaired by Juan Bertrand Mata—president of *Catalana de Gas* and director of *Banco Urquijo*—and included one representative from each company. This new organisational structure reflected the waning influence of Ricardo Margarit, who, at the age of 72, had served as executive director since before the Civil War. In contrast, as Fàbregas points out, a young man of 35, Pedro Durán, emerged; in 1958, he was appointed a member of the board of CFE and became the consensus executive among the various parties (Fàbregas, 2014, pp. 42–43).

3 Personal Relationships and International Perspectives

The discoveries of natural gas in various countries propelled the initial steps towards the future implementation of this energy source. The fields in the Po Valley (1949), Lacq Valley (1951), Algeria (1956), Groningen (1959), and the North Sea reserves represented a pivotal contribution to the development of this energy (Ballestero, 2017, p. 21). Simultaneously, the evolution of cryogenic technology and the construction of methane carriers for gas transport offered a high-quality, low-pollution alternative, not to mention the energy contribution this represented for Europe. Almost at the same time, nuclear energy began to become more visible. *General Electric* and *Westinghouse* commissioned the first reactors for their respective plants.

Pedro Durán's connection with Algeria was a decisive element in his professional and business career. In fact, his contacts with members of the National Liberation Front (NLF), when the country was still under French rule, allowed him a privileged relationship with prominent figures such as Abdelaziz Bouteflika, with whom he maintained a long and profound personal friendship; Bouteflika would later serve as President of Algeria between 1999 and 2019.

Upon his joining the *French Euro-African Mining and Industrial Association* (*Asociación Euroafricana Minera e Industrial*—ASSEMI), he began his relations with the Algerian government. This organisation had been created by Georges Picot in 1955 through the union of several private industrial companies from various European countries, including Germany, Belgium, the Netherlands, Italy, Luxembourg, and Switzerland. Companies such as *Société Générale of Belgium*, *Brown Boveri*, and *Fiat* participated in this conglomerate. The objective uniting these companies was the exchange of information regarding the different possibilities for industrial activities in the African regions under European influence. The French officer, with deep roots in the country, promoted an industrialisation policy alongside projects that fostered stability and peace in the region. He led the *Société d'études pour l'équipement minier et industriel* (SEPEMI) and promoted other French and European capital companies specialising in diverse products: iron and manganese exploitation (SENAF), nitrogen fertilisers in Colomb-Béchar (SETAZ), and construction materials for the Sahara (SENAM). The studies carried out revealed the necessity of establishing relations with foreign industry to open channels for marketing and financial resources to cover the required inputs. The discovery of natural gas fields in Algeria in 1956 represented a culmination of these projects and a greater involvement of European countries (Ballestero, 2017, p. 22).

The liberalising movements of the dictatorial regime in Spain in the late 1950s fostered certain relations with European politicians. José Solís, Secretary-General of the Movement, invited Maurice Lemaire in February 1959 to deliver lectures in Madrid and Barcelona on the Eurofrigaz project for the transport of gas to Europe. The former French Minister of National Recovery and member of the Council of Europe addressed the continent's heavy dependence on external energy and highlighted the need to import a basic energy source such as natural gas. The plan was to build a pipeline from Algeria to Essen—2600 km—passing through Barcelona, Lyon, and Paris. It would have the capacity to transport 10,000 million cubic metres of gas per year, with the Spanish market potentially receiving 10% of that volume.

In this context of new expectations, the ASSEMI Council of Delegates held in Paris on 27 June 1960 accepted the entry of *Banco Urquijo*, represented by Pedro Durán and Jaime Mac-Veigh Alfós. Consequently, from November of that year, *Catalana de Gas* participated in the European Industrial Committee for the Utilisation of Saharan Gas, an organisation in which other companies such as *Rhurgas*, *Distrigaz*, the *Italian Methane Society* (*Sociedad Italiana del Metano*–SOCIM), *Montecatini*, and *Gaz de France* also participated.

As Fàbregas notes, from that moment, Pedro Durán became part of one of the most exclusive groups in Europe for the promotion of natural gas across the continent. The Catalan engineer came from the electricity industry, but it was clear that electricity generation could have gas as its basic source. Furthermore, *Catalana de Gas* faced a crossroads in terms of change and adaptation to new technologies (Ballestero, 2017, p. 22; Fàbregas, 2014, pp. 48–49).

Pedro Durán's character is distinguished by his ability to maintain good personal relationships with all kinds of political, economic, and social figures. This skill enabled him to establish contact with prominent bankers and politicians during the years of the dictatorship, to the extent that his potential appointment as a minister was even discussed due to his knowledge of and dealings with the Head of State, Francisco Franco.

Throughout the twentieth century, *Banco Urquijo* occupied a prominent position in the field of industrial investment and promotion. Within this context of personal relationships, the bank served as the meeting point between Pedro Durán and Leopoldo Calvo-Sotelo, also a civil engineer and top of his class. For years, Calvo-Sotelo was administrator of *Explosivos Río Tinto*, a company partly owned by *Banco Urquijo*, and later served as President of the Spanish Government during a particularly turbulent period in national politics (Lafuente del Cano, 2017).

The notable closeness with Juan Lladó, an executive of *Banco Urquijo*, led to understanding with Minister Gregorio López Bravo. To a large extent, the Catalan executive's influence on the industrialisation of Catalonia and his ascendancy in Spanish industrial policy can be explained by the intense and long friendship he maintained with López Bravo and the forward-looking vision they both shared. Their affinity arose from a dinner at Juan Lladó's house, to which Leopoldo Calvo-Sotelo was also invited. Durán himself recounted this encounter, which marked the beginning of a deep friendship (Álvarez Morales, 1988, p. 103).

López Bravo completed studies in naval engineering and began his professional career at the *Spanish Shipbuilding Company* (*Sociedad Española de Construcción Naval*—SECN) in Sestao. After several years at the *Matagorda Shipyards* in Cádiz, he returned to the Sestao shipping company as director in 1956. Politically, he served as Director-General of Foreign Trade in 1959, and Director of the Spanish Institute of Foreign Currency (*Instituto Español de Moneda Extranjera*) in 1960. Subsequently, in 1962, he was appointed Minister of Industry at just 39 years of age, and in 1969, Minister of Foreign Affairs.[1]

4 A Young Executive for New Times

The management of *Catalana de Gas*, founded in 1843, followed very traditional parameters. A review of the Board of Directors' Minutes Book is sufficient to perceive the course of decision-making and the objectives set by its members. Ricardo Margarit Calvet led the company and had a long trajectory within it (Fàbregas, 2014, p. 53). The president was Juan Bertrand Mata, heir to the prominent textile entrepreneur Eusebio Bertrand Serra.

In the 1940s, Lladó promoted the involvement of distinguished businessmen with *Banco Urquijo*. Juan Bertrand was one of those selected, to the extent that he

[1] The friendship with Pedro Durán was so close, and there was such excellent harmony between them on economic matters, that the Minister of Industry even offered him a position at the Development Plan Commission (*Comisaría del Plan de Desarrollo*). On that occasion, as well as on others during the early years of the democratic period, Durán declined to enter political life (Álvarez Morales, 1988, p. 104).

was incorporated into the boards of both the aforementioned bank and *Banco Hispano Americano* (Fàbregas, 2014, p. 54).

Pedro Durán's good relations with *Banco Urquijo* facilitated his appointment as a director. Gradually, the Catalan executive became one of the most representative figures in Spanish industry throughout the 1960s. From his appointment at HECSA and later at *Catalana*, it was evident that he was Juan Bertrand Mata's trusted confidant. The elderly president passed away in 1965, and from that moment, Durán became a cornerstone of industrial modernisation and assumed the presidency of *Catalana*.[2] The shareholders appointed him as the visible head of the company group. A manager had become the leader of one of the country's major companies. Ownership had ceded to the executive. A significant change and a new form of management were penetrating Spanish companies. The eras in which ownership and management were conflated were coming to an end. Small and medium-sized textile firms, abundant across Catalonia, began promoting greater professionalisation in management. New managerial techniques were being introduced into the Spanish business sphere. The era of engineers had begun (Torres Olivares, 2015).

Pedro Durán's presidency at *Catalana de Gas* was particularly marked by the incorporation of new organisational patterns and the innovative transformation of the entire group. For example, *Gas Natural, S.A.* (1965) emerged under his initiative with the intention of bringing this raw material to Spain; he also presided over HIFRENSA, created by HECSA in collaboration with other electrical companies, with the aim of constructing Catalonia's first nuclear power plant.

In February 1966, he was appointed director of *Banco Urquijo*, filling the vacancy left by Juan Bertrand and fostering closer ties between the engineer and the financial institution. This alignment was reflected in the creation of Spain's first investment fund that same year, with *Gesfondo, S.A.* as the initial managing company, of which Pedro Durán was president and Ramón Trías Fargas, the CEO. This initiative placed the bank at the forefront of investment fund management (Fàbregas, 2014, p. 62).

The significance of *Banco Urquijo* was evident in the stable investments it maintained in various companies: *Catalana de Gas*, *Unión Eléctrica Madrileña*, and *Gas Madrid*. Within this exchange of positions, Durán was also appointed director of *Banco Hispano Americano*, filling the vacancy left by Félix Escalas Chameni, the historical representative of *Banco Urquijo* in Catalonia. Holding these significant posts provided key positioning for direct knowledge of the Spanish economy and industries.[3]

The new management team at *Catalana de Gas* prioritised gas production over the electricity business. In his recent position, Durán promoted several far-reaching

---

[2] *Catalana de Gas y Electricidad* (CGE), Board of Directors' Minutes Book, 11 August 1965, pp. 108–109.

[3] At that time, it was difficult to foresee that the financial institution would disappear within a few years and that mergers would become the prevailing trend among electricity and gas companies. From the merger of *Catalana de Gas* and *Gas Madrid* emerged *Gas Natural SDG*; and subsequently, together with *Unión Fenosa* –the successor to *Unión Eléctrica Madrileña*– *Gas Natural Fenosa* was established in 2014 (Fàbregas, 2014, p. 63).

projects. Firstly, the modernisation of gas factories, replacing coal with catalytic cracking lines of light naphthas.[4] Secondly, he promoted greater quality control in gas production and measurement. Thirdly, he established various provisions relating to financial policy, tariffs, management, and employees. In the latter, he proposed technological redundancy for more than 500 people. The automation of the new factories required a substantial reduction in workforce. Durán himself stated that the reorganisation of *Catalana* and the consequent elimination of the significant losses it had accumulated were achieved with a 40 % reduction in organisational structure and the efficiency of the new plant fuelled by naphtha (Ballestero, 2017, p. 29; Pániker, 1967).

Between 1963 and 1964, the new production lines at the San Martín de Provençals and Barceloneta factories began operations.[5] These were the first in Spain to apply this cutting-edge technological innovation. This policy initiated a process that would lead to the absorption and acquisition of other small gas factories and distributors, for example, those in Vilanova i la Geltrú, Manresa, Mataró, and Sitges. Subsequently, in 1965, he acquired the *Compañía Española de Electricidad y Gas Lebon*, the third-largest gas company in the country, with factories in Cádiz, Granada, Málaga, Santander, Murcia, and Valencia (Fàbregas, 2014, p. 56; Fernández-Paradas & Sudrià, 2018, pp. 135–136). With this strategy, *Catalana* aimed not only to reconvert its facilities and improve service quality, but also to achieve near-total market control, acquiring new customers and extending its reach to regions such as Andalusia, Cantabria, and the Levante (Fàbregas, 2017).

Pedro Durán's entrepreneurial capacity, already demonstrated in the construction of the Pyrenean plants and his management at HECSA, is further highlighted by his involvement in Eurofrigaz. This collaboration brought him into contact with the American company *Esso* and its efforts to export liquefied natural gas from Libya to France and Italy, while also providing him with greater knowledge of the technology in this industry. The refusal of General de Gaulle to entrust foreign companies with France's energy supply allowed Durán to envisage the possibility of introducing natural gas to Spain, with the consequent improvement of the distribution network and a significant investment in the construction of a regasification plant. Despite the project's scale, he obtained the support of President Juan Bertrand and the shareholders, including *Banco Hispanoamericano*, *Banco Popular*, and *Banco Urquijo*. As Ballestero (2017, p. 31) notes, it is likely that Gregorio López Bravo was aware of the project: its magnitude and the close friendship between the two men underpin the minister's knowledge of the initiative.

At the end of 1964, *Catalana de Gas* requested administrative authorisation from the Ministry of Industry to import, store, regasify, distribute, and sell natural gas in Barcelona and several surrounding municipalities. The justification was based on the scarcity of naphtha for manufactured gas and the feasibility of implementing

[4] CGE, Board of Directors' Minutes Book, 2 March 1962, p. 34; 11 April 1962, p. 37.

[5] CGE, Board of Directors' Minutes Book, 17 April 1964, p. 80; 13 January 1966, p. 128; 13 October 1966, p. 147.

natural gas. Technological advances enabled the transport of liquefied gas by methane carriers and the installation of a regasification plant in the port of Barcelona. Consequently, it was necessary to establish a fiscal regime similar to that for naphthas used in manufactured gas production. The application proposed transferring the concession to a company—largely owned by *Catalana*—that would carry out the project. Authorisation was also required to construct facilities to separate the propane and butane associated with the Libyan gas, which would be sold under a monopoly regime (Castro-Valdivia & Matés-Barco, 2020).

Simultaneously, throughout 1964 and 1965, *Catalana de Gas* established contacts with *Esso*[6] to involve the company in the enterprise.[7] On 9 November 1965, the agreement was signed. The American company participated with 35 % of the capital of the new company, and the agreement stipulated the sale, over fifteen years, of 1300 million cubic metres per year of gas from Libya. The product consisted mainly of methane (natural gas) and 300 million cubic metres per year of propane and butane. These components were to be separated at the Barcelona port facility.[8]

Gas Natural, S.A. was established in Barcelona to advance this project on 28 December 1965, with a share capital of two million pesetas, represented by 2000 shares.[9] Most were subscribed by *Catalana* (1980 shares) and the remainder by two employees: José María Lozoya and Pedro Giró, to meet the requirement for three shareholders. Subsequently, following a capital increase, *Esso* and the aforementioned banks joined (Ballestero, 2017, p. 32). The new company resulted from the association of *Catalana de Gas y Electricidad*, *Esso*, *Banco Urquijo*, and *Banco Popular Español*. Essentially, it involved importing natural gas from Libya—later Algeria—contracted with *Esso*, and constructing a regasification plant in the port of Barcelona, while establishing a commercial network in the region. Pedro Durán was appointed the company's first president, with Pedro Grau Hoyos as CEO, both from *Catalana de Gas* (Fàbregas, 2018, pp. 263–264). *Esso* asserted its participation with several appointments: technical and commercial directors, the head of Human Resources, and Paul Temple as Vice President of *Gas Natural* (Ballestero, 2017, p. 38).

The 1962 government included a wide range of political families, and the INI, the main instrument of the government's industrial policy, depended on the Presidency. In this context, López Bravo promoted an industrial policy removed from the autarchic principles of INI officials. State intervention was intended as a

---

[6] Affiliated with *Standard Oil Co. of Spain*, which had adopted the name *Esso Standard Española, S.A.* since 1955.

[7] CGE, Board of Directors' Minutes Book, 14 October 1964, pp. 90–91; 18 December 1964, p. 97.

[8] There is evidence of a similar project promoted by the *Compañía Ibérica de Petróleos*, a semi-state company with participation from the Ministry of Finance, *Banco Exterior*, and the Fierro Group. In 1955, the company proposed the construction of a gas pipeline to transport gas from Algeria to Europe via Spain. The proposal included the construction of a branch to Jaén to supply gas to the *Land Rover Santana* plant in Linares. For various reasons, the project was not implemented (Ballestero, 2017, p. 22).

[9] CGE, Board of Directors' Minutes Book, 13 January 1966, p. 129.

subsidiary element, not hindering private enterprise and allowing a modern and competitive industry. Differences with the Falangist groups, defenders of autarky, regulation, and interventionism, were evident during his tenure at the Ministry.

This conflict between technocrats and Falangists highlighted the differing conceptions of energy policy and the role of the State. López Bravo's appointment as Minister of Industry represented a profound change in energy policy and the subsidiary role of the INI relative to private initiative. With Juan Antonio Suanzes' resignation in 1963, the emphasis on industrial and technological self-sufficiency was abandoned. This new policy reduced the INI's prominence, partially paralysed its activities, and slowed investment policies. State contributions were substantially reduced, and its financial structure deteriorated significantly. As Ballestero notes (Ballestero, 2017, p. 30), this change prevented the introduction of natural gas in Spain from being driven by the INI (Martín & Comín, 1991; Schwartz & González, 1978).

5 Conclusions

Understanding and analysing the life trajectories of entrepreneurs allows for the incorporation of experiences and situations into business organisation. This set of actions enriches decision-making within companies, as individuals make choices in highly complex circumstances, independently of variables or organisational structures. Furthermore, immersion in entrepreneurial biographies facilitates an approach to economic reality, since understanding successes and failures requires acknowledging the inherent fluctuations of business activity. This prevents a static view of economic processes and commercial enterprises, regardless of their size. The study of companies and their founders provides insights that integrate economists' theoretical reflections with experiences developed in concrete contexts. Additionally, it is necessary to examine not only the general theoretical framework but also the organisational structure of firms, their various divisions, and the innovations they have undergone throughout their existence.

In this context, the study of Pedro Durán Farell is of particular importance. His biographers describe him as a person of great maturity, leadership capacity, tireless work ethic, boundless imagination, action-oriented, a promoter of major projects, possessing considerable fortitude in taking risks, and endowed with exceptional interpersonal skills. Durán's presence in the business world was extensive: not only in the gas and electricity sector, but also in banking—including *Banco Industrial de Cataluña* and *Banco Urquijo*—as well as in highways, RENFE, and companies such as *Auto Electricidad* and *La Maquinista*.

Of particular note is his drive in technological change applied to the gas industry, as well as the development of new industrial projects to expand natural gas in Spain. The study of his business activity demonstrates the importance of personal relationships, the relevance of engineers in corporate leadership during the 1950s and 1960s, and the role of banks in that industrial development. Furthermore, it is instructive to analyse the interrelation among different business groups, as illustrated by the exchange of directors on the respective Boards of Administration.

Competing Interests The authors have no conflicts of interest to declare that are relevant to the content of this chapter.

Sources Historical Archive of Gas Natural. *Catalana de Gas y Electricidad* (CGE), Board of Directors' Minutes Book, 1960–1969.

References

Álvarez Morales, M. (Coord.) (1988). *Gregorio López-Bravo visto por sus amigos. Laredo.*

Ballestero, A. (2017). *El gas natural en España. LID Editorial.*

Burdiel Bueno, I., & Pérez Ledesma, M. (Coords.) (2000). *Liberales, agitadores y conspiradores. Biografías heterodoxas del siglo XIX*. Espasa Calpe.

Carreras, A., & Tafunell, X. (2018). *Entre el Imperio y la Globalización. Historia Económica de la España Contemporánea*. Crítica.

Castro-Valdivia, M., & Matés-Barco, J. M. (2020). Catalana de Gas y Electricidad (1960-1969): Las transformaciones de una década. In M. Fernández-Paradas, I. Bartolomé-Rodríguez, & J. Mirás-Araujo (Eds.), *Cercanas pero distintas. La desigual trayectoria de la industria del Gas en las regiones del sur de Europa* (pp. 215–239).

Díaz Hernández, O. (1998). *Los Marqueses de Urquijo. El apogeo de una saga poderosa y los inicios del Banco Urquijo, 1870–1931*. Eunsa.

Fàbregas, P.-A. (2014). *Pere Duran Farell. Biografía*. RBA.

Fàbregas, P.-A. (2017). La estrategia de la implantación de la industria del gas en España (1826-2010). In I. Bartolomé, M. Fernández-Paradas, & J. Mirás-Araujo (Eds.), *Globalización, nacionalización y liberación de la industria del gas en la Europa latina (siglos XIX-XXI)* (pp. 21–44). Marcial Pons.

Fàbregas, P.-A. (2018). *Naturgy. 175 años de compromiso con la energía y la sociedad. Planeta-Naturgy.*

Fernández-Paradas, M., & Larrinaga Rodríguez, C. (2021). *Business history in Spain (19th and 20th centuries)*. Peter Lang. https://doi.org/10.3726/b17988

Fernández-Paradas, M., & Sudrià, C. (2018). La transición de la industria del gas de carbón al gas natural: dos modelos, España y Cataluña. *Revista de Historia Industrial, 71*, 121–149.

Hernández-Andreu, J. (2019). Santiago Pons Quintana y Jaime Mascaró: Dos grandes empresarios menorquines del calzado. In J. M. Matés-Barco (Ed.), *Empresas y empresarios en España: De mercaderes a industriales* (pp. 303–315). Pirámide.

Lafuente del Cano, J. (2017). *Leopoldo Calvo-Sotelo y Europa. Historia de una convicción política y económica*. Sílex.

Maluquer i Sostres, J. (Coord.) (2001). *Pensamiento, reflexiones y escritos de Pere Durán Farell. Laia.*

Martín, P., & Comín, F. (1991). *INI. 50 años de Industrialización en España*. Espasa-Calpe.

Matés-Barco, J. M. (Coord.) (2019). *Empresas y empresarios en España. De mercaderes a industriales. Pirámide.*

Matés-Barco, J. M., & Caruana de las Cagigas, L. (Eds.). (2021). Entrepreneurship in Spain. A history. Routledge. https://doi.org/10.4324/9781003126973.

Núñez García, V. M. (2013). La biografía como género historiográfico desde la Historia Contemporánea Española. *Erebea, 3*, 203–226. https://doi.org/10.33776/erebea.v0i3.2305

Pániker, S. (1967). *Conversaciones en Cataluña*. Kairós.
Schwartz, P., & González, M. J. (1978). *Una historia del Instituto Nacional de Industria (1941–1976)*. Tecnos.
Torres Olivares, B. (2015). *Los orígenes del IESE*. LID Editorial.
Torres Villanueva, E. (Coord.) (2000). *Cien empresarios españoles del siglo XX. LID Editorial.*.
Tortella, G. (2000). Prólogo. In E. Torres (Ed.), *Cien empresarios españoles del siglo XX* (pp. 13–14). LID Editorial.
Tortella, G., & Quiroga, G. (Eds.). (2013). *Entrepreneurship and growth*. Palgrave Macmillan. https://doi.org/10.1057/9781137033352
Urrutia, J. (Coord.) (2018). *La bolsa y la vida. La esfera de los libros.*
Vázquez-Fariñas, M., Ortúñez-Goicolea, P. P., & Castro-Valdivia, M. (Eds.). (2021). *Companies and entrepreneurs in the history of Spain. Centuries long evolution in business since the 15th century*. Palgrave Macmillan. https://doi.org/10.1007/978-3-030-61318-1

Juan Manuel Matés-Barco is Professor of Economic History and Business History. Director of the Department of Economics at the University of Jaén (Spain). He holds a degree in Geography and History from the University of Zaragoza and a PhD in History from the University of Granada. Research focused on public services and the economic development of contemporary Spain. He has conducted research stays in Italy, France, and Portugal. Director of the journal *Agua y Territorio/Water and Landscape*. Principal Investigator of GEHESE-UJA. Coordinator of various research projects and editor of several collective works published by prestigious national and international publishing houses.

María Vázquez-Fariñas is a Lecturer in History and Economic Institutions at the University of Málaga, having previously taught at the universities of Jaén and Cádiz. She holds a degree in Business Administration and from the University of Cádiz and a PhD in Social and Legal Sciences from the University of Cádiz. Her research focuses on contemporary public services and networked companies in Spain, and in the nineteenth-century Cádiz, including the wine industry, trade, the port, and slavery. She has published extensively in national and international journals and with prestigious publishers such as Brill, Routledge, Palgrave, and Springer. She has participated in numerous international projects, conferences, research initiatives, and editorial and scientific committees.

Mariano Castro-Valdivia is a Lecturer in History and Economic Institutions at the University of Jaén. He holds a degree in Economics from the University of Valencia and a PhD in Economics from the University of Jaén, with research stays at Sapienza University of Rome, Université Bordeaux Montaigne, and the University of Salamanca. Researcher in national I + D + i projects and member of the Historical Studies on Business Research Group (GEHESE-UJA). He researches the teaching of economics in Spanish universities and the management of networked public services. He has published extensively and edited works with Palgrave, Marcial Pons, and Tirant lo Blanch.

Business History in Times of Change: Cycles, Crises, and Recovery at *Construcciones Calderón*

Francisco Cabrera-Gallardo

Abstract This chapter examines the evolution of the construction sector in Spain through the case of *Construcciones Calderón*, a family business founded in 1949 that managed to adapt to the profound economic and social transformations of the country. Over seven decades, the company went from carrying out small local projects to participating in large infrastructure and urbanisation projects. The text analyses how *Calderón* navigated the sector's cycles of boom and crisis, especially during Franco's developmentalism, the real estate boom of the 1990s and 2000s, and the subsequent recession after 2008. It highlights the company's ability to adapt through diversification, professionalisation, and intergenerational management. In addition, the chapter reflects on the contemporary challenges facing the sector—sustainability, digitalisation, and new forms of financing—based on the specific experience of this company. Overall, it offers a microhistorically view of a key sector for the Spanish economy.

1 Introduction

This chapter examines the history of a Spanish construction company in the context of the contemporary evolution of the industry. Adopting a microhistorical approach, it analyses how the sector has been shaped over the past seven decades, providing insights into its structural and cyclical dynamics.

Construction in Spain represents a significant sector for the national economy. Macroeconomically, it contributes to GDP, while at the microeconomic level it supports a broad secondary industry. Over the years, and in the face of multiple economic crises, the sector has proven to be volatile, subject to cyclical fluctuations

F. Cabrera-Gallardo (✉)
Department of Economics, University of Jaén, Jaén, Spain

PhD Program in Economic and Business, University of Málaga, Málaga, Spain
e-mail: fcabrera@ujaen.es

M. Vázquez-Fariñas, F. Cabrera-Gallardo (eds.), *Business Trajectories in the History of Spain*, Frontiers in Economic History,
https://doi.org/10.1007/978-3-032-16214-4_10

and strongly influenced by the real estate market and broader economic conditions (Carreras & Tafunell, 2010; Comín Comín, 2011).

The company analysed here is *Construcciones Calderón*, with research based primarily on primary sources, including writings and documents by one of its founding partners, José Calderón, as well as internal company records, allowing a detailed and reliable reconstruction of its history.

With more than seventy years of activity, the company, founded by three brothers, has continued to pursue the same core business it began in the mid-twentieth century. Over the decades, operating in a highly competitive market, the company has experienced successive stages of expansion, internationalisation, and adaptation to technological advances, while successfully navigating challenging periods such as the 2008 financial crisis, which led to the bankruptcy of numerous construction firms in the aftermath of the property boom. Today, it is considered a medium-sized enterprise operating across both the secondary and tertiary sectors, reflecting the diversification of its business activities.

In its business strategy, the company has evolved from executing basic infrastructure and construction projects within its immediate geographical area to developing business lines focused on cutting-edge or highly specialised projects for the preservation of historical heritage. This evolution has been accompanied by a policy of continuous reinvestment of profits, enabling the company to meet the constant challenges of the market with a sustained commitment to innovation. As a result, it has become a robust enterprise, providing a compelling case study for understanding the transformation of the construction sector from the perspective of contemporary economic history.

2 History of *Construcciones Calderón*

In the late 1940s, three brothers from the Spanish province of Jaén decided to start a construction business that would become *Construcciones Calderón*. The company now has more than 70 years of experience in the industry and has grown from a company created to provide self-employment for its founders to a family business that is a benchmark in the sector in Spain.

This long history has allowed the company to witness different stages of Spanish economic history since the mid-twentieth century. This helps us to contextualise and analyse certain milestones that have marked the economy of Andalusia and Spain.

Thus, through the chronology of *Construcciones Calderón*, we can see a real example of how Spain went from Franco's autarchy and international isolation to progressive trade liberalisation, leading to the integration of the Spanish economy into the international system.

The beginnings of *Construcciones Calderón* date back to 1949. That year, brothers José, Eduardo and Cristóbal Calderón Carmona decided to join forces professionally and embark on a business venture dedicated to the construction sector.

They began by carrying out small projects for individuals and local neighbours in Jaén, at a time when the post-war economy was beginning to recover.

The construction industry offered opportunities for entrepreneurship, as Spain was in need of housing and new infrastructure to rebuild the country (Carreras & Tafunell, 2010).

A few years later, in 1952, after three years of growth in orders and work to be done, they decided to formalise their working relationship through a commercial company called *Construcciones Calderón S.A.* For this new business phase, they had the financial support of their parents, which made it easier for them to take this step.

Focusing on civil engineering, they began to diversify their business model and devote themselves to the conservation of historical and religious heritage. Thus, they specialised in the restoration and rehabilitation of this type of property with high cultural value. This commitment, as we will see throughout the chapter, has been a major factor in the success and recognition of this company, as it coincided with a situation in which public administrations were making significant investments in this field of preservation.

Thus, the initial stage of the company was marked by rapid growth, driven by the award of significant public contracts worth large sums for the time. One such contract was awarded in 1953 for the construction of three bridges in the rural area of Jaén for 82,000 pesetas, paid for by the Provincial Council of Jaén. With this and other projects aimed at remedying the lack of basic infrastructure in the interior of the peninsula, *Construcciones Calderón S.A.* managed to carve out a place for itself in the sector, becoming a reliable company for contractors, which in turn led to a higher ratio of contracts awarded.

Thus, the second half of the 1950s was a time of consolidation for *Construcciones Calderón S.A.* In a national context in which public works were increasingly taking central stage as the driving force behind territorial modernisation, this company was securing more public contracts, mainly from the Provincial Council of Jaén, which ensured its workload, profitability and, in turn, financial stability. This public civil engineering work mainly consisted of the construction of roads, sewers, bridges, paving, etc. Today, we might consider these types of projects to be of a low standard, but we must understand the context of the time, with very primitive machinery and technical and technological limitations.

The expansion of *Construcciones Calderón S.A.* continued apace. In 1958, an important milestone in the company's history occurred. One of the three founding brothers, José, whom we will discuss in more detail in a later section, fell ill and was forced to take a six-month leave of absence. Upon his return to work, the three brothers agreed that José would take charge of the administrative side of the company, which was growing steadily and had until then been delegated to an external company called Gestoría Palacios, located in Jaén.

From this point onwards, management and accounting are centralised within the company itself. The administration department is developed, five specialised workers are hired, professionalising this area, which in the long term will be beneficial for the company's growth, resulting in greater control over the financial and bureaucratic aspects of the business.

They acquire state-of-the-art trucks and excavators, which, with this strategic investment, allows the company to be more competitive in public tenders, as well as reducing construction times and operating costs, resulting in greater corporate profits.

By the end of 1959, *Construcciones Calderón S.A.* had almost 200 employees, including operators, experts, architects, and draughtsman, making it a major company in the construction sector in the Andalusia region.

The 1960s were an important decade for the company. With a heavy workload and many contracts, it actively participated in projects related to Franco's first Economic and Social Development Plan, which increased public spending and the expansion of civil engineering as a means of rebuilding and modernising the country. This led to a significant increase in state investment, which resulted in an expansion of the construction sector (Comín Comín, 1988).

The Franco regime gradually opened up the economy, moving from an autarkic model to more inclusive and technocratic development strategies (Carreras & Tafunell, 2010; Comín Comín, 2011). As a result, public works became a profitable market sector, with financial stability and no volatility, thanks to government contracts. This was a crucial element in an economy still characterised by uncertainty and a lack of private investment (Catalan, 2002).

Focusing on Jaén, where *Construcciones Calderón S.A.* was predominantly active, on 17 July 1953, the Spanish government approved the Plan for Works, Colonisation, Industrialisation and Electrification of the province of Jaén (BOE, 1953), also known as the Jaén Plan (BOE, 1957). Its objective was to reduce the high levels of backwardness in this area compared with other regions of Spain by correcting the structural imbalances of a predominantly agricultural and scarcely industrialised province. This involved undertaking new works and additional public procurement with significant funding.

This, in turn, attracted demand from the private sector for residential and industrial projects. According to the company's internal information, it not only built hundreds of houses between 1952 and 1967, but also agro-industrial facilities, such as oil factories.

The economy of the province of Jaén during the late Franco era continued to be based on olive farming, which had an impact on the workforce during the olive harvest season, as construction workers temporarily left construction to focus on agriculture (González de Molina Navarro, 2014). This led to a shortage of construction workers, causing the construction industry to temporarily grind to a halt.

To remedy this situation and sustain the company's economic activity, the three founding brothers of *Construcciones Calderón S.A.* decided to diversify the business to occupy their time during the agricultural harvest months. They began transporting olives harvested on farms to agricultural cooperatives. They also transported pomace at night to processing factories, for example, to the pomace factory in Torredonjimeno.

In the early 1960s, as part of a vertical integration strategy, they set up an aggregate plant to supply material to construction sites. They made a substantial investment, but the project did not achieve the expected profitability and was closed down.

In 1961, against a backdrop of widespread population growth in cities, internal migration, and a structural housing shortage (Naredo, 2014), *Construcciones Calderón S.A.* began the construction of more than 1200 houses in Jaén, one of the most ambitious projects the company had undertaken in its history. The failure of this project caused a huge financial setback for the company, and at the end of 1967, *Construcciones Calderón S.A.* was dissolved.

Faced with this situation, the three founding brothers were forced to embark on new professional projects separately. Years later, in 1969, two of the brothers, Cristóbal and José, together with an external partner, Manuel Cañada (Calderón Carmona, 2018), and supported financially by friends and relatives—reflecting the typical form of post-war family business financing, based on interpersonal trust and self-financing due to the limited banking penetration among SMEs (Valdaliso Gago, 1999)—decided to relaunch their venture through the establishment of a new company, *Construcciones Calderón S.L.*

They quickly regained the trust of contractors. One of them was the Bishopric of Jaén, which hired them for several religious projects during 1970. All of this shows a synergy between private enterprise and ecclesiastical actors within the context of religious development promoted by Catholic institutions during the Transition (Botti, 2008; Casanova, 2001; Martín de Santa Olalla, 2006).

During those years, the new company continued to expand its business lines and reached a very significant agreement with Banco Popular Español that would last for several decades for the maintenance and construction of bank branches nationwide, reflecting how construction was gradually moving towards the tertiary sector with the aim of modernising service infrastructures (Matea Rosa & Sánchez, 2006).

In other attempts at diversification, the company opened a blind factory and a building materials warehouse. Both projects were less successful than expected based on the investment made and were sold. With these unfortunate business ventures, the shareholders decided to focus fully on the company's core business, construction.

Between 1982 and 1987, there were several changes in the share capital of *Construcciones Calderón S.L.*, resulting in the two Calderón brothers becoming the sole owners, thus returning the company to being exclusively family-owned.

Business was going well in the late 1990s. The company was recognised in the construction sector at the national level, as it had the capacity to carry out a wide range of types of work, giving it stability. This was further boosted by Spain's accession to the European Economic Community in 1986, which increased investment in housing, conservation, and infrastructure (Torres Villanueva, 2009).

It was in 1999, against this backdrop of maturity for the company, that the generational change took place: brothers José and Cristóbal Calderón Carmona, founding members of the company and sole shareholders since 1987, retired, handing over the reins to their sons Jesús and Cristóbal.

This stage took place in the context of a common trend among Spanish family SMEs in the second half of the twentieth century, in which generational transfer not only ensured business continuity but also maintained the founding values and bonds of trust established over decades (Serrano Cañas, 2013). In this case, with a dual direct line succession involving the children of the two founders, reinforcing unity among shareholders and the family legacy (Belausteguigoitia Rius, 2017; Gallo & Amat, 2003).

3 Transfer of the Company to the Heirs

With the transfer of power at *Construcciones Calderón S.L.*, and now under the management of the second generation as a family business, led by Jesús and Cristóbal Calderón, they continue to expand the business.

After two decades at the helm of the company, the heirs have continued to consolidate the company in the construction sector and have advanced its development through internationalisation and structural expansion. For example, in 2017, they opened a branch in Granada with the aim of improving the management and monitoring of projects carried out in this Spanish province.

In order to undertake this type of project in Spain, public certifications issued by the Spanish Ministry of Finance (2020) are required, which qualify the company for such specialised activity. For this reason, *Construcciones Calderón S.L.* has had to comply with demanding regulations that require high technical qualifications and compliance with strict legal procedures according to Ley 9/2017, of 8 November (2017).

One of these certifications is the K7, which allows the company to carry out interventions on properties protected as cultural or heritage sites, thus enabling it to undertake projects on historic and emblematic buildings of enormous artistic value. This has positioned the company as a leader in heritage restoration, in line with the Sustainable Development Goals (SDGs), especially regarding the protection of cultural heritage (UN, 2015).

This gives rise to commenting on some of the most important projects that have already been carried out in the second generation of this family business.

In the civil sector, they have built various residential housing developments through the Andalusian Public Land Company, called Empresa Pública de Suelo de Andalucía (AVRA) in the province of Jaén. They have also had the opportunity to work on the construction of the "Olivo Arena" Sports Palace in Jaén, which, with an area of more than 41,000 square metres, can accommodate 6500 people.

Works related to religious heritage have become a hallmark of the business history of *Construcciones Calderón S.L.* Examples of this are the repair of the roofs of the cathedrals of Jaén and Granada, as well as the restoration of the Major Seminary in the latter city. They have not only carried out projects in this field in Andalusia. They have also worked in Moralzarzal (Madrid), with the construction of the church of the Cistercian Convent of Calatravas.

Continuing with the restoration of historic buildings, it is worth highlighting the restoration work carried out on the Sacromonte Abbey in Granada and the Torre de la Vela tower at Almojíar Castle (Málaga).

In terms of healthcare facilities, the company has built private physiotherapy and dental clinics and refurbished areas of large healthcare centres such as the Virgen Macarena Hospital in Seville.

Another major project, one of the largest and awarded by the Bishopric of Granada, was the construction of La Inmaculada University School of Education in this city, which was carried out between 2009 and 2012. This project was allocated €24 million to build an educational space consisting of classrooms, offices, sports halls, a library, a church, conference rooms, etc., covering more than 8000 square metres.

These projects are some of the most significant among those undertaken, illustrating the company's entrepreneurial capacity to win public and private construction contracts against other competing companies, as well as reflecting its territorial presence. They also serve as an example to understand the variety of construction types in which this second generation has diversified the business today.

In a process of crossing borders, the business expanded into the African continent, mainly to Algeria and sub-Saharan Africa. There, the company has undertaken construction and infrastructure rehabilitation projects linked to educational development, carried out within the framework of international cooperation programmes. In this way, *Construcciones Calderón S.L.*, while enhancing its competitiveness, also contributes to the United Nations Sustainable Development Goals (UN, 2015), specifically SDG 4 (Quality Education) and SDG 9 (Industry, Innovation, and Infrastructure).

Following the retirement of the founders, the new generation initiated a process of internationalisation, seeking to secure long-term growth through geographical diversification (Fernández Rodríguez & Nieto Sánchez, 2005).

The founders' children, after taking over the reins of the company, have always followed the idea that the company should have a strong presence in the territory through Corporate Social Responsibility actions. They implement these in areas such as education, culture, sports, and institutions. As Cristóbal Calderón (son) mentioned in an interview with Revista Económica de Andalucía (2017), this reflects the social, cultural, and sporting commitment they have made in the geographical areas where they operate.

Some of these initiatives include collaboration with universities such as the University of Cádiz, through the sponsoring of the master's degree in Hospital Engineering and Architecture, thereby reducing tuition fees for students, and with the University of Jaén, via an annual contribution of €25,000 to the "Cátedra Arqueólogo Manuel de Góngora. Empresa familiar Calderón", which focuses its activities on heritage conservation and restoration, as well as academic and educational initiatives (Construcciones Calderón, 2025).

In support of sport, it has sponsored major events in the city of Jaén, such as the San Antón Night Race and the Half Marathon, thereby helping to consolidate the sporting and cultural identity of the area.

With the presence of *Construcciones Calderón S.L.* in Africa, the company established an educational project called the Calderón Institute for Technical and Professional Training (ICAF), which promotes the transfer of knowledge and technical training within the African region, aiming to generate social impact through education.

According to information obtained from sources such as Einforma (2020) and Empresite (2020), and based on the rankings established by the Ministry of Digital Transformation and Public Function in its official classification of SMEs (2005), *Construcciones Calderón S.L.* falls into the category of medium-sized enterprise, as it has between 50 and 249 employees, a turnover of less than 50 million euros and a balance sheet of less than 43 million euros.

If we continue to examine the structure of the company, we find that it is a privately owned company with an international presence, which places it within the model of internationalised SMEs, a trend that has been on the rise since 2000 (Fernández Rodríguez & Nieto Sánchez, 2005). Furthermore, we can point out that it is a company mainly dedicated to the secondary sector (construction industry) but also active in the tertiary sector through its real estate and service provision activities. This diversification between productive sectors is common in second-generation family businesses seeking new market niches from which to generate income (Belausteguigoitia Rius, 2017; Gallo & Amat, 2003).

4 José Calderón as an Entrepreneur

To understand the business figure of José Calderón Carmona (1932–2024), in addition to considering the factors outlined above, it is necessary to situate him in within the context of his personal circumstances and unique experiences.

He was born in Jaén (Andalusia, Spain) into a large, hard-working family. Despite the difficult circumstances of his childhood during the Spanish Civil War, he received an education and had early job opportunities in the construction sector, which would ultimately shape his future as an entrepreneur (Calderón Carmona, 2011).

A prominent figure in Jaén society, Vicente Oya Rodríguez, who served as the Official Chronicler of the City of Jaén between 1975 and 2016, describes him as "a perfectionist in his work, who knew how to earn the affection, consideration, and trust of authorities, official bodies, businesspeople and workers" (Calderón Carmona, 2013). This outgoing personality was decisive in establishing a wide network of contacts and thereby opening doors for his business.

His brothers Cristóbal and Eduardo, who together with José started the *Construcciones Calderón* project as partners in 1949, are fundamental to understanding the character of this businessman, as they accompanied him in his corporate decisions, which helped the company to prosper in a sector such as construction, with many options for the future in a Spain that, after the Civil War, was about to be rebuilt and developed.

His early career within the company was temporarily halted in 1954, as José had to complete his compulsory military service in accordance with the regulations in force at the time. As he was assigned to a military barracks in Córdoba, a city not far from Jaén, this allowed him to continue his work in construction during his periods of leave, even if only for a few days.

Another important milestone in the life of this entrepreneur, as mentioned above, occurred at the end of 1958. He fell ill and had to take 6 months off work. In 1959, he and his two partners, his brothers, decided that José should train in managerial and administrative tasks and take charge of these matters in the company. This marked a turning point for the company and for José, as this new role opened up new business horizons with the professionalisation of this department of the company, which would improve day-to-day management at the administrative level.

As José Calderón himself mentions in his writings, he estimates that during his active career he has built around three thousand homes with his companies, in addition to generating countless thousands of jobs and boosting the economy through his business activity.

In such a long entrepreneurial career, there have been successes and failures, as is natural in any type of business. In the latter case, the documentation consulted, which was written by the entrepreneur himself, highlights some projects, mentioned previously, that were a fiasco but which, despite this, were able to move forward through business diversification, profit reinvestment, and a relentless search for improvements in the means used to increase long-term profitability, enhance efficiency in the work, and ensure the ability to meet project deadlines. This gives *Construcciones Calderón* a better corporate image of reliability in the sector and, in turn, increases the chances of obtaining new private and public sector contracts.

Doing business with the public sector was a strategic decision, as José Calderón points out in his writings, because the option of bidding for public works contracts helped to stabilise the company, guaranteeing a steady flow of work and predictable profitability, with profits being reinvested to constantly modernise the company (Calderón Carmona, 2013).

A fundamental factor that determines the likelihood of success is that, throughout all these years, this entrepreneur has been constantly evolving in the sector, which has allowed him to remain at the industry forefront. This meant that his company was able to adapt to changing macro and microeconomic environments, surviving major crises and bringing the company to the present day to hand it over to the second generation. In addition to the business side, José always kept in mind his social commitment through Corporate Social Responsibility actions that he promoted on a personal level and through *Construcciones Calderón*, with the aim of giving back part of the profits to society.

When the time came for him to retire in 1999, this new generation took over the reins of a company that was well established in the construction sector, specialising in new areas of business and with promising prospects for the future.

In recognition of his long and fruitful business career and social commitment, José Calderón has been honoured during his lifetime with, among other awards, the "Gold Medal for Merit in Work", awarded in 2011 by the Spanish Government, the

Order of Civil Merit from the Spanish Ministry of Foreign Affairs, and the "Silver Medal for Commercial Merit" from the Ministry of Economy. At the local level, a street in his hometown of Jaén is named after him.

Being able to learn about and study the biographies of people with long business careers who have dedicated much of their lives to their work can be a useful and valuable tool in decision-making for new generations who decide to start entrepreneurial projects.

5 Conclusions

This chapter has shown how a company in the province of Jaén (Andalusia, Spain) has grown over more than seventy years, from a small local business to a major player in the construction sector, not only at the regional level, but also nationally, and even internationally with several projects currently underway.

Looking back at the history of *Construcciones Calderón*, we can identify three phases: the first covers the period from 1952 to 1967 and involves the initial collaboration of the three brothers who created an unincorporated partnership and its subsequent dissolution; the second phase began in 1969 with the incorporation of a limited company; and the third phase saw the transfer of the company to a second generation of entrepreneurs, namely some of the founders' children.

As we have seen, this company, which began as a self-employed venture by the three founding brothers, has expanded its business areas over the years through various entrepreneurial projects within the construction sector. Thus, sometimes successfully, sometimes unsuccessfully, they launched a number of projects: a window blind factory, a sand quarry, and a building materials warehouse that served as a self-service store and sold to competing companies.

Focusing on the industry, *Construcciones Calderón* has diversified its business portfolio by carrying out and specialising in different types of work at all levels: civil construction, restoration of religious buildings, new educational, sports, and health centres. In order to undertake so many different types of work, the company has had to obtain external certifications and authorisations from public bodies for the restoration, protection, conservation, and rehabilitation of heritage sites.

These more than seven decades of business projects have led to the creation of numerous jobs, the revitalisation of the economy where the works have been carried out, and the completion of numerous and diverse construction projects. This is a summary of how a local company has been able to overcome the numerous economic crises that have hit this sector hard in Spain over time, especially that of 2008, and become a benchmark in its sector at regional and national level through sustained and diversified business growth.

Competing Interests The author has no conflicts of interest to declare that is relevant to the content of this chapter.

References

Belausteguigoitia Rius, I. (2017). *Empresas familiares: dinámica, equilibrio y consolidación.* McGraw Hill.

BOE. (1953). *Ley de 17 de julio de 1953 por la que se aprueba el plan de obras, colonización, industrialización y electrificación de la provincia de Jaén.* Retrieved July 11, 2025, from https://boe.es/buscar/doc.php?lang=es&id=BOE-A-1953-9814

BOE. (1957). *Plan de Obras, Colonización, Industrialización y Electrificación de la provincia de Jaén.* BOE n° 195, 13 de julio de 1957, pp. 5792–5794.

BOE. (2017). *Ley 9/2017, de 8 de noviembre, de Contratos del Sector Público, por la que se transponen al ordenamiento jurídico español las Directivas del Parlamento Europeo y del Consejo 2014/23/UE y 2014/24/UE,* de 26 de febrero de 2014. BOE n° 272, de 09/11/2017. Retrieved September 15, 2025, from https://www.boe.es/buscar/act.php?id=BOE-A-2017-12902

Botti, A. (2008). *Cielo y dinero. El nacionalcatolicismo en España 1881–1975.* Alianza Editorial.

Calderón Carmona, J. (2011). *Recuerdos de mi infancia y juventud en el Puente de la Sierra.* Gráficas La Paz.

Calderón Carmona, J. (2013). *Historia de una construcción a lo largo de sesenta años de vida.* Gráficas La Paz.

Calderón Carmona, J. (2018). *Encuentros con la historia a través de sus protagonistas.* Gráficas La Paz.

Carreras, A., & Tafunell, X. (2010). *Historia económica de la España contemporánea (1789–2009).* Crítica.

Casanova, J. (2001). *La Iglesia de Franco.* Biblioteca de Bolsillo.

Catalan, J. (2002). Franquismo y autarquía, 1939-1959: enfoques de historia económica. *Ayer. Revista de Historia Contemporánea, 46*(2), 264–283.

Comín Comín, F. (1988). Evolución histórica del gasto público. *Papeles de Economía Española, 37*, 78–99.

Comín Comín, F. (2011). *Historia económica mundial: De los orígenes a la actualidad.* Alianza Editorial.

Construcciones Calderón. (2025). *Official website of Construcciones Calderón.* Retrieved in September 2025. https://construccionescalderon.com/

Einforma. (2020). *Datos generales de Construcciones Calderón SL.* Retrieved August 25, 2025, from https://www.einforma.com/informacion-empresa/construcciones-calderon

Empresite. (2020). *Informe de Construcciones Calderón SL.* Retrieved August 25, 2025, from https://empresite.eleconomista.es/CONSTRUCCIONES-CALDERON.html

Fernández Rodríguez, M. Z., & Nieto Sánchez, M. J. (2005). La estrategia de internacionalización de la pequeña empresa familiar. *Cuadernos de Economía y Dirección de la Empresa, 22*, 107–125.

Gallo, M. A., & Amat, O. (2003). *Los secretos de las empresas familiares centenarias claves del éxito de las empresas familiares multigeneracionales.* Ediciones Deusto.

González de Molina Navarro, M. (2014). *La cuestión agraria en la historia de Andalucía: nuevas perspectivas. Cuadernos de Andalucía en la Historia Contemporánea.* Fundación Pública Andaluza Centro de Estudios Andaluces.

Martín de Santa Olalla, P. (2006). La Iglesia durante el franquismo. *Un debate abierto. Historia del Presente, 7*, 127–148. https://doi.org/10.5944/hdp.7.2006

Matea Rosa, M. LL., & Sánchez, C. (2006). La construcción en España. *Boletín económico - Banco de España, 3*, 45–62.

Ministry of Digital Transformation and Public Function. (2005). *Definición de microempresas, pequeñas empresas y medianas empresas.* Secretaría General Técnica. Retrieved September 19, 2025, from https://portalayudas.digital.gob.es/artemis/Normativa/DocumentosNormativa/Normativa%20General/Definici%C3%B3n_PyME_CE.pdf

Ministry of Finance. (2020). *Consulta de clasificaciones otorgada por la Junta Consultiva de Contratación Pública del Estado en vigor*. Retrieved August 7, 2025, from https://serviciostelematicosext.hacienda.gob.es/DGPE/Contratistas/paginas/ListadoEmpresas.aspx

Naredo, J. M. (2014). El modelo inmobiliario español y sus consecuencias. *Boletín CF+S, 44*, 13–28.

Revista Económica de Andalucía. (January 26, 2017). *Construcciones Calderón refuerza su actividad en Granada con la apertura de una delegación*. Retrieved July 27, 2025, from https://andaluciaeconomica.com/construcciones-calderon-refuerza-su-actividad-en-granada-con-la-apertura-de-una-delegacion/

Serrano Cañas, J. M. (2013). *El cambio generacional en empresas familiares*. Marcial Pons.

Torres Villanueva, E. (2009). Las grandes empresas constructoras españolas. Crecimiento e internacionalización en la segunda mitad del siglo XX. *La internacionalización de la empresa española en perspectiva histórica, 849*, 113–127.

UN (United Nations). (2015). *Objetivos de Desarrollo Sostenible*. Retrieved August 21, 2025, from https://sdgs.un.org/goals

Valdaliso Gago, J. M. (1999). Orígenes y desarrollo de la historia empresarial en España. Príncipe de Viana. *Suplemento de ciencias sociales, 17*, 91–117.

Francisco Cabrera-Gallardo is an Interim Assistant Professor of History and Economic Institutions in the Department of Economics at the University of Jaén (Spain). He holds a degree in Business Administration and Management, having been awarded the Platinum Curriculum Prize by the University of Jaén. He holds a Master's Degree in Business Administration (MBA). For one year, he was a fellow at the Spanish National Research Council (CSIC). He is currently working on his doctoral thesis in the field of Economic History, in the Doctoral Program in Economics and Business at the University of Málaga.

www.ingramcontent.com/pod-product-compliance
Ingram Content Group UK Ltd.
Pitfield, Milton Keynes, MK11 3LW, UK
UKHW020912180926
475648UK00003B/34
* 9 7 8 3 0 3 2 1 6 2 1 3 7 *